WELLS NEXT THE SEA
A small port and a wide world

For Helena

Further details of Poppyland Publishing titles can be found at
www.poppyland.co.uk
where clicking on the 'Support and Resources' button will lead to pages
specially compiled to support this title.

POPPYLAND
PUBLISHING

Wells next the Sea

A small port and a wide world

Roger Arguile

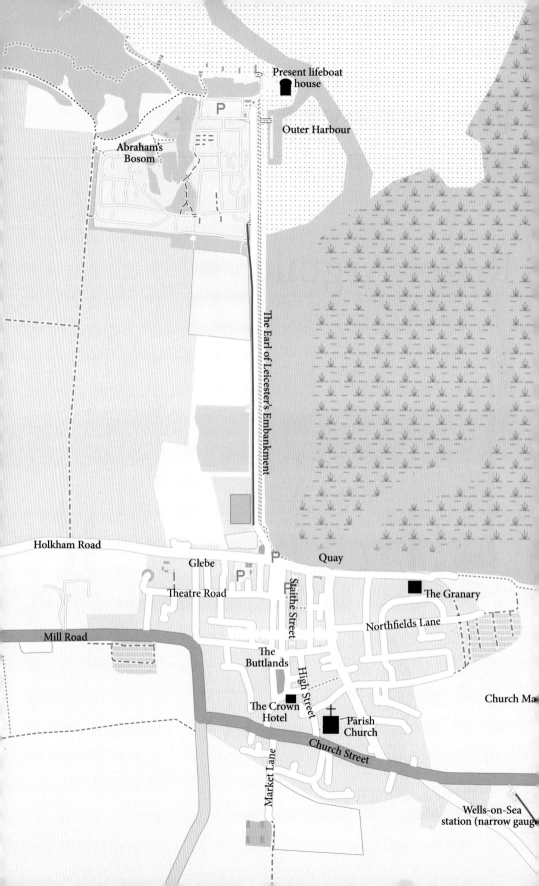

Present lifeboat house

Outer Harbour

P

Abraham's
Bosom

The Earl of Leicester's Embankment

Holkham Road

Glebe

Theatre Road

P

P

P

Staithe Street

Quay

The Granary

Northfields Lane

Mill Road

The
Buttlands

High Street

Church Ma

The Crown
Hotel

Parish
Church

Market Lane

Church Street

Wells-on-Sea
station (narrow gaug

Opposite: *A map of Wells next the Sea, indicating the position of some of the places mentioned in the text.* Top: *The Granary, the iconic building of the quayside, no longer just a granary. The picture is at high tide and boats float freely in the harbour.* Bottom: *Wells is a 'drying' harbour, with just a narrow channel remaining at low tide. Many vessels, as this former lifeboat, simply sit on the sand or mud and refloat as the tide comes in on its twice daily cycle.*

Previous pages: *The tug* Marie *and a steam coaster make their way down the channel at Wells.*

ISBN 978 1 909796 10 2 (hardback)
ISBN 978 1 909796 11 9 (paperback)

Published by Poppyland Publishing, Cromer NR27 9AN

Picture credits

Author: 5 (top), 22, 24, 30 35, 38, 40, 49, 50-52, 54, 63, 93, 99, 101, 131(top), 165, 176
Author's collection: 33, 45, 47, 118, 125, 160, 161 (top), 167 (top)
Holkham Archive: 95
David Cleveland: 167 (top, bottom)
Robin Golding: 104
Robert Malster: 105 (top), 161 (bottom), 164 (top, bottom)
Robert Malster Collection: 2-3, 130 (top, middle), 131 (middle, bottom)
Norfolk Record Office (will of John Tydd, 1514, NCC will register Coppinger 69) 56
Norwich Cathedral 16
Open Street Map and contributors: 4
Mike Page: Front cover, 169 (bottom)
Poppyland Collection: 16, 82, 131 (middle), 135 (bottom), 141 (top)142
Poppyland Photos: 5 (bottom), 8-9, 12, 36, 103, 137, 141 (bottom), 168-169, 173, 178
Michael Stammers: 13
Graham Taylor: 161
John Tuck Collection: 30, 85, 113, 132-133, 135 (top), 147-148, 156-157, 166 (top
    and middle), 172 (top)
Guy Warren Collection: 136, 146 (top), 166 (top)
Mike Welland: 82,
Susan Wild: 151

Foreword

Wells next the Sea is known to the of thousands of visitors it receives every year. On a summer weekend the streets are packed with people who come to enjoy the beaches, the cafés and the pubs which line the quay. Some will wander into the local museum and some will look at the older buildings and perhaps even the church. Behind this modern façade Wells has a fascinating and complex history, the subject of this new book by Roger Arguile. The book traces the history of Wells from the early Middle Ages to the present. It follows the growth of Wells' fishing industry in the Middle Ages and its growing importance as one of the trading ports for Norfolk's increasingly vibrant agriculture. We see the town in the eighteenth and nineteenth centuries as it grew in prosperity as a centre of the grain and malt trade; and we witness its 'decline' in the twentieth.

Throughout the book the author balances the local story with the national picture showing how, even in the Middle Ages, Wells was not a world apart but always influenced by national events. The book presents the local and the visitor alike with a clear and well written account of the history of Wells which manages to combine enthusiasm, local knowledge and good research into a thoroughly readable and accessible account.

Professor Alun Howkins
Honorary Professor of History, UEA
Emeritus Professor of Social History, Sussex University

Preface

This work began as a reworking of Arthur Purchas' book *Some History of Wells-next-the-Sea and District*, published in 1965; my copy has been well thumbed for the sources it provided. Since then much more information has become available and access to it is now so much easier. A short version, *Wells-next-the-Sea: A Little History*, was published by Poppyland Publishing in 2013 and the research which this required seemed to justify a larger work. The late Michael Stammers and Guy Warren gave me encouragement in beginning it.

The sources are many and various. Digitised copies of early sources from the University of Iowa have been plundered. Histories both general and specialised have provided background. The publications of the Norfolk Record Society, particularly in their work on the papers of Nathaniel Bacon, put everyone in their debt. Many individuals have been helpful. Mike Welland of the Wells Local History Group has been enormously helpful: his knowledge of Wells is encyclopaedic and he has generously shared it with me. Susan Wild let me see her biography of her grandfather Sam Peel before it was published; Dr Evan Jones generously made his research notes on cod fishing available to me; members of the Brewery History Society helped with the history of malt. Graham Taylor of Crisp Maltings lent me the Directors' minute books of F. & G. Smith. Ian Blanchard shared his forthcoming

Tourism and the enjoyment of the beach and sea is vital to the town of today – and the sea has been core to the town's development in the past.

book on the twelfth century; Derek Keene kindly responded to my interrogations. Bridget Nichols did some translating for me. I have had many conversations with people whom I have asked to dig into their memories and lend their materials, among them Brian Barker, Roger Bishop, Peter Bowles, Bob Brownjohn, John and Diana Claxton, David Cox, Peter Elphick, Ted Everitt, David Perryman, Tom Sands, David Sizeland, John Tuck and John Tyson. Photographs come from a number of sources, some of which are part of the History Group archive. John Tuck and Guy Warren have generously shared items from their collections. Several people have read the typescript and made suggestions including Alison Bowles, the late Freddie Hetherington Sims, Amanda Howe, Ken Rose, Joyce Trett and my wife Helena. My own researches into the enclosure movement in Wells, on the Poor Law, on mediaeval wills, the various episodes of rioting, malting and mid-Victorian legislation have been included, so it is not entirely a work of borrowing. Nevertheless, my debts to the above are huge.

My thanks are due to everyone who listened as well as those who pointed me in new directions. In particular I want to thank the Wells Library staff who have been magnificent in ever-smilingly finding books from all manner of sources, and my wife who has suffered from my daily preoccupation for over two years.

Roger Arguile
Wells, July 2014

Contents

1. Introduction

The chalk ridge on which Wells stands is a natural reservoir for rainwater. The many wells once dug into the chalk provided its people with sweet water from earliest days. Its name at the time of the Domesday survey, Guella, is probably the dog-Latin version of an Old English word meaning a spring of water. Most ancient documents refer to 'Welle', 'Wellis' or some similar formulation. Most of the wells have now been filled in or covered over; in the ages of unchecked disease natural sources of clean water were a valuable commodity which may account for the comparative longevity of its people and the early success of the town. Its other asset, the sea itself, is entered via a channel which winds its way through the marshes to its north. These formed behind the dunes thrown up by wind and tide. As the silt brought in by the tide was deposited behind the dunes, little by little, century by century, the marshes with their fragile ecosystems built up. The channels carved by the outgoing tide offered both access and protection to sailing vessels. All these elements have contributed to making the town what it is.

Wells was, in the Middle Ages, one of a number of little ports from which fishing and trade were carried on. It is virtually the only one to remain. Others, like Thornham, have largely silted up. Holkham harbour has quite disappeared through the process of land reclamation of the marshes for agriculture. The long spits of sand which choked Blakeney, Cley, Wiveton and Brancaster have not affected Wells. Numerous attempts have been made, so far with some success, to keep the harbour open largely by ensuring a good flow of water to scour the channel from the harbour to the sea. The various schemes produced huge arguments some of which ended up in court. The concerns to keep the harbour open for marine traffic have been longstanding.

As for fishing, the vagaries of fish stocks and of the market have been the story all along, beginning before the thirteenth century when herring were the major catch. That fish stocks fluctuated wildly was recognised but not understood; the fishermen nevertheless benefitted from living in some of the richest fishing waters in the world.[1] Trade was always international. Men from Wells fished off shore, in the Dogger Bank, and as far away as Iceland as long ago as the fifteenth century, a feat to make modern mariners quake. Cod were landed already air dried or salted and, because their supply exceeded the needs of the town, they were exported either inland or to other towns and cities by sea. It was taxation which helped to destroy that trade. Oysters came and went in the nineteenth century; sole and brill likewise. Sprats were fished out in short order in the twentieth century. There were always arguments about overfishing, clouded by the lack of data and the assumption of each generation that what it first experienced was the norm. The ocean as much as the land has a history and the long decline of fish stocks over hundreds of years is a story which also needs telling. Matters have been complicated by government regulation and market fluctuations right from early days even until the present.

Wells' role as a trading port goes back a long way too, possibly to the early thirteenth century when corn was sent to Flanders; the town occasionally met London's grain needs in the fourteenth century. It imported coal from the north east by the late fifteenth century and probably much earlier to meet the shortage of fuel as the felling of woodlands proceeded apace. Later

The parish church of St Nicholas, in part the oldest building in the town but substantially rebuilt after the fire of 1879. The story is on page 147.

still, ships from London and the continent brought all manner of commodities, the grocery and hardware trades of the day. Facing the continent it vied with larger ports; the nineteenth century saw the town at its most prosperous – apparently self-contained, it supplied London brewers with malt and traded with the world.

Wells was also a manufacturing town even until sixty years ago. Looking at it now that may seem hard to believe, but for more than two centuries it made the malt which was supplied variously to Holland, then London and then to the Midlands. In the mid-eighteenth century, one third of the country's malt exports went through the books of Wells harbour. By the nineteenth century probably twelve maltings dominated the town, rising as high as its windmills, another lost feature.

The peculiar character of the soil and climate of north Norfolk provides the wherewithal for the growing of barley, from which malt is made. Barley is still grown widely and its products drunk in pubs near and far. The land once supported large numbers of sheep whose droppings fertilised the soil and on which once upon

A contemporary model of Henry Tyrrell's shipyard in the town from the mid 19th century; shipbuilding is further described on pages 71 and 125.

a time England's prosperity depended.

Not everything produced in the town went out by ship, but the harbour was focal to it; it was a gateway to the world. There were few good roads until the eighteenth century, most of them Roman (though the Pilgrim's Way from London to Walsingham was one of the half dozen great roads of mediaeval England.) Even in good weather when the roads were passable, ships could carry more tonnage and more quickly.

The combination of productive land and access to the sea made Wells an important place. It may seem to stretch credibility to claim that Wells was at different times of national importance. If what is contained in this book is at all accurate, that case can be made. (Local Acts of Parliament certainly claimed so.) It had its moment of fame. The combination of the coming of the railway, siltation and the greater accessibility of other ports brought about its relative decline. Even so, it experienced a revival of its sea trade in the years after the Second World War until larger vessels and changes in governmental regulations brought about its demise. From earliest days the demands of government were an ambiguous factor in influencing the prosperity or otherwise of the town.

The maltings have gone; the coal coastal trade has gone. The produce of the fields no longer goes out of the harbour in ships. The fishing, if it is to be sustainable, will remain a shadow of its former self.

In recent years the town has found two new sources of income. The first, tourism, dates from the early part of the nineteenth century; tourism has mushroomed and now produces an income of something around £23 million a year. Many of the old houses and some commercial properties such as the Granary have become second homes and the bed and breakfast and self-catering trades have grown enormously. Most recently, vessels engaged in the building of wind farms have brought employment to townspeople and income for retailers. A new outer harbour has been built to shelter the vessels, just a stone's throw from Abraham's Bosom where boats sheltered from adverse wind and weather eight hundred years ago.

In telling the story I have drawn on sources wider than the town itself. No single place can have its story told without reference to wider events. No place reveals all its secrets. During the early period there are great gaps in the sources. For that reason it has sometimes been necessary to generalise from events known from elsewhere. Sometimes it has seemed useful to write about national events which then help to explain why things happened here; single reports often only make sense when you know their context. Even so, it is remarkable how often the name of the town appears in public documents. Local history may be a minor genre in the business of historical endeavour but it could be said to offer a corrective to the tendency in more general histories to snatch data from different places, sometimes from different centuries in the same breathtaking paragraph.

Finally, I like to think that, whether readers know the town well or not, they will find what follows interesting as part of the story of England and that they will be sufficiently absorbed, as every writer hopes, to want to turn the page.

2. The Making of a Community

The Conquest and before

Norfolk has been continuously inhabited for thousands of years; some of the earliest arrivals after the Ice Age apparently walked from the continent across the grassy plain that was to be swamped by rising sea levels eight and a half thousand years ago. It became the North Sea.[1] Wells had to wait for that sea to arrive for its chalk ridge to overlook a harbour. The oldest visible marks of habitation locally are Iron Age earthworks. Warham fort, whose remains can be seen a couple of miles from Wells, was built probably in the second century BC by the Iceni tribe. Holkham fort, also an Iceni artefact, is dated later, just into the new millennium. It lies within the protected nature reserve just to the south of the Pinewoods which fringe the beach. Boudica was the most famous daughter of the tribe, a charioteer by all accounts. Her battles against the invading Romans were fought further south, mainly around Colchester. The fort at Brancaster, only discernible from the air by crop marks, is Roman; coins and pottery are regularly dug out of the soil. Some remains have recently been found within the town itself. When they departed, the Romans left behind, apart from many items of interest to archaeologists, an international language from which several European languages would develop, a complex culture and a religion which was to influence the whole of European culture even until now.

When they departed in the sixth century, England was the subject of a series of wars and invasions: the Angles and the Saxons came, giving a name not only to this part of England but to the country as a whole. From the sixth century until the eighth, the kingdom of East Anglia was a stable, civilising presence in what was effectively a peninsula bounded by the sea to the east and the fens to the west; but this did not entirely prevent its being intermittently at war with the neighbouring kingdoms of Mercia and Northumbria. Thereafter, much of Saxon East Anglia's cultural heritage was lost by the destruction wrought by the invading Danish Vikings; towns and villages, churches, monasteries and their libraries were all burned. England was for a while part of a kingdom which included Norway and Denmark. The Danish king Cnut (Canute) brought peace but on his death England was divided and, before long, invaded again by other 'Northmen' whom we know as Normans.

In the years after that most famous date in English history, 1066, William of Normandy, having invaded Kent, fought his way across England. The years were bloodstained and it took him ten years or more to quell the hostile Saxons. This progress through the fens was slow and resistance fierce. The name of Hereward the Wake is still known as one who is said to have led the resistance in the east until his death in 1072. The fens were not yet drained, with Hereward's redoubt, the Isle of Ely, standing in the midst of them; it took until 1086 for William to subdue it.

The Battle of Hastings as depicted in the Bayeux tapestery

The Normans changed some things but not others. They found, and did not much alter, the forms of agriculture already being developed by the Saxons. These differed across the country but hereabouts the 'open field' system had been introduced, in which very large fields were divided into strips each worked by a different tenant and crops rotated between the fields.[2] The origins of the strip system are much disputed; it meant that tenants had a share of better and worse land; it enabled common ploughing; it may have been the result of tenants acting together to clear marginal land and then dividing the proceeds of their labours; it is said to have derived from partible inheritance rules. In any case it was still being introduced in some places in the thirteenth century.[3] What the Normans did was to alter the system of ownership. Everyone was a tenant of the king, either directly or down a chain of tenancies, ending with the villeins who did not even own themselves. He then proposed to itemise all objects of value, which he did in the famous Domesday survey.

Domesday, manors and monasteries

There were actually two Domesday books. The first, or Little Domesday book, more closely recorded the most valuable part of the country, East Anglia; the rest of the country was covered in less detail and in some cases not at all. The little community of Wells was clearly in existence by this time; its land was ploughed, its Saxon manorial lord oversaw the work of his tenant farmers who worked their land and tended their livestock. Like everywhere else, it was itemised because it had economic value.

The survey was not however just a record of the assets of each community; it records in many cases how matters stood 'in the time of King Edward' as it says (the letters T.R.E., *Tempore Regis Eduardi*, occur in most entries). Thus, in short order we have something about the value and ownership of land before the Conquest (established by the examination of panels of jurors, Saxons whose knowledge was relied on, sworn under threat of dire punishments). Here at 'Guella', the Saxon Ketel was deprived of his five-carucate[4] manor and the Norman Aldit took his place, in spite of the fact that Ketel was 'a free man'. What he took over is described: there were five villeins, unfree tenants who nevertheless held between them a carucate, and seven borderers or serfs who had none. He himself farmed two carucates. The number of pigs had increased since the Conquest from four to sixteen, the sheep flock from sixty to 200. There were four cows. There was a mill, a source of income for the new lord: the villagers were bound to bring their corn to be milled by him – at a cost. (Private hand mills were common but illegal.) There were in addition nineteen sokemen, free tenants, holding the remaining two carucates between them. In spite of the growth in the manor its value had fallen from £5 to £4.[5]

The existence of such a number of free tenants, sokemen, seems to have been an East Anglian pattern. It has been suggested that the greater reliability of harvests and the fact that most communities were in the hands of several manors created a more mobile, more market-oriented society less dependent on great lords, but no convincing explanation has been found.

At any rate, the itemising and valuation had more than an economic purpose. The new regime, struggling to impose its will on a sometimes violently resistant local populace, created a system designed to ensure loyal military service at the behest of the monarch. 'The general imposition of a military burden on the aristocracy contributed to a revision of social relationships at all levels, to a regrouping of land

and men into units with a prime responsibility for maintaining the members of a feudal army.[6] The Normans were a militaristic if devout people (and when they eventually ran out of European wars to fight, they directed their attention, and that of their retainers, to the Crusades).

There is no mention of a harbour; presumably it was, like the Church, not thought to be of any economic or military value at the time. (It was to become so.) That there was a church is likely, possibly built of wood. Meanwhile, the king himself claimed large amounts of land nearby in Fakenham and around Wighton, the latter consisting of twelve carucates, something like 1,500 acres, some of which lay within Wells. Other land, part of the king's manor at Stiffkey, with its four borderers, four sokemen and more than a carucate of land, was also within the town. As for those whom the king had rewarded with land, so-called tenants in chief, apart from Aldit there was Alan, Earl of Richmond who held two carucates of land in Wells, Warham and Holkham; the Bishop of Thetford had twelve acres of land here, part of his manor at Hindringham; and there was outlying land of Binham manor which had been awarded to Peter, Lord Valoins. Norfolk, unlike many other parts of the country, was so divided as to land ownership that few townships or communities lay in the hands of only one manorial lord. This was to be of significance later as the hand of a lord was weakened by his lack of the ability to control a community.

These dispositions and the nature of land ownership, remote in time as they are, are still with us. The highest form of land ownership, absolute title, is short for 'fee simple absolute in possession' which is, in theory, a tenancy from the Crown. Historically, until less than a hundred years ago, sales of some land in the town, called copyhold, had to be registered in the manorial court (usually held in a solicitor's office or even a pub); and just over two hundred years ago in 1813 the enclosure award refers to four former manors, the Dukes, Normans, Binham Priory and Walsingham Priory whose successors were then claiming to be allotted land as part of the enclosure process (of which more later).

Wells Manor came into the hands of Walter Giffard, made Earl of Buckingham by the Conqueror, from whom it was inherited by the de Clares; their influence on the future of the town may possibly have been determinative. The de Clares owned huge amounts of land having received nearly two hundred manors as a gift from the Conqueror. These were known collectively as the Honor of Clare, mostly distributed in Norfolk and Suffolk and including Wells. The de Clares were held to be pious folk. This did not prevent them from protecting their interests. Just as the king wished to value everything for the purpose of taxation so the lords would do. In 1286 Gilbert de Clare, the then Earl, claimed ownership of any boat wrecked off the shore. The rule apparently was that if all the sailors drowned, down to the last dog, the Earl had a full claim. Otherwise he shared it with those who had undertaken the rescue. It appears that the Earl's bailiff threatened the locals so that they dared not assist the survivors.[7] He had the right to any rabbits – 'free warren' as it was called, a welcome change from salted meat or fish which seem to have been the major source of protein of the locals, at least in winter.

Gilbert was the last of his line, dying at the battle of Bannockburn in 1314. His lands were divided between his three sisters one of whom, Margaret, married Hugh de Audley, Earl of Gloucester. Their sole daughter, also Margaret, was abducted and married by Ralph, Lord Stafford, possibly because of her personal charms but more likely because of her inheritance. This gross action was nevertheless endorsed by King Edward III as a reward for earlier service to him by Ralph against the Mortimer family who had successfully deposed Edward's father, Edward II. The manor was then to come into the hands of Thomas Howard, Duke of Norfolk, who had married into the family, but also following the execution for treason of Ralph's descendant Edward, the seventh Earl, and third Duke of Buckingham, five generations down the line.[8] Sometimes called Stafford's Manor, it came eventually to be styled 'the Dukes'.

An outlier of the manor of Stiffkey appears to have come into the hands of the de Clares at some time and was therefore absorbed into their manor.

The second manor, 'Normans', remained in the King's hands until the reign of Henry I, when it was granted to Robert son of Ernisius (but it was then forfeited from his grandson who rebelled against King John). John then granted it in 1209 to Geoffrey Fitz Piers, Earl of Essex. Its tenancy thereafter disappears from view for several hundred years. At the Reformation it came into the hands of Ralph Symonds of Cley. Eventually it came via Christopher Curteis, a merchant of Wells, into the hands of the Coke family, of whom much more anon. How it came to have the name Normans is another matter. The lord of the manor of Wighton in the late thirteenth century, William de Ken, who was known as the Norman, sold off parts of his demesne land and when his son was deprived for treason, parts of the manor were given to Philip de Albini 'as the lands of the Normans'.[9]

The last two manors mentioned in the enclosure award were held by religious orders. There was a custom adopted by pious landowners of giving land to monasteries and other religious houses, partly as an act of thanksgiving for the blessings of their life and partly so that the monks would then pray for their souls. Mediaeval people lived violent lives – wars both at home and abroad – but they had a sense of their accountability to God. Those who took part in the battle of Hastings were thought of as having done a good work because Harold had broken his oath.

Nevertheless they were made to do penance for their acts of slaughter. This notion of making satisfaction, the theological version of paying one's feudal dues, was widely believed in.[10] Binham manor, some of whose lands extended into the town, belonged to Roger Lord Valoins as we have seen. He gave them to Binham priory[11] which he founded about 1104 dedicating it, as a daughter cell of St Alban's abbey, to the Blessed Virgin. Other lands were given to it over the years. Part of Wells Marsh was given to Binham by Norwich priory. (At the dissolution of the monasteries in 1539 it was granted to Sir Thomas Paston.)

Walsingham priory also held lands in the parish. Predating the Conquest, it was refounded by Geoffrey de Favroches in 1169 as the site of a vision of the Virgin Mary by his mother, Richeldis. It rapidly became a place of pilgrimage. Whereas Binham was Benedictine, Walsingham belonged to the order of Augustinian canons. The distinctiveness of the order was described by Pope Urban II, who declared that the Augustinians restored a balance to the religious life. Whereas the Benedictines brought order into whole countrysides through their agriculture and settled form of life with their substantial foundations, the Augustinians 'sought in a humble way to repair the ruins of the world'.[12] They rebuilt ruined churches; they re-established religious communities; they gathered together misappropriated tithes and applied

The Norwich Domesday recorded tithes payable to the several ecclesiastical manors.

them to religious purposes, for the relief of the poor, the sick and the infirm. They were very popular: one can imagine how Geoffrey de Favroches supposed that they would be the right people to care for a site of pilgrimage to which folk might come for the health of both body and soul. More modest in their lifestyle and aspirations, such houses were also more within the means of magnates of moderate means such as he was.

Manors received income both from the lands which they held in each parish and also in the case of religious houses a tithe or tenth of the estimated income from parishes of which they were patrons. The tithe had been made compulsory in the tenth century (and continued until the twentieth). It was to be paid initially to the priest as his income from the lands in the parish and was charged on all produce of the land, grown or manufactured. Over time monasteries, in order to improve their income, had impropriated the livings of many parishes. In theory this operated for the benefit of both parties in that the monastery provided the local parish priest and also cared for the church building. In many cases however the parish was merely a source of income. The greater tithe, which became a fixed sum, was paid to the monastery while the local priest received as his income the lesser tithe consisting of the tenth of the actual fruits of the harvest after the greater tithe had been paid; it was inevitably the more difficult to collect. It appears that the greater tithe was payable to Binham priory. A visitation of the parishes of the diocese was undertaken in 1291 in order to assess their income, both in terms of tithe and of the *taxatio temporalis*, the manorial duties owed to the various religious houses. This 'secular' tax on the land was divided between the two religious houses who owned manors in the town, and the Prior of Norwich. All this was recorded in what came to be called the Norwich Domesday, a thirteenth-century account of the income of Norwich diocese produced at the behest of Pope Nicholas IV.[13] (Payments to secular landowners are not recorded.)

Religious houses depended upon endowments, acts of generosity by the nobility. These normally consisted of the gifts of land, though monasteries also appropriated the tithes from parish churches. Some, like Creake Abbey, also an Augustinian house, were hospitals to which the king might send elderly retainers and which otherwise cared for the local sick, elderly and infirm. People came to Walsingham from all over the country and from Europe in order to pray at the shrine. Lynn was known to be a port through which European pilgrims came and it is possible that they came through the port of Wells as well.

Something else that came by sea was the stone for the building of religious houses. None of it could be procured locally, and while parish churches were largely built of knapped flint – a craft very ancient indeed – places like Walsingham and Binham acquired the stone of which they were largely built from Barnack in Northamptonshire or from France; it was then brought by river and sea in barges. The River Stiffkey via Blakeney was evidently the major route of choice; Wells or Holkham would be more appropriate for Burnham and Peterstone. (Even parish churches needed stone for the openings, mullions and transoms of windows and for the quoins at the corners and buttresses; round towers were one solution to the shortage of dressed stone – they did not need it – but Wells had a square one.)

Apart from the Benedictine and Augustinian houses, there came the newer houses of the friars. The Friars – the word means brothers – originated from reform movements within the Church which encouraged missionary preaching.[14]

They were disliked by parishes and monasteries alike. Preaching was popular and attracted both crowds and money which drew people from the parishes and older monasteries. Thus in 1241 a house of Carmelite Friars would be established at Burnham and another at Blakeney in 1296; in 1347 the Franciscans would come to Little Walsingham against some resistance from the Priory. Much more modest than great places like Binham, they were to become part of the variegated religious landscape of the country. The controversies which they engendered tell us a good deal about the life of the Church at that time: Norwich, at that time the second city of the country, was a centre of intellectual debate based on its Cathedral Priory; preaching was important to this process and the reform of the church was of concern on all sides. It was the prescriptions that differed.[15] It was also a time and a place in which mystical writing flourished. Julian of Norwich's *Revelations* written in 1373 and an autobiography of Marjorie Kempe of Lynn written a decade or so later are both in print today.

The smaller religious houses would not always survive. Peterstone, an Augustinian house whose remains can be seen only as part of some cottages next to Holkham, was to be amalgamated with Walsingham in 1449; Creake was to suffer a devastating fire in 1483 and its members perished from 'the sweating sickness' in 1506.[16]

A manorial society

Records of these early times are patchy. Descriptions, taken from various sources, nevertheless give some indication of the kind of the world in which the people of Wells lived. Lords, lay and ecclesiastical, often owned many manors, distributed in widely separated parts of the country. It was therefore impossible for them to attend in any detail to local affairs. Practice undoubtedly varied. The lord's deputy, the seneschal or steward, would, in large estates such as those of the de Clares, act for the lord. Individual manors or, if they were small, several of them

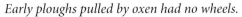

Early ploughs pulled by oxen had no wheels.

together, would be the responsibility of the bailiff. The standard system supposes a bailiff appointed to administer the affairs of the manor and a reeve appointed by the tenants to represent their views.[17] Because the two sides needed each other negotiation was necessary but this tidy arrangement was not always in place. In any case, familiarity with the rentals and the customary practices or bye-laws of the manor and the services due from each tenant were all essential to the work of the bailiff. Manorial land was never confined to one place. The strip farming system meant that each manor consisted of land distributed between fields and between villages; this required good record keeping.

When it came to communications with the town in respect of the harbour and the vessels which traded or fished from it, it was 'the bailiffs and the community of Welles and Holkeham' to whom the monarch addressed himself. He did so in the expectation that the bailiffs would communicate with the masters of the vessels and attempt to secure their compliance with commands. They might be expected to make their vessels available for war or to comply with regulations in relation to trade or fishing.[18] How good a knowledge the king actually had of local conditions is not known, but by 1285 statute had required that Edward I's commissioners be supplied with the names of every village and hamlet; from at least the 1270s seigniorial stewards and bailiffs were meant to have written down the names of every male over the age of 12, to be read out twice a year when the sheriff visited. In theory therefore the king knew the number and even the names of the inhabitants of Wells.[19]

The administration of the various manors was through a six-weekly meeting of the various manorial courts. Every male over the age of twelve had to attend unless he had an acceptable excuse. The court was the means by which the economic and social relations of the community were adjusted. Everything of value was taxed, from the sale of bread and ale to the use of the mill. Transfers of tenancies were approved by the manorial court (as they would be until 1925); disputes over land were resolved; annual yields were recorded for the purpose of tithe as well as manorial dues. The court also acted in criminal matters and Gilbert had, and presumably exercised, the power of life and death,[20] certainly over thieves caught on his own lands (infangthyof),[21] who would be hanged by his own bailiff. Such powers were disliked by the king's courts and gradually over time were taken away; clearly they were exercised by the lord in the thirteenth century.

The proceedings of the manorial court had to be recorded in writing. Initially in Norman French, English rapidly superseded it as the most comprehensible language. Latin was for the church, French for the king's court, but English for the conduct of local affairs. Those who could read were at an advantage; they could take on official roles, that of bailiff or reeve. Likewise clergy and members of religious orders needed to be able to read; many clerks thereafter sought secular employment. Monasteries were centres of such teaching. Partly because the majority of literature was religious, reading was regarded as a holy act; many more could read than could write.[22] Education in parishes was sometimes conducted by chantry priests, sometimes, reputedly, by mothers of small children.[23] Some parish priests could barely read, while some lay people could read tolerably well: as always there was much variability in their competence. Grammar schools, so called because they taught reading and writing, were rarities, though there was one at Coxford in the thirteenth century and one at Aylsham in the fourteenth. How long either lasted we do not know. The canons of Walsingham priory taught literacy but only to clergy.

Ceres presides over the land (from a 16th–century German woodcut)

'Maybe half the population could read, in mediaeval England . . . if by reading is meant the ability to recognise the written words of the best known prayers.'[24] The number who could read fluently would have been far fewer but the bailiffs of Wells and Holkham could not have done their jobs without an ability to read. Ralph Grigge, a local ship-owner, would have been at a disadvantage without it.

Wells was part of North Greenhoe Hundred. The hundred originated as an administrative area covering a hundred 'hides' of land; it predated the Conquest. (A hide was an area supposed to support a peasant family, variously computed as between forty and a hundred and forty acres.) The relation of the hundred courts to those of the manor, the court baron and the court leet, varied from place to place:[25] in some the manor restricted itself to economic matters, leaving the hundred courts to deal with crime; in others the lord or his bailiff would exercise a wider judicial function, as we have seen. (The Hundred Rolls, where they survive, provide an invaluable insight into the varied patterns of local administration. Hundreds have never been formally abolished but their importance lessened over time and nineteenth-century local government legislation deprived them of any significance.)

The Normans had imposed a more ordered system of governance, but many factors lay outside their control: most obviously and immediately it was the harvest, when everyone worked all hours; the lord was likely to demand 'boon works', compulsory favours from his tenants to get the crop in. Upon the harvest would depend survival through the winter when little grew and domestic animals could not be adequately fed from summer crops; cattle were either slaughtered and salted or kept semi-starved until the spring. A series of indifferent harvests would bring the threat of starvation. Whole villages were abandoned.

Agrarian change was driven by a number of factors. In good times, people married earlier and population grew. More land was then put to the plough, thus reducing the availability of pasture for oxen required for ploughing as well as the quantity of manure required to keep the land in good heart. This caused a fall in output. Tenants responded by clearing and/or draining land for new pasture, what was called assarting. The overall effect of these developments was the growth, between 1086 and 1315, of the population which more than doubled from 1.2 million to 3 million.[26] Far from being a period of stability, the twelfth century was one of rural change which was to set off other developments.

Population growth did not occur evenly either through time or across the country. The greatest growth appears to be towards the end of the thirteenth century; the prime areas of development included the extensive lands of Ely and Ramsey abbeys south of the Wash, which between them were responsible for the draining of lands around them.[27] Norfolk, adjacent to them, seems to have been affected. The light lands of west Norfolk were susceptible to increased ploughing though, as even now, it was better for growing barley than wheat, therefore better for beer than for bread. The greatest proportion of peasant calorific intake was derived from grain, partly eaten and partly, in the form of beer, drunk.[28] For the rest, dried or salted fish, peas, cheese and eggs made up their diet.[29] Sheep were valued more for their wool than their meat; it was, in those early days, more often plucked from their coats, even from dead animals, rather than shorn. Pigs, which could look after themselves, were a bonus.

Greater production also increased the opportunities for trade. During the last part of the twelfth century, weekly markets began to appear especially along the Norfolk coastlands. The first reference to Wells weekly market is in 1202; it had undoubtedly existed as an informal event for some years before that. It was one of dozens which sprang up along and near the coast.[30] There, manufactures, including locally-made cloth, implements of iron and wood, would be exchanged for produce. Money would become important, enabling as it did much more flexible means of exchange: men might engage in specialist trades, eating what they paid for rather than what they grew. Fairs, which took place annually on feast days, were an opportunity to sell to outsiders; they might run for several weeks – Holkham had an annual fair at the feast of the Beheading of St John Baptist at the end of August; Burnham Overy had one at the feast of St Barnabas in June; Blakeney a

St Nicholas Fair in December. There were others. To these might come merchants buying grain or fish or even draught animals now required in greater numbers to speed the plough. Norfolk and Lincolnshire became, together with Sussex, the most commercially active regions in the country.

The origins of the harbour

The harbour must have had a role in all of this though little concrete evidence survives. The first record of the harbour is the story of Hereward the Wake, who after the end of the siege of Ely took ship at Wells with some of his adherents in making his escape. This would have been about 1070.[31] There is no reference to the port in the Domesday survey; its commercial significance came later.

There seem actually to have been two ports here, Wells and Holkham. Entry to Holkham lay via a wide channel known as Micklefleet Wash,[32] through Holkham Gap: that to Wells around the Point was much as at present. (The outer channel at Wells altered its course over time, as it still does, and was known to run out as far west as Holkham and as far east as East Hills, becoming quite dangerous when there was any north in the wind.) Several creeks ran into Wells channel, notably the East and West Fleets which drained the marshes on each side. The latter connected with the Holkham channel via Abraham's Bosom.

That Wells came to be important was due to a number of factors, some to do with trade, some with the fishery and some with the aims of government. Sea ports had begun to take over from harbours up rivers; Boston, Lynn and Wells from Lincoln and St Ives. As the word port implies, they were gateways, capable of dispatching and receiving cargoes but also increasingly acting as instruments of government control and providing for the king's war needs.

The growth of maritime trade depended on the means of transport. There is some evidence of the development at this time of vessels of deeper draught (cogs, they were called), which required better harbours. Of large capacity they were essentially cargo vessels, probably of Dutch origin, single masted and, when fitted with a keel, true deep-sea traders.[33] It has been said that 'after 1200, most port towns were founded for the quality of their harbours and less for the nexus of transport their location offered',[34] which may account for the rapid development of ports. The development of Boston and Lynn took place about this time; it appears that Lynn's quays, which have been the subject of detailed archaeological excavation, were then built as the town itself expanded. Wooden quay walls, revetments, were built on the banks of existing channels which were then infilled to create a flat loading dock and a vertical wall against which vessels could tie up. In the course of time, such wharves would extend further into the centre of the channel where the water was deeper, the land behind them being then populated with tenements.[35] There is reason to believe that something of the sort took place in Wells. How it happened is a matter of speculation.

There is a longstanding belief that the original harbour lay beside the Church. The land there is very low lying and a stream runs through it out to the east bank where it runs through a sluice. Undoubtedly, before the North Point bank was built the sea would flood the church marsh from time to time, as it did when it broke down the bank in 1953. Various attempts have been made to justify the conviction, based on the claimed needs of monastic traders aided by the de Clares, or on archaeological remains of boats, that the earliest port was safely snug south of the town ; equally strong denials have pointed to the lack of coercive evidence. As we have seen, the earliest ports tended to be up river; churches are a good sign as to where settlements originate. Nearby Walsingham was provided with a new street plan, as Wells is claimed to have. The story is told that at this same period the king, who would have been King John, granted a charter to Ramsey Abbey to make of Wells a trading port for its considerable output of corn, salt and reeds and for the import of wax and building materials. The lords of the manor, the de Clares, were to be asked to build a new town on the north side of the chalk ridge and therefore closer to the sea than the church staithe.[36] It was to be laid out in a grid pattern with streets at right angles to each other. If this is true, there may have been two communities, the old village surrounding the church to the south and the newer one nearer the sea where the present Quay is.[37] It is possible that as the old harbour silted up, possibly by the fourteenth century, it would have been replaced by the new Quay, past which a much larger body of water flowed out, thus scouring the channel. Doubtless only archaeological excavations would lay the ghost or prove the theory.

Whatever the truth of the story, and it has to be said that hard evidence for it is lacking, this would have been the time when Wells began to need a harbour, for it was to become, as it would remain for a long time, a provider of grain both coastwise and overseas.

The narrow strip of land adjacent to the coast with its abundant crops and many little harbours seems likely to have supplied the Flemish merchants routinely and the English capital more occasionally with grain. William de Warenne, First Earl of Surrey, who held Holkham among well over a hundred manors in Norfolk, was married to a Flemish noblewoman, Gundrada; he is unlikely to have kept his political connections with the continent distinct from his commercial interests. (Such was the value of the trade between East Anglia and Flanders that it continued in spite of a royal ban when the two countries were at war.[38])

As for London, its population had risen to more than 70,000 in the late thirteenth century, higher than it would be for some time thereafter. It relied for grain increasingly on its hinterland, the Thames valley, Sussex and Kent but also, in times of dearth, perhaps one year in six, upon East Anglia. In what was almost a military operation, London cornmongers scoured the southern counties seeking alternative supplies.[39] Norfolk was at the extreme end of the supply line but because transport by sea of bulky goods cost about a twentieth of transport over land, this compensated for the greater distance the corn had to travel. Individual peasants might have only a small surplus, but it was plainly to their advantage to increase yields where there was market for it; together they might fill a ship or two. The cornmongers, operating from various London markets, had apparently learned from their king how to command supplies for large populations – he for his armies, they for a city.[40] Local agents dealt with demesne bailiffs or with small farmers through local markets to provide for their needs. Their intelligence would have been of most importance when local supply failed as happened in the years after 1315; the merchant Thomas Birle of Brancaster is mentioned as one local who supplied the Mayor of London with eighty quarters of grain. He was undoubtedly not alone. That more than a few of the cornmongers were also ship-owners who dealt with East Anglian ports, helps to complete the picture.[41]

A different issue, one of many, which is often raised but is not easily resolved, is whether Wells took part in the early wool trade. Wells manor had over two hundred sheep at the Survey; sheep would be an important part of the agricultural economy for hundreds of years. But because the town was, for most purposes, treated as merely a 'creek' of Lynn, there are few records. Lynn, not an ancient borough, had grown through the expansion of agriculture in the fens by monastic orders and in particular in the production of wool.[42] Because it was important nationally as an earner of revenue, wool had been taxed since the thirteenth century and in order to regulate the trade and prevent smuggling the coastline was divided into thirteen areas and a Custom House built at the principal port in each area,[43] one of which was at Lynn. In the decade 1280 to 1290 Boston, the largest, exported annually over 9,600 sacks of wool. Lynn with an average of 1,350 sacks was in the third rank. Local wool was of a middling quality, not as fine as that of Leicestershire, Lincolnshire or the Cotswolds; it was said to be good enough for the export trade. Wool exporters bought the fleeces at local fairs to which sheep farmers had brought them,[44] but it does not appear to have been exported from the harbour. In any case, the indigenous weaving industry was increasingly taking wool from local markets to be made into cloth in Norwich from whence it was exported via southern ports, not apparently from Wells or even from Lynn.[45]

Thus, when in 1363 a ship laden with wool arrived in Wells, probably seeking refuge in a storm, because it was not 'cocketed', i.e. recorded for customs, its cargo was forfeited.[46] In 1377 it was reported that wool, possibly from Scotland, was being landed in ships 'brought to or found in the parts of Wells in that county' without licence (and therefore without customs payment). The merchants and mariners were not named but those complicit in their being released from custody, John Holkham and Thomas Silk, most certainly were.[47] The wool churches of the Cotswolds, of Lincolnshire and Suffolk became famous; but Wells was not one of them. It seems more likely to have been a 'fish' church.

There is no mention of sea fishing in the Domesday survey, only of eels. Most fish eaten were fresh water species, pike, perch, bream or tench; or fish like salmon that began and ended their lives in rivers. Archaeological evidence from middens shows that consumption of sea fish was negligible. Fish weirs, U-shaped walls of stakes, had long been built on river banks to trap the fish; because they became a hazard to shipping they were eventually banned 'except by the sea coast'.[48] Along the shore, men took advantage of the tides: as the tide ebbed fish would be trapped by stakes or stones. Weirs were still in use in the early fourteenth century in Wells[49] (and indeed continued in some East coast harbours until the nineteenth century). Shellfish were picked up by hand at low tide.

Sea fishing from boats became important in the twelfth century. It appears to have been first introduced by St Wilfred in Sussex,[50] lowering nets over the side of boats, but it was the rapid population growth of the twelfth and thirteenth centuries which encouraged the emergence of commercial fisheries. Fresh water fisheries were in decline: sewage, animal waste and industrial effluent from the new communities combined to degrade fish habitats, rivers and lakes. Mill–dams stopped migrating fish and slowed river flow.[51] Whatever the causes, the fishing ports were in a good position to benefit. The numbers and variety of fish were huge – ling, whiting, haddock, plaice, thornbacks, skate, mackerel, hake, dogfish and pollack – though herring and cod were most highly prized. Herring, an oily fish, deteriorated quickly, unlike cod which could be air dried or salted. Any fishing trips would be for one or two nights, rarely for three.[52]

Fishing harbours were developed. In 1252 Scarborough obtained permission to build a stone and timber quay, charging mercantile vessels but also fishing boats to raise the funds for the work.[53] Lynn was carrying on trade in fish with Norway by 1275.[54] Wells had its harbour by then. Clearly methods of preservation had developed: salting the herring in barrels. By the early fourteenth century both

The invention of the barrel enabled fish to be transported in quantity with ease.

Scarborough and Great Yarmouth held fairs for the sale of their wares; that at Yarmouth ran for 43 days from late September to mid November when herring and cod would be bought and sold in huge quantities, much of it exported to Europe.[55] Possibly 1,000 vessels converged on the port.

England was at that time a fish-eating country and East Anglia was in a position to supply it. In October 1313, Edward II put in his Christmas catering order from the counties of Norfolk and Suffolk for consumption by the court and Parliament: twenty lasts of red (smoked) herring; 10,000 cod; 20,000 stockfish and twenty barrels of sturgeon – to be paid for out of debts owed to him by the sheriff of the two counties.[56]

Apart from the plentifulness of its supply there was another reason why communities ate fish – the fast days of the church. The Benedictine diet had been largely vegetarian; in Norman England the transition was made to fish, with lay people increasingly expected to follow suit. The number of fast days when meat was to be avoided increased to a theoretical 182 days a year. Not only Friday but Saturday and, by custom, Wednesday, were non-meat days, not to mention Lent and Advent.[57] The concentration of fast days was between the beginning of Advent to the end of Lent, December to March, before the return of the fish shoals. It therefore became important to develop the means of preservation of fish, cured, wind-dried, salted or smoked. Salted (white) and smoked (red) herring were sold inland, competing with freshwater fish which tended to be more expensive. Lynn had access to the Great Ouse and thus to Cambridge, Ely and even Bedford; Yarmouth to Norwich and Bury. Wells was less accessible. On the other hand fresh herring was transported surprisingly long distances, depending on the weather, in baskets slung over packhorses and wrapped in seaweed or canvas. Moreover, the other little harbours, of which Blakeney was the largest, were able to catch fish far in excess of the needs of the local community. Increasingly from the early fourteenth century fish too were taken to London, whose appetite for fish was insatiable and where 'Blakeney' was known for fish. The term actually included other fishing towns from Wells to Cromer. The rewards were considerable: a catch could be worth twice as much as the value of a vessel and its gear.[58]

The newer ports assumed a quite different importance in the king's name. King Edward I may not have established the chain of coastal harbours but he soon took advantage of it. In 1297 he wrote to the bailiffs here (as well as to Holkham, Yarmouth, Blakeney, Thornham, Wainfleet, Burnham, Lynn and Boston and many dozens of other ports around the country) asking for information about any letters being passed 'out of the realm' by sea, demanding that such letters be brought immediately to the King. Any vessel leaving these shores required a licence and without one would be arrested. This looks like an attempted act of counter-intelligence, to prevent the French from knowing about British war intentions or the disposition of their forces. It was followed on 27 April by the requisition of all vessels of more than forty tons burden to be at the port of Winchelsea by midsummer's day in the King's service. Vessels were required for the carrying of horses among other things. A third request to the same ports in July demanded that ships trading with Gascony should join the fleet. All of this relates to an abortive attempt to prevent the annexation of Flanders by the French King, Philip IV, by means of naval intervention. In spite of the vigorous efforts, the hostilities ended in a truce because Edward I ran out of money.[59]

An apparently similar request for ships was made by Edward II in 1324 'that they shall be ready to set out in the King's service on three days', again of vessels of forty tons or more. Edward was fighting for his life quite literally; the plot against him came from his estranged wife, Isabella, in France. Two years later the request was for vessels of fifty tons or more but in addition, smaller vessels were forbidden to leave the port 'for the sake of fishing, trading, or for any other cause' on pain of forfeiture.[60] The instruction would ensure that all vessels on the high seas were either those in his service or were those of the King's enemies; it may have made life easier for the King but, as so often, it made life much harder for fishing communities. That episode ended in the flight of the King, his capture and death.

Weighty as these matters were from the point of view of dynastic politics, they raise the more domestic question as to whether there were at that time in Wells vessels of more than forty tons. It may be that larger vessels visited the harbour for trade but a list of all vessels which were able to sail out to sea only thirteen years later, in 1337, compiled for the King by William de Wardale, indicates that the boats then were much smaller. The town had thirteen fishing boats and Holkham nine.[61] John Belneyt of Holkham and Ralph Grigge of Wells owned three boats each, and four others owned two each, capable of carrying between twelve and twenty tons.[62] Whether they were large enough to be used as naval transports is uncertain; they were likely, in any case, to have been coastal vessels. The King no doubt sought assistance from every port which might conceivably have vessels for which he had a use. On the other hand, a specific request for a Wells boat 'with men and victuals to furnish it' was made the following April as also to neighbouring ports including Blakeney. Clearly some boats which were deemed not fit for war service were 'arrested' in the process and application had to be made for them to be allowed to fish.[63] Doggers and other little fishing boats were discharged but it appears that larger boats, of which Wells was only required to supply one, were to be arrested for war service.

The sea had become a highway, a source of food and a frontier, but it remained trackless and uncontrollable. It belonged to nobody. Fishermen were hunter-gatherers, competing with each other as with the elements; it was wilder and less subject to order than the land. Fishing was seasonal work: in summer North Sea cod were caught; in the autumn coastal herring as the shoals migrated south; lobster were part of the haul in Lent. The risk of wreck was constant – in winter the seas are heavier – and there was the opportunity to take advantage of it. Trading vessels passing along these shores would be driven on to the treacherous sandbanks when the wind was in the wrong quarter.

These conditions, which could blow up without warning, were an opportunity for those who lived by the sea. The harvest of the sea was a term which could be widely interpreted. Men preyed upon vessels carrying wool from the Wash ports to France and Spain. The richest sheep country lay in the Lindsey division of Lincolnshire. So in 1275 one Peter de Sancto, merchant of Cahors in France, complained that when his ships laden with wool and other merchandise were wrecked on Holkham beach and had been unloaded 'certain men of those parts carried off fifty two sacks of wool and other merchandise to the value of 700 marks'.[64] In 1308 seven local men boarded a ship belonging to Walter Abraham at Burnham, tied him up 'bound his hands behind his back until the blood gushed out at the nails', and carried away the cargo and thereafter took away and broke up his boat.[65]

Piracy presented the opposite danger. Lacking coastal defence vessels, the monarch had to call upon those such as the bailiffs of port towns to assist in dealing with pirates' vessels, which might not always be of foreign origin. Henry III had to call upon the good men of Yarmouth, Lynn, Blakeney and other ports to supply ships 'with all speed, fitted with armaments' to pursue malefactors and disturbers of the peace of the Cinque Ports.[66]

The trade with Norway was likewise lucrative and therefore subject to predation. In 1300 a ship from Norway sailing by Holkham was attacked and goods were carried off into Holkham. One Geoffrey de Whymbergh was brought before the Assizes and tried for the offence.[67] Nothing is known of the cargo but the Norwegians had by this time more or less given up agriculture, relying on the sale of stockfish to make a living. East Anglian vessels from an early date sold grain in return.

From time to time, the sea disgorged of its own. Whales, which were once common in the North Sea, were washed up on Norfolk beaches from time to time. Whaling had been conducted by the Basques since the eleventh century; whales arrived hereabouts of their own accord but were sufficiently prized by manorial lords and local people that those who cut up whales on the beach at Burnham and took away their fat for oil were pursued with the authority of the law.[68] By the sixteenth century they had all but disappeared.

Bad weather, plague and revolt

Inland, Norfolk's wheat country lay to the east; on the north and west coasts the soils were lighter and barley grew better. Sheep flocks were essential to the fertility of the land; supplemented by a certain amount of dairy farming[69] they aided the growing of barley. Manorial organisation had long begun to decay, with money services replacing the provision of labour, though many feudal incidents such as the need to pay a fine in order to marry remained. Boon works at harvest were often still required. Where the lord was remote from some of his manors, he would be likely to sell the produce and buy locally for his estate needs. In the late thirteenth century three-fifths of the population of the country was of unfree status overall but locally there was a growing number of small freeholders, over half the total.

As we have seen, the various agricultural improvements such as manuring and marling increasingly put land under the plough. These were the days of what was called 'high farming' with which was associated the growth in the corn trade. A change in weather patterns brought it to an end. The period from 1315 to 1322, and for some time after, sometimes called the Great Famine, was marked by a series of poor seasons following one after the other: summers were cold, winters wet so that land could not always be ploughed when necessary; grain grew poorly, hay could not be made. Coastal flooding inundated thousands of acres of land.[70] The abbot of Ely had noted in 1316 that 'a great part of the land [around the Wash was] submerged by the sea'.[71] Twelve such events apparently occurred between 1250 and 1350.[72] From our earlier account it is plain that London was the more eager to obtain necessary supplies from hereabouts in such circumstances. We cannot know whether the capital's cornmongers found surpluses in Norfolk or whether it simply outbid local people. Its financial muscle would be a recurring problem to provincial markets.

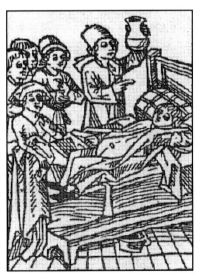

A contemporary woodcut depicting treatment for disease.

To add to this, epidemic disease spreading from Europe killed plough oxen and dairy cattle

33

alike. Many people were driven to the point of starvation; marriages were delayed sometimes for years. We may guess that access to fish would have been vital at such times. Such hardship turned people against outsiders, and drove them to desperate remedies. Criminal gangs were recorded roaming the countryside. North Norfolk was a difficult area to police; the marshes and their little ports were good places in which to hide. Thus in 1317 John de Thorpe, 'a conservator of the peace', was commissioned to enquire into the activities of certain 'disturbers of the peace who are accustomed to land on the sea coast between Lynn and Blakeney where they are received and entertained and to hold conventicles of the malefactors of those parts, passing to and fro between town and town to commit trespasses threatening the people with death.'[73]

Whatever the problems of high food prices resulting from poor harvests (and London's greater ability to suck in grain supplies even at the risk of starving local people) they were as nothing compared with the coming of the Black Death in 1349. The disease was carried by fleas that live on rats, probably bubonic plague. It was brought over on board ship, the first case being at Weymouth in June 1348. It carried off over a third of the population of Europe and had its effects locally. It also marked a watershed in the life of rural communities. Suddenly there was a huge shortage of labour. (The epidemic can scarcely have left mariners alone either.) The land was often untilled and labourers, forbidden by the Statute of Labourers 1351 from demanding higher wages, nevertheless did so. The disease seems to have been virulent locally; most of the parishes suffered the loss of one or more of their clergy. Warham lost its priest; Wighton lost three in two years. Philip de Handbury, who had been appointed vicar of Wells in 1327, was spared; he lived until 1366.[74] Bishop Bateman of Norwich wrote to the pope that he had lost over a thousand clergy in 1349; he asked for a dispensation to license sixty youths of but twenty years of age to hold the benefices to which he had instituted them.[75] All this gives some clue as to the effect on the communities which they served.

The disease recurred in subsequent years,[76] emptying houses but also giving opportunities to those who survived. Empty dwellings could be used to house animals in winter; land left untilled could be added to another man's use. Some of the survivors prospered. There is some evidence of a revival of the sea trade. By 1370, vessels from Wells, Blakeney and Holkham were engaged in the trade in wheat, barley and malt.[77] The visitation of the parish by the archdeacon of Norfolk in 1368 revealed a parish not utterly in disarray. The rector reported that he had a full set of vestments and vessels, missals and prayer books. He even had a copy of the popular new priest's manual, *Pupilla Oculi*, which showed he was very up to date.[78] Published in three volumes, it provided instructions on everything from the taking of services, the answering of religious questions, tithes, baptisms, marriage, confession, baptism and the burial of the dead. Hearing confessions was an important part of the duties of parochial clergy in which the relationships between landlord and tenant had come to be of concern. Clergy were expected to ask whether excessive demands were made of the latter and whether they were lax in their performance of their duties to the former. Of all the local matters in which posterity is bound to be tantalisingly ignorant, the words of penitent and confessor are most properly no one else's business.

Some men were opportunistic; others were desperate. It was a time of almost unprecedented change. Men once tied to the land by their status as villeins simply went in search of work elsewhere, now freed from their fealty. The manorial system, already loosened, began to break down and with it the system of taxation. Half a million taxpayers had simply disappeared. The new system of poll tax, a tax upon people, fell most heavily on the most populous region of the country, East Anglia.[79]

One effect was the so-called Peasants' Revolt of the summer of 1381. Initially focussed in London, it rapidly affected the eastern counties including Norfolk, and the warlike bishop of Norwich, Henry Despenser, was called upon to quell the uprising. The conflagration spread rapidly, carried, it appears, by men on horseback travelling from village to village locally in the name of a dyer from North Walsham called Geoffrey Litster. The violence was at first directed at the tax collectors, but became more diffuse; Flemish merchants in Norwich and Yarmouth were made scapegoats so that a number of them were killed though they had nothing to do with the initial causes of the revolt. Some actions were directed against those against whom there were specific grievances: there were attacks on law officers and on the holders of manorial records which held them in thrall, the records of their status as villeins. Binham Priory was attacked and its records destroyed probably for just this reason; likewise, a Justice of the Peace near Walsingham was pursued in peril of his life so that he boarded a boat and was chased as far as Burnham.[80] Perhaps this was the message that spread so quickly – that such actions would give them their freedom. In some cases, charters were not merely destroyed; they were replaced. Other property was not, by and large, attacked; nor in the countryside were lives taken.

The revolt ended as quickly as it had begun. Like a strong wind it blew itself out. Superficially, the old order was restored but the revolt was a symbol that the back of the manorial system was broken. In the years that followed a new class of prosperous tenant farmers arose, some of them even literate and interested in education. The average size of holdings increased as rents fell. The lords became rentiers rather than agriculturalists; even demesne land, that farmed by the lord himself, was rented out. Thus occurred 'the silent revolution by which the administrative initiative in the vill[age] passed from the manor to the parish.'[81] With the loss of manpower, tenants tended to turn arable land into pasture for sheep.

The rise in wages at first caused food prices to increase but the overall effect of the fall in population was to bring them down. It was one factor in the decline of the East Coast fishing industry during these years. Prices did not recover; the herring fishing suffered from falling catches; Icelandic cod fishing was dangerous and expensive. It would be some time before there was a significant recovery.[82]

Conditions were not helped by the recurrence of floods. In 1416, Peterstone priory declared that they were in sore straits from the inundation of 1378, and the still more serious inundation of 1387[83] which must have included the marshes and low lying properties of the town. (For the priory buildings to have been reached by the water

Binham Priory – a Benedictine foundation.

would have meant that the tide would have risen half way up Staithe Street in Wells.)

With the gradual weakening of the old manorial order and its courts, even before the Black Death, the king's justice was more and more claimed as supreme. The first Justices of the Peace had been appointed in 1327, the power reconferred and the title given in 1361. These were local men appointed to administer justice but they owed allegiance to the Crown not to the manorial lords. Petty Sessions in Wells were held in alehouses.

Opinions differ as to how successful they were. England in the fourteenth century was not a law-abiding country: good order was not helped by the fact that, for purposes of war, every male from the ages of fifteen to sixty was required to possess arms which, even in the case of the poorest, meant a bow and arrow and a knife. 'To arm the population entailed arming its numerous criminals . . . able bodied men of the village, trained to act as a military unit, could without difficulty organise themselves in defiance of the law'.[84] By 1388 six justices were appointed to the county, raised to eight in 1390. The king's judges had visited on circuit (in eyre) since the twelfth century hearing cases presented by local people; the new justices were a permanent presence and were to have an increasing importance in the life of the community.

3. The parish and its world

The change from a manorial society to one based upon the parish (and, increasingly, on towns) in the early years of the fifteenth century was slow and uneven. The Black Death had not immediately altered the pattern of relationships but the recurrence of the disease, notably in 1361 and 1375, increased the pressure for change. Those who had owed the king knight service – the duty to provide military assistance – had long converted that obligation into a money payment, no more than a rent; their successors were to become the new gentry. Likewise there were villeins who had land which they dealt in and acquired more who were becoming yeoman farmers.

As for the artisan classes, one feature was the increase in the number of men who were no longer employed exclusively or at all on the land. These were craftsmen and tradesmen who made and repaired carts, who worked in metal, shoeing horses and mending ploughs. As coal replaced charcoal as a means of heating iron so the work became more sophisticated. There were weavers and millers and those who worked for them. The houses of the gentry required skilled carpenters and builders – brick became a building material in these years. Above all there was a need for men to service the fishing, whether by building or repairing boats or by servicing the tackle. Much would be done within families and few people could manage without a variety of skills. Wells would have provided largely for itself. Little by little trade produced greater degrees of specialisation.

The development of the fishery

When the fishing boats came into Wells harbour, the sight of a sail on the horizon would set off a flurry of activity. By the time a vessel came up the winding channel to the harbour, dozens of folk would be waiting. As the fish were landed in baskets the buying and selling would begin, bargaining and arguing as the fish were piled high on the strand. The stewards or bailiffs of the great manorial and monastic households would buy directly as the fish was landed. Ordinary townsfolk may have been less lucky as dealers attempted to buy up the catch. Increasingly trade was done by middlemen. Most fishermen would not engage in trade; if they could they would sell the fish from the dock and were encouraged by authority, the bailiffs, to do so.

In some places the merchants would forestall those wishing to buy off the Quay by sailing out to meet the fishing fleet to buy the fish and resell them at higher prices. Those living inland were even more vulnerable to 'forestallers' who might buy the whole catch in order to sell at markets when higher prices could be commanded. So widespread was this that legislation was passed requiring that fish should only be unloaded in Blakeney haven and by daylight and only after prices had been agreed.[1] Attempts were made to divert fish from recognised markets in order to avoid tolls. Eventually, in 1534 an Act of Parliament would outlaw the selling of fish to merchants on shore or even to the ship-owners. This was intended to prevent unscrupulous merchants from systematically buying up the stocks of fish and inflating their price at the three East Anglian fish fairs at Ely, St Ives and Sturbridge. The trouble was that it hindered the fishermen from making a quick return and

 reduced the viability of the fishery. Its repeal in 1543 seems initially not to have improved matters.

As bigger vessels were built fishermen became more and more adventurous. On the other hand, the further out to sea the fishing boats ventured the more likely they were to encounter competition.

Herring Fishing from Olaus Magnus Historia de Gentibus Septentrionalibus 1555.

During the fourteenth century, England found herself engaged in two international conflicts over fishing: against the merchants of the Hanse over herring and against the Danes over the Iceland cod fishery.

The Hanse, the Hanseatic League of German merchants, was the formalisation in 1356 of a series of trade alliances between German cities associated with Bruges, Lübeck, Visby, Rostock and as far away as Novgorod. It controlled trade and defended the interests of its members. Its influence extended as far as Bergen and included Danzig as well as many inland cities. Because of its monopolistic power it was able in 1369 to ban English merchants from salting and barrelling locally herring caught off the Norwegian coast. In 1371 English merchants, trying to buy the local produce, the so-called Scania herring, were prevented from trading it for English cloth rather than with ready money. Scania herring was a highly sought-after product; it had driven the poorer East Anglian version from the market. Being gutted and packed between layers of salt in wooden casks, and then repacked in fresh brine, its shelf-life was of up to a year. This made it a preferred product when inland transport was slow and difficult.[2] English merchants were therefore happy to obtain it but its import did nothing for the home herring fishery. Eventually, the art of salting herring was learned by English fishermen too.

Had the league been a mere trading organisation with monopolistic powers matters would have been difficult enough. As it was the lawful activities of its traders was accompanied by acts of piracy and murder. An agreement finally reached by Henry IV and merchants of the league, that compensation be paid for various acts of piracy, indicates that the ports of the north Norfolk coast were the major victims. Lynn and its adjacent ports as well as Cley and Wiveton were among those most affected. Ships were boarded and taken to the Norwegian port of Marstrand where their cargoes and gear were removed. In 1412 it was reported that a hundred fishermen of Cromer, Blakeney and other towns of the coast of Norfolk were murdered after having fled the privateers of the Hanse to the port of Wynforde in Norway; they were bound hand and foot and thrown into the sea.[3] Gradually, relations became less violent if not more cordial. The Hanse established premises in Kings Lynn and secured exemption from local taxes.

Government regulation and taxation were constant factors as attempts were made to obtain revenues from a continually changing but at times very profitable enterprise. The protection of the fishery in time of war was one element of this. One example was the instruction in 1374 by Edward III that no taxes were to be levied on fish landed in Wells and other nearby ports provided it was not sold on out of the country. The local fishermen had petitioned the king to be relieved of this 'subsidy' – the word means tax – and they were clearly heard.[4] Sometimes government sought to protect foreign merchants, as we shall see in relation to the wool trade, but one pressure exerted at this time was that England was at war with France and fish was a valuable source of food.

Apart from human interference, there remained the intrinsic variability of the behaviour of the fish. The herring shoals seemed unaccountably to have altered their behaviour and disappeared from their Baltic feeding grounds. Cod was eaten by the Royal Household in the fourteenth century, supplied by the Norwegians. Again the Hanse proved an obstacle. By 1357 there was an active cod fishery working from Blakeney, Cley and Wells, initially off the Dogger Bank which had become known as a rich fishing ground. By 1383 they were fishing off Norway. Sometimes they stayed away for as long as six months; selling fish abroad or dispatching them to England by smaller boats or, increasingly, air-drying them to preserve them. Certainly by 1408 Englishmen were fishing off Iceland. It was a perilous trade. The voyage, which took about a fortnight to complete, took ships through the violent waters of the Pentland Firth off the Orkneys, 'the most daungerouse place of all Christendom',[5] where strong currents and frequent storms took their toll. Twenty-five vessels were sunk off Iceland in a single day in a storm in April 1419. East Anglian vessels were slow to establish a regular fishery, but the greater demands placed on mariners pushed forward developments in boat design and technology. Initially they sailed in vessels of ten to fifteen tons burden, tiny vessels by later standards. Contemporary

accounts tell of the trade in 'stokfishe', cod caught and air dried before being sold by Icelanders to the English.[6]

The background to the venture is that Iceland, having become a Norwegian dependency in 1262, was then, by the Union of Kalmar of 1397, united with Sweden and Denmark, the

Cod fishing with lines from Olaus Magnus Historia de Gentibus Septentrionalibus 1555.

latter country being the dominant partner. The Danes were apparently not much interested in their distant possession, failing even to send the promised six vessels a year with the necessary supplies to supplement the island's scant resources. The Danes insisted nevertheless that all fish exports should pass through the staple town of Bergen on the Norwegian coast. When the English appeared off Iceland in 1412, its people were at first hostile to the English fishermen but they began to recognise that they could both sell and buy from them. The doggers from East Anglia came to fish but also to buy dried 'stockefish' from Icelanders and then, in response to need, to bring the grain which the locals could not grow and the metal goods which they had not the fuel to smelt. They brought wood for building and for boats, good cloth to dress them and much else which their home country had failed to supply. Merchants' vessels now accompanied the fishing fleet. They ignored the prohibitions coming from the mainland. It came to be known to the Icelanders as 'the English century'.

Eventually, seeing the decline of Bergen as a result of this trade, a new Danish governor imposed a more restrictive regime.[7] Where hitherto the Icelanders had scarcely seen a merchant vessel, over the last quarter of the century its harbours became crowded with vessels mostly from the Hanse, eager to sell a variety of commodities and to buy a single commodity, fish. Attempts by the Danes to restrict and then prohibit trade had been longstanding, as far back as 1430. They tried to get the English crown to enforce their prohibition, but to little avail. So great was the prize in fish that what was forbidden by law was ignored by the fishermen themselves and even the licensing system which allowed the English a certain degree of trade was largely ignored by both fishermen and merchants. From Scarborough, from Lynn, from Dersingham, from Burnham, from Wells, from Cley and from Cromer they went.[8] Edward IV issued licences indiscriminately. Relations deteriorated such that in 1467 the governor of Iceland, Bjorn Thorleifsson, was killed by Englishmen as he tried to enforce the regulations.[9] This led to a full scale Baltic war[10] which, combined with Hanseatic interference, brought the fishery to a halt.

Forced to look elsewhere, the West Country ports like Bristol turned to Newfoundland for fish; but with East Anglia it was different. The securing of a treaty in 1490 allowed the fishery to resume. Fishermen from Wells, Blakeney, Cley and Wiveton began again to undertake expeditions to Iceland. Relationships improved; and when Henry VII received a further complaint about the conduct of English fishermen from his cousin the king of Denmark, he instructed local fishermen effectively to pay for what they took and not to drive too hard a bargain.[11] By 1528 no fewer than 149 vessels were making the voyage to Iceland, almost all of them from Norfolk and Suffolk; a small proportion, six, were from Wells.[12] Vessels ranged in size between twenty and ninety tons, a fleet in the region of 8,500 tons burden in total.

The conduct of war

Something has already been said about the use of fishing vessels in war. Given that we are an island nation it may seem strange that England has not at all times had a standing navy, particularly as England was on bad terms with its neighbours over much of the period. Naval fleets were created to meet need. In the ninth century King Alfred's navy was a major factor in uniting the country against the Danes; the success of the Norman invasion turned on the fleet William had assembled. To meet the threat of invasion by the French, in 1209 King John spent £5,000 on building fifty-four ships – mostly oared galleys similar to Viking ships.[13] The defeat of the French at the Battle of Sandwich in 1217, 'one of the most decisive mediaeval naval battles in northern waters,[14] ended the threat for the time being.

However, this left the English with a single French possession, Gascony to the south, while the coastline opposite southern and eastern England was in French, usually hostile, hands. Under the circumstances it is remarkable that the maintenance of a standing navy was considered too expensive and the fleet was allowed to decay. If the realm were to be defended, let alone aggressive action against the French mounted, merchant and fishing vessels would have to be used, both to transport troops and to engage with enemy ships. The requisitioning of ships from harbours around the country became a feature of government demands. We have already seen Edward I's use of his power of requisition in his dealings over Flanders.

The Hundred Years War with France, usually dated 1337 to 1453, marked the change from defensive requisitioning to aggression. Edward III had resolved to become king of France. Throughout his reign, and through five reigns in all, occurred the spectacular resurgence (and eventual collapse) of English influence in mainland Europe in which probably every community was involved.

In the conduct of warfare both on land and at sea, the use of the longbow was a most important factor. Every community was required to train men in the skill of using it; long practice was required in order to become proficient. Demand from the King was high. The difficulty was that men could not both shoot arrows and sail ships; the latter was sometimes the greater need. Arguments have run to and fro about whether the Buttlands, the local green space in the centre of town, was used for such a purpose; it is said to have been too small. Locals must have trained somewhere; Wells archers were called for service in 1338, but then allowed to stand down because, instead, the Admiral of the Fleet, Walter de Mauny, wanted a ship for the King's service with men and victuals to serve it.[15] Previously in 1295 the king had sought to recruit 8,000 archers from the counties of Norfolk, Suffolk, Cambridgeshire and Huntingdonshire, part of a force of 25,000.[16] In any event the naval battle that followed at Sluys off the Dutch coast in 1340 resulted in the destruction of almost the whole of the French fleet of some 198 vessels.

Naval warfare in those years was conducted at close quarters, not hugely different from land battles, with bows and arrows the main weaponry. Square sailed vessels could not sail effectively to windward; oared vessels called, at different times, galleys or balingers were more manoeuvrable but having a lower freeboard they were overlooked by the taller cogs whose crews could pelt their crews with stones or shoot them with arrows.[17] When vessels came alongside, they might be held together with grappling hooks, when cold steel and, by the fifteenth century, hand guns became the weapons of choice. So-called 'ship killers', cannons, were only in the process of being developed, making more noise than producing destructive effect.

The most successful land battle of the war was the battle of Crecy in 1346. It was preceded by the largest seaborne invasion of mainland Europe before D-Day. A fleet of more than 1,000 ships was assembled at Portsmouth, summoned in secret and including trading and fishing boats from ports all around the country. Remarkably, unlike almost every other great campaign of the period, almost nothing appears in official records. So obsessed was Edward by the fear of espionage that the invasion took the French completely by surprise. Such was its scale, involving some 14,000 men not to mention horses, supplies and the new secret weapon, the bombard, an early form of cannon, that Norfolk men, vessels and probably archers were engaged in some numbers.[18] Crecy, Poitiers and Agincourt marked the high points of the war; the victory at Agincourt in 1415 was followed by a series of poor diplomatic decisions and lost battles ending in the less well-known battle of Castillon in 1453. This was the final reverse.

Not only its men but the town's ability to supply the troops with victuals was in demand. Thus it is recorded that in 1327 Richard atte Wode, the king's Serjeant at Arms, was deputed to purchase victuals for one month for the maintenance of forty men at sea 'who lately set out with Robert de Scales in the King's company upon the sea for the defence of the realm and the repulse of the King's enemies in France' including three heifers from the constable of the town of Wells.[19]

The demands of war also included money. The cross channel wool trade had been hard hit. The king sought to raise money from the shires but also to borrow it, largely from Italian merchants. It is a reminder of how international was trade in those days, largely as a result of the Italian appetite for English wool. Bartholomew Bardi, merchant of Florence, is described as one of the king's merchants. He it was who financed the release of the manors of Wells and Warham in which one Hugh de la Palice held a life interest.[20] Without such sources of liquidity the king simply could not conduct business. Later, prior to Agincourt, huge sums of money and victuals were assembled from all over the country.

The king's demands placed considerable pressure on local resources at once fragile and variable. The peremptory requisitioning of vessels impeded trade, halted fishing and, as a result, deprived coastal communities of their means of subsistence. The frequent demands for the use of vessels, softened only in the case of vessels away in Gascony, evidently drove local fishermen and merchants to passive and sometimes active resistance. It is not therefore surprising that in April 1380 Wells mariners, when arrested by the serjeant-at-arms with their boats to serve the Admiral of the north, 'besieged [the serjeant and his officers] in a barn, threatening to kill them, until they were rescued' and released. The miscreants were brought before the king and Council.[21] Much later, in 1437, a number of Norfolk mariners persuaded the king's council to release from military service a number of fishing vessels, 'having shown to the king and the council that the principal season for fishing is between Easter and Michaelmas' .[22] The loss of a fishing season was not merely economically damaging; it was life-threatening. It seems unlikely that the government did not know when the fishing season was but government priorities were different.

On the other hand, fishermen, going about their lawful business, were always at risk from attack and might require assistance from others. Local fishermen had for some time protected themselves by sailing in convoy. The escalation in attacks demanded a better response and in 1377 after French attacks on local fishing, some Norfolk men fitted out five ships to chase the French away.[23] Later, this was to become more organised still. In 1469, the Duke of Norfolk was being paid up to 20 shillings per vessel for offering protection to fishing vessels.[24] In the early 1480s Crown protection against Scottish and Hansard attacks was arranged for East Anglian boats fishing in the North Sea. So in 1484 East Anglian vessels sailing for Iceland were ordered to assemble in the Humber and proceed only as an escorted convoy. This process, called 'wafting', continued until the reign of Henry VIII.

The ships

As to what kind of vessels sailed from Wells in those days we only partly know. There were over sixty names for different kinds of vessel, but none of them are described with any accuracy in contemporary accounts.[25] There is no space to write of ships, barges, crayers, doggers, cogs, hulks, carracks, galleys, carvels, balingers, lodeships, farcostas, cobles and the rest but even if there were, we know little enough about them. We have to rely on the scant evidence of the seals of towns such as that illustrated here and occasional survivals dug out of the harbour silt by archaeologists. The first distinction often made is between the keel-less hulk (which has been described not unfairly as shaped like a banana) and the cog. The latter, as it developed, became the trading vessel of choice for nations on both sides of the North Sea. Originally without a keel, its stem and stern posts and deep draft gave it great carrying capacity and it was simple to construct. With its straight bows and deep keel, it was, as it was sometimes said, most sea-kindly.

But when we look in the records of fishing vessels plying off Wells we find no mention of cogs, only of 'doggers', 'crayers' and 'lodeships'. 'Doggers' were undoubtedly fishing vessels, usually small, apparently up to eighteen tons but often much smaller. Even so they were used for long voyages. In 1383, cod were being sought off Norway by Blakeney doggers, spending up to six months away from home; they claimed that they were unsuitable for naval service (because they were too small to carry horses).[26] (Later they would be built up to eighty tons.) 'Crayers' on the other hand were single-masted trading vessels between twenty and fifty tons. Both are recorded in the Patent Rolls of 1449 as sailing out of Wells.[27] 'Lodeships', which feature heavily in the lists of 1437, appear to be pilot vessels, which suggests that they were small, though apparently large enough to be requisitioned for war service. John Grigge was a Wells owner of several such vessels.

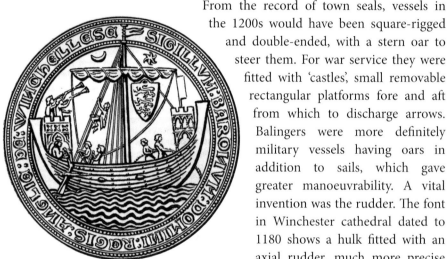

The seal of Winchelsea showing a single–masted vessel.

From the record of town seals, vessels in the 1200s would have been square-rigged and double-ended, with a stern oar to steer them. For war service they were fitted with 'castles', small removable rectangular platforms fore and aft from which to discharge arrows. Balingers were more definitely military vessels having oars in addition to sails, which gave greater manoeuvrability. A vital invention was the rudder. The font in Winchester cathedral dated to 1180 shows a hulk fitted with an axial rudder, much more precise and effective than a stern oar; that development was, like many others, slow and irregular; without it long voyages would have been well nigh impossible. Vessels also carried a primitive compass; like the rudder it was invented by the Chinese: both reached the west by the twelfth century. When first used the compass had been merely a piece of wood mounted with a needle floating in a tub of water. The needle had to be rubbed with a lodestone before each use. The pivoted compass permanently magnetised, with a card showing the points of sailing, came only in the fifteenth century. Before the compass, sailors had had to rely on various means for ascertaining their position; one was the presence of birds as indicating land, a perilous enterprise almost beyond belief. It was no wonder that most vessels hugged the coasts, thus, of course, increasing the distance they had to travel. Storms at sea were greatly feared and, in reality, sailing close to the coast was often more dangerous. More widely used was the sounding lead to measure the depth of water under the ship; a hole in the bottom of the lead was filled with tallow to which samples of the sea floor might adhere, thus giving a clue as to the vessel's position.[28] Lead lines were particularly useful in the shoal waters hereabouts.

Most vessels were of dual use, carrying cargo and fishing; the main difference was between undecked inshore boats and larger vessels, fully decked, used for long voyages. The latter were better at keeping the water out, always a fundamental objective.

As to where they were built, we must guess. Lynn was certainly a place where boats were built in the early fourteenth century but it seems likely that boats were built either in Wells or in one or more of the Glaven ports; they must have been repaired locally. As we know from nineteenth century shipbuilding, the sites were inland, up narrow rivers, sheltered from the sea.

The striking advance in ship design came in the 1400s with the development of two-masted vessels. The mainmast was square rigged as before but the mizzen was provided with a three cornered lateen sail, set fore and aft, enabling vessels to sail closer to the wind.[29] This was to have a dramatic effect on average sailing speeds. Secondly, the 'castles' were now integral to the vessel, the prow higher allowing vessels to take the sea better. Average speeds varied hugely. Under ideal conditions vessels were capable of up to eight knots; but speeds to windward were less than a knot even if sailing was possible and, on the run to Bordeaux, vessels tended to hug the coast and to seek harbour in the face of storms. The round trip would take between 93 and 150 days, an average speed of just over half a knot. Travelling in convoy reduced vessels to the speed of the slowest.[30]

Coal, barley and sheep

As we have seen, the Iceland fishery brought with it trade. Much of it came to be dominated by foreign vessels of the Hanse, but the coastwise trade, particularly in coal and grain, was carried on by local ships. Sea coal, as it was called, had been picked off beaches of the north-east of England or recovered from shallow drifts into cliffs for centuries. A more advanced method of extraction was the sinking of vertical shafts into the earth. Bell pits, so called, were vertical shafts sunk down to the seam some feet below and expanded in all directions as the coal was removed in buckets. As the area of extraction grew wider so grew the risk of collapse. When this seemed likely (or after it had happened) a fresh shaft was dug a distance away. From as early as 1228 there was a trade in coal between the north-east and London.[31] By 1508, there was a regular trade between Wells and Newcastle, as many

Graffito of a 15th century sailing ship.

as three shipments on the same tide. As the coal was delivered, the boats were loaded with barley, rye, wheat, malt, herrings and meslin (a mixed grain of wheat and rye) to take north. Wells was the largest importer of coal of any of the ports on the north coast, with over seventy movements over a three year period; interestingly, Burnham, in the early 1500s, imported more coal than Blakeney. The Wells vessels made the trip very irregularly, sometimes once a fortnight, sometimes not for six months; some, like the *George*, made only one trip over a three year period. They were, presumably, engaged in other trade or fishing the rest of the time. Hugh Tydd, whose devout family figures at various times in the life of the town, and John Atkins were among the masters who engaged in the trade. It is likely that, as with Kings Lynn, they were members of one of the gilds, which might then corporately have taken an interest in the harbour.

The vessels themselves carried thirty tons or more; the measurement then in use was the chauldron which, in the case of coal, was a measure equivalent at that time to twenty-one hundredweight, just over a ton.[32] The twin purposes of the trade were the import of coal for burgeoning manufacturing and the export of grain to feed the miners of the north-east. Unlike those of many other ports, Wells vessels rarely made the northward trip in ballast, in other words, loaded with stones or sand to stabilise the vessel. Apart from the fact that ships arriving in Newcastle were penalised for their trouble by having to pay for its discharge, Wells vessels had wheat, barley and malt to bring.[33]

That this was the case gives the lie to the claims later made that north Norfolk was, before the nineteenth century enclosures, a wasteland where, it was said, two rabbits would fight over the same blade of grass.[34] In fact, the combination of sheep and corn, so-called sheep corn husbandry, had been operated by peasant farmers in East Anglia for centuries, making the light soil ideal for the growing of corn, particularly barley. Sheep were put on the stubble after the harvest and remained until it had to be sown or, if it was to be fallow, the whole year, fertilising the soil with their dung. During the growing season, the sheep would be moved onto the marshes or the common. Thus it was at Holkham[35] and probably at Wells too. The areas of foldcourses, land set aside for sheep after the harvest, were fixed leaving some of the arable land for the tenants' cattle. Tenants at Holkham were also able to share the heathland for their horses, cattle and pigs. All of this required close cooperation between landlord and tenant. If land was overstocked or the limits of the foldcourse were exceeded; if flock-owners let their sheep onto tenants' winter corn or if shackage (the right to pasture on stubble after harvest) was refused, the arable farmers would suffer.

The new breed of yeoman farmers, those who had done well out of the dislocation occasioned by the Black Death, were just the men to destabilise the system. They were more inclined to drive hard bargains and to engage in those practices which made the foldcourse system more difficult to make work. Men like John Townshend of Raynham would become both sheep farmers and merchants, buying grain from local monasteries and acquiring land. When Coxford priory got into financial difficulties, John Gygges of Wighton was given the task of administering its property. These men were both socially and geographically mobile. So John Pepys, the son of a Cambridgeshire yeoman, settled in South Creake and bought a manor at Holkham. Some sent their sons off to train as lawyers – they rose up the social scale, but the source of their wealth was sheep. '[I]n West Norfolk sheep rearing was at least as important as grain production with which it was so closely linked'.[36] Different interests made for conflict.

Increasingly sheep were sold for their meat but it was wool prices which determined the size of flocks. As they rose in the 1460s so flocks increased. In 1516, Roger Townshend had 18,000 sheep in his many flocks across the county. When prices fell after 1534, his flocks shrank to fewer than 5,000. Records of sales show that most of it was sold locally, occasionally as far as Bedfordshire, Hertfordshire and Northamptonshire. Many of Townshend's customers were parish gilds; others were butchers, including several of the pilgrimage town of Walsingham.[37] Unlike grain, the processes by which wool was turned into clothing was complex, requiring a range of skills most often exercised by different people often in different places. Shorn or plucked wool passed into the hands of a wool-brogger (broker) and from him to a clothier who organised its manufacture into cloth.[38] The wool had to be cleaned, oiled, sorted, carded or combed and then spun. It would then be woven, after which it would be fulled (pre-shrunk), dyed, its nap then removed with shears before it could be sold. Some of Townshend's wool may have found its way to the Norwich worsted weavers.

As for the barley, some was turned into malt. Farm malting for local consumption was normal though some undertook malting under contract. The Townshends sent their malt to Cromer, Cley and Thornham and beyond, often by sea. Wells, as the most convenient port, with a considerable fleet of traders, was the preferred route for the distant trade. Townshend's accounts for 1476–77 refer to the cost of transporting sixty quarters to a ship waiting in Wells harbour.[39]

The parish at prayer

Norfolk is full of churches; of the 900 known to have existed over 650 remain. Great men had them built and extended; the affluent among the tenantry regarded them

North Barsham parish church, 13th century.

as a source of local pride; monasteries saw them as a source of income and local influence; parishioners saw them as the gate of heaven, in token of which they put their money into them.[40] The earliest church in Wells is likely to have pre-dated 1200; the Norman lords built churches in every settlement. Few of them remain as originally built but North Barsham gives a clue as to the style: a two room building with a nave and chancel with tall narrow windows. In 1251 the Wells advowson, the legal right to appoint the priest of the church, was given to the de Clares by the Abbott of Fonteney in France.[41] The first known vicar of was John de Syderstone, presented in 1302 by Gilbert the last of the de Clares. The church was worth thirty one marks (£21) in 1291 and paid tithe to Binham priory of £2 2s 8d.

Most churches were altered and added to at various times over the four hundred or so years of church building before the Reformation. This was often done in grand style, particularly in the latter half of the fifteenth century and the early part of the next. They were the years of the Wars of the Roses but also the years of rebuilding. The luxuriantly ornate 'Decorated' style of architecture had dominated the thirteenth century. By the fourteenth it was replaced by a more austere style, later called Perpendicular, because of its larger straight mullioned windows, ideal for stained glass; it produced more splendid towers, loftier naves and stone roofs. Not only biblical scenes but the arms of the patrons might be displayed on the windows. In Wells church the great east window carried the arms of Lord Stafford, impaling those of the Duke of Gloucester as well of those of Stafford and Neville.[42]

The de Clare line failed in 1314 with the death of Gilbert at the battle of Bannockburn. His estates were divided up between his three sisters and their husbands, one of them being Hugh de Audeley first Earl of Gloucester. As we have seen, their daughter, Margaret de Audeley was abducted by Ralph, first Earl of Stafford and taken in marriage. Their grandson, Edward the fifth Earl, married Ann, daughter of Thomas of Woodstock, Duke of Gloucester in 1398. In turn, Edward and Ann's son Humphrey married Ann Neville. All of this was represented in the church's windows by the depiction of their arms. (Because they were secular, the windows survived the Reformation at which all religious imagery, whether in windows, on fonts or walls, was defaced or smashed on the grounds that it was idolatrous. The windows were eventually lost in a storm in 1810.)

All the manorial lords who were patrons of the church were royally connected; all were to be directly engaged, one way or the other, in the Wars of the Roses, which occupied virtually the whole of the second half of the fifteenth century. Humphrey, who became Duke of Buckingham and who appointed Thomas Bradley as incumbent in 1446, was one of the largest landowners in the country. He took the side of the Lancastrians and died at the battle of Northampton in 1460, defeated by the Earl of Warwick, another member of the Neville family. Humphrey's grandson, the second duke, was beheaded by Richard III for treason. Both of these, or rather their widows, acted as patrons for the parish. A third widow, Catherine, Duchess of Buckingham, was the sister-in-law of Edward IV. She appointed John Danby in 1495.

How far the heady brew of politics and nobility, alliances and betrayals, wars and executions, impinged upon the life of the community of Wells is hard to tell. With the decline of the manorial system the new breed of gentry assumed greater powers. From local wills it appears that small landowners and mariners constituted an alternative power base to that of great lords. Their devotion to the church, to its worship and maintenance is clear from their testamentary dispositions.[43]

The fifteenth century was to be the last flourish of mediaeval church building which was taking place right across Europe. In this country it was aided by the relative prosperity brought about by Edward IV's peaceable policies after his return from exile in 1471. (Edward had usurped the saintly Henry VI in 1461, and was himself ousted in 1470 by the old king and his determined queen Margaret of Anjou; he returned under arms a year later, and had his predecessor murdered to ensure that there were no further embarrassments.) The years that followed until his sudden death in 1483 produced the finishing

The 19th century rood in South Creake church.

touches to the church. Completed in one style, large but not excessively grand, with its wide chancel, its side aisles surmounted by clerestories and its fine square tower, it tells us that this was a modestly prosperous town, though one which was, even in those days, at risk from inundation. Over the south door the story of the flood was painted, and over the north door the story of Jonah.[44]

The church was at that time dedicated to All Saints.[45] The chancel was rebuilt during the incumbency of that same Thomas Bradley who was rector from 1446 to 1463;[46] the nave dates from the same period, around 1460.[47] Its rood screen in the chancel arch was surmounted by a loft following the East Anglian pattern, with the exception that the stairway to the loft was contained in a hexagonal turret on the outside of the north wall of the church, both doors being however within the church (it survived the fire of 1879). Roods were large crosses carrying a statue of the crucified Christ and attended by statues of the Virgin Mary and St John; they dominated the naves of mediaeval churches. They were mounted on platforms, called rood lofts, high above the congregation in the chancel arch. (They were to be the target of the Reformers' destructive zeal. Not one survives.) The rood was the focus of the Holy Week liturgy when the Passion gospel would be read from it on Good Friday. The church's low pitched roof carried figures of angels with extended wings on the wall plates between the mouldings as well as angels with shields or swords on the intersection of the ribs and principals, all of them painted with bright colours.[48] As well as stained glass, the walls were painted with pictures of biblical scenes, most probably of Christ's Nativity and his Passion, devotion to which was typical of the period.[49] Lit by numerous flickering candles casting smoky light upon the many figures of the angels and saints at the various altars, it must have been an extraordinary sight.

The church boasted several gilds or fraternities, each of which had an altar dedicated to its saint set around the aisles. One was dedicated to St Nicholas, a second to St George, a third to the Holy Ghost, a fourth to St Thomas, a fifth to All Saints, a sixth to Our Lady,[50] the seventh to the Holy Trinity and the eighth to the gild of St Mary Magdalen.[51] (Not all of them necessarily existed at the same time.) Gilds were popular: Kings Lynn had seventy gilds; Yarmouth nineteen; even little South Creake down the road had seven. Contrary to widespread belief, gilds were

An illuminated antiphoner from Ranworth in Norfolk.

primarily devotional organisations, dedicated to the altar in the church whose lights they would keep burning on Sundays and the many feast days. In some places, like Lynn, they had large gild halls; in others they were more evanescent groupings, sometimes of young men sometimes of 'maydens'. They brought together religious devotion with the more mundane concerns for which they have become known. Any organisation attracts those of like interests, the harbour and the fishery being among them, but a motive force was the observance of the seven corporal works of mercy: feeding the hungry, giving drink to the thirsty, clothing the naked, harbouring the stranger, visiting the sick, ministering to prisoners and burying the dead. These partly derived from the gospel injunction that when such tasks are performed, they are not only done for the needy person, but are acts of service to Christ.[52] Charity on such a view could not be divorced from devotion. Some gilds kept roads and bridges in good repair, often marking them with wayside shrines,[53] demonstrating once again that our modern distinction between sacred and secular was unknown to them. Some kept livestock; others united men of a particular trade. The Holy Trinity Guild at Lynn came to dominate the seaborne trade of the town.[54] The Wells gilds brought together ship-owners, merchants and mariners.

We have no idea how assiduous they were in their works of charity but obsequies over the dead and prayer for the repose of their souls were mediaeval pre-occupations. During those years, most churches in Norfolk rebuilt or extended their roods. Wells was no exception.[55] Gilds played a major part. Men and women believed as much in heaven, hell and purgatory as they believed that their king reigned. Superstitious those times may have been, but church life was thriving.[56]

One of the reasons for this was that much of it was led not by the clergy but by lay people. The various fraternities were often jealous of their role even so far as not tolerating clerical interference.[57] They vied with the gentry in making contributions towards the refurbishment of churches and the provision of the accoutrements of worship. The visitation lists of vestments and plate, not to mention the work of beautifying and making visible the devotional life of the church, all testify to an energy which derived from lay initiative.

Hugh Tydde, possibly the father of the ship owner, who died in 1471, was typical. He left money for candles to be lit at the several altars in the church. As well as the gilds of St George and St Thomas he left money for the shrines of St Cecilia, St Peter, St James, St Clement and St Erasmus. William Clubbe, part owner of two vessels, the *Mary* and the *Thomas*, left money to three of the gilds and a jewel or ornament for the church to the value of £10. Thomas Fuller left money for the light of St Katherine. This was no short term fad: Richard Sutton a hundred and fifty years before had left money for the light of St Nicholas.[58] Moreover, the character of these images also gives an indication of the inextricable link between the church and the community in its various aspects. St Peter and St James were fishermen; St Nicholas, St Clement and St Erasmus were all patron saints of sailors. There was also a pre-occupation with martyrdom; virgin martyrs such as St Katherine and St Cecilia often feature.[59] In an age without analgesia when medicine was primitive, the pains of the sick might be alleviated by the intercession of those saints who had suffered martyrdom. The connection with the land was no less real. Hugh Tydde left money

King Henry VI depicted on the rood screen at Barton Turf.

for the 'plough light', a candle placed before the rood which was a sign of prayer for a good harvest.[60] Plough Monday at the beginning of January was the beginning of the cycle of seasonal observances related to the land. The religion of that time was expressive of the complexity of human life in the town in which the saints were friends and helpers.

The senior Tydde left money to several of the religious houses in the district and to the church. Finally, before disposing of his major assets among his family, he asked that a 'discrete priest [be asked] to celebrate for [his] soul and the souls of all [his] ancestors in the church of All Saints, Wells for three whole years'.[61] Similar dispositions were made as late as 1532.[62] That the living should pray for the dead seemed natural. Heaven and earth were not that far apart.

Local devotion also extended (only a few years after his death) to King Henry VI (1422–71) who was widely regarded as saintly. In his case, it was the king's prayers that were sought for benefit of the living. The process of his canonisation was never completed but his celestial aid was widely sought. Wells was one of a number of local churches to include a shrine to him.[63]

Not everyone agreed. Erasmus, the great Dutch scholar, who had visited Walsingham on two occasions, was subsequently scathing about the relics of saints which were the subject of devotion there. Debate there had always been; that it questioned the very roots of devotion so widely was new. How far it penetrated the life of the parish is hard to say. Edward Lee, who was ordained deacon and given the title of Wells church in 1502, was to become a controversialist and senior churchman: he eventually became Archbishop of York. He was notable for his literary attacks on Erasmus's views, taking a traditionalist line. How much time he spent on our lovely coast, we cannot, of course, say. Parochial posts were sources of income for scholars, and curates often did the actual job. (According to the 1499 diocesan visitation, just under 10% of parishes in the diocese were held by absentees.) Lee resigned in 1532 and died in 1544.[64]

4. The Breaking of the Mould

The world of mediaeval Wells was never stable. There were the vagaries of the seasons and the size of the catch, not to mention the French wars. On the other hand, the commonality of faith produced a kind of internationalism epitomised by the arrival of continental pilgrims to Walsingham through our ports. At any rate fresh causes of dispute generate fresh divisions, and these fresh causes were to come thick and fast.

The Walsingham conspiracy

The sixteenth-century process of the breaking up of the Roman Catholic Church, usually called the Reformation, had a huge effect on ordinary people. What some historians think of as inevitable and predictable came to people like the citizens of Wells as a shock. It changed the pattern of their lives not just on Sundays but on every day of the week. Henry VIII's disagreement with the Pope over his marriages was never the heart of it. His efforts to secure an heir were driven by a desire for stability. What made the break so startling was the change in church life imposed by a government whose ministers were heavily influenced by new thinking about the Bible from the continent. Early manuscripts of the Bible had become newly available; translations from them were at variance in important respects with the authorised Latin version; reform, advocated by many on all sides, took on a particular path. After the break with Rome in 1534, the next step was transfer of all dues formerly paid to the pope to the king. This taxation, called first fruits and annates, was based on the wealth of each church or monastery. There followed a survey of the possessions of churches called the Valor Ecclesiasticus.[1] Shortly after, the decision was taken to demand not a proportion of the income of monasteries but the capital itself. The smaller monasteries were suppressed and, three years later, the larger ones, the proceeds of sale being confiscated. The purposes of some of Henry's reforming ministers and his own need for money for war coincided. The monasteries were not as unpopular as is sometimes thought; many of them lacked piety but fears of the impending closure of Walsingham Priory produced a conspiracy so threatening to the government that the eleven men convicted were hanged, drawn and quartered all in different parts of the county as an example.[2] As in many places there were different opinions: most of the canons of the priory had subscribed the oath of supremacy of the king in 1534, but not all. The prior, Richard Vowell, was complicit; his sub-prior, Nicholas Mileham, was one of the conspirators. The rebels were first brought before Sir Roger Townshend and Sir John Heydon, local Justices, from whence they were taken to Norwich castle before sentence. Mileham was hanged in the village at what became known as Martyrs' Field. A Wells man, Richard Malyot, who was tried for the crime of misprision for his complicity in the conspiracy received a sentence of imprisonment for life. The statue of Our Lady of Walsingham was taken to London in 1538 and burnt. Two years later when a Wells woman claimed that the statue had nevertheless worked a miracle, for voicing her belief she was put in the stocks and then paraded round the town in a cart and children were encouraged to pelt her with snowballs.[3] Binham went the same way; its properties, including some in Wells, were sold by the king to Thomas Paston in 1541.[4] What would have happened had Roger Townshend, a Catholic in his youth, acted differently is anyone's guess.

The effect of the changes upon ordinary people was practical. Most of the saints' days, on which days men could hope to have some time off the labour in the fields, were abolished, allegedly because they interfered with agriculture. The king, who reckoned himself to be something of a theologian, was an inconstant reformer

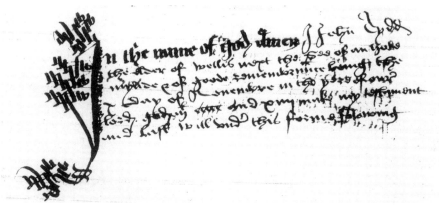

The title page of the will of John Tydd, ship-owner, who died in 1514.

and the Latin Mass was retained until after this death in 1547. Sunday mornings remained the same for the moment, but the increasing uncertainty as to where the future lay and the draconian nature of reprisals against resistance fuelled the fears of the parish. Hew Tydde, ship-owner, who died in 1543, left money to the church for tithes he had 'negligently' failed to pay, for a 'plough light' and a light for Our

Lady, but he did not give money to any of the gilds or ask for prayers for his soul. The change seems to have been sudden. John Clubb had left money to the Trinity gild in 1514; John Tydd left money to St George's gild in the same year; as late as 1532 Thomas Waddilove left money for 'a trental [thirty] masses [to be] celebrated by any honest priest', presumably to shorten his time in purgatory.[5] Godly these men and women may have been but their interest was to make dispositions which would carry the force of law. They assumed that this would be the case.

The local church

It was when Henry's weakling son, the nine-year-old Edward VI, came to the throne that events occurred which affected everyone. Edward Seymour, the king's uncle and Earl of Hertford, a hearty Protestant, was named protector of the realm. He lost no time in pursing the reform agenda. Henry died on 27 January 1547. By the summer Injunctions were issued requiring the destruction of all relics, images, pictures and paintings, including the great rood which dominated the church, standing as it did in the chancel arch. Commissioners were appointed to enforce the destruction.[6] The gilds were abolished; the gild altars with their images of the various saints were no longer to be permitted; they were ripped out.[7] The removal of images of the saints, much preached against, in Henry's reign, had begun in 1538; now it was to be universal. The wall paintings, traces of which were still discernible in the 1850s, were whitewashed out. Stained glass was a more difficult matter; the injunctions forbade destroying them if to do so would leave the church open to the weather. All painted glass with religious imagery eventually went. The church, once frequented daily by those who would come, as they saw it, to see their Maker revealed in the form of the bread consecrated at the altar, was now empty except on Sundays. In 1549 the old Latin Mass was to be replaced by an English language service, in which all references to the Pope, to Purgatory and to the saints had been removed. (Quite different from the old service, some called it 'a Christmas game'.) One version of the truth, which is always perceived somewhat differently by different people, was imposed by government fiat.

The churchwardens lost no time. Whereas the 'idolatrous' statues had been put in place lovingly, they were ripped out crudely, leaving not only vacant spaces but also considerable damage to the fabric which needed to be repaired. After midsummer they had begun to sell what they did not need, perhaps fearing that it would otherwise be confiscated. They sold a silver censer, an incense boat and a silver cruet, worth together £10. They proceeded to sell other items: a silver cross, a chalice, a chrismatory (used in baptism), a pax brede and a number of vestments and copes – the garments worn by the clergy at the celebration of the mass. Their certificate setting out these sales declares that the money, the considerable sum of £62, had already been spent – £40 on church repairs, £10 upon the purchase of an organ and £6 'for the maintenance and keeping of our haven'.[8] The rest of the money would be spent on whitewashing and repairing the church, they said. They declared finally that all was done 'with the consent of the whole parish there'.[9] This formula was typical. State confiscation was hitherto unprecedented; parishes had been largely independent units, answerable to bishops but not to kings; now their controversial actions, which would have included the sale of items given by benefactors or by groups within the parish, needed to be justified. It was not before time either. In February 1549 sheriffs and justice of the peace were required to demand lists of instruments of worship to be lodged with the Custos Rotulorum, the keeper of the county records, together with a declaration by the churchwardens that they acknowledged that they had been forbidden to sell any 'plate, jewels, ornaments or bells from henceforth'.[10]

The Commissioners finally arrived in Wells on 3rd September 1552. They had come, apparently, merely to catalogue the instruments of the old worship; they had no power of confiscation. But no one was deceived.[11] Confiscation would come soon enough. The list even mentions that two items, a chalice and a bell, were 'reserved', a sure sign that the rest would soon be taken. By this time the holders of the office of churchwarden had changed. One can imagine the arguments which must have taken place earlier as items bought out of money raised, perhaps by gild members, were to be sold. The parish got through two sets of wardens during this period, Henry Goldsmith, William Heyer, Hugh Sabb and John Neve. We may guess that the decisions taken over what to sell in order to defeat the government's desire to take its valuables from the parish were taken with difficulty. In some places the wardens hid, or bought for themselves, items which otherwise would have been sold. Huge profits were made by tradesmen who bought, at knockdown prices, the fabrics and precious metals which were coming onto the market in large quantities.[12] Interestingly, organs were normally the subject of confiscation; the earlier wardens may have made a misjudgement therefore in buying an organ with the proceeds of the sale of sacred vessels and vestments. Who knows whether they were allowed to keep it? As for the rest it was declared that they intended to repair, whitewash and mend the church as need required. Thus were to be covered over the wall paintings which had hitherto adorned churches across the land. The walls between the aisle windows were then covered with inscriptions from the psalms in English.[13]

The interpretation of human actions is never certain but the fact remains that between 1547 when government enthusiasm for the new religion became clear, the parish sold only some of its plate and vestments, apparently continuing to practise the old religion, retaining enough items to allow them to do so. This was typical even in places like London where reformers were more in abundance; in Wells, as in most places, obedience to the king and fear of consequences, rather than enthusiasm for the new faith was what drove the Reformation. Many if not most parishes continued in their old ways of taking the services as if they were the old Mass.[14]

On 16th January 1553 the King's Council at last ordered the general confiscation of all church goods except a cup or chalice, a covering for the communion table, the necessary prayer books and a surplice. Now the rector, William Thurkyll, and the churchwardens, James Tydd and Ambrose Fiske, handed over what remained: a chalice, a silver pax brede, and the three bells with their clappers from the tower, several copes and a red satin and a green vestment.

Uncertainty and division

Ironically, within six months Edward was dead and his half-sister Mary was swept onto the throne in a wave of popular enthusiasm. Initially she was unsure how to act and she was short of money so the income from confiscated goods was welcome. By the autumn she had resolved on a policy of modified restoration. By then it was too late to recover much of what had been taken.[15] Some silverware was returned; sometimes what had been taken was re-allocated on a somewhat random basis because its origin could not be determined. The Latin Mass was restored; vestments were put into use, some emerging from private houses where they had been secretly stored. Roods and altars were rebuilt, often makeshift and crude. John Rayner was vicar during Mary's short reign, dying conveniently just after his Queen, in November 1558; the register describes him as 'a good keeper of hospitalitie for ye poor'.[16] Richard Brewerner followed him. What had been begun under Edward was now completed under Queen Elizabeth.

The new regime saw itself as somewhat embattled: the return of Queen Mary and her reinstatement of the catholic polity had shown that the future was not safe for Protestantism. Elizabeth's attempt to reinstate a moderate form of reform after her accession in 1558 was met with strong and differing views. Some wished for the old regime to be retained; others wanted the reform continued. These Puritans would not be happy until bishops, priests, even the prayer book were all swept away. Others were to come to love the beauty of the prayer book whose words became part of the English language.

Everyone was required to attend church on Sundays so control of the church was a means of communicating and regulating behaviour. Some men, like Fermor Pepys in South Creake, went to church while their families went to mass; others paid the fines exacted from non church attenders. Nathaniel Bacon, JP of Stiffkey and MP for Lynn, on the other hand was an ardent Protestant, taking over a year to secure the appointment of a 'sound' co-religionist, John Percival, as vicar of his home village in 1574.[17] He and fellow JP William Heydon did the same at Fakenham, Wiveton and Holt.[18] Catholic practice was to be rooted out and recusants – those who still adhered to the Catholic cause – pursued. Bacon was said to be a man easier to admire than to like; his brand of Protestantism was austere and demanding (though he was not above gaming at cards) and he fell out with those like Heydon when the latter seemed to have lost his zeal. There was a softer and more emotional version of the faith, focussing on sociability, but the theme of flesh against spirit was ever present.

Not everyone was keen to pursue dissidents. Local people, the so-called juries of presentment, were apparently reluctant to disclose their neighbours' religious opinions. And if local people were reluctant, the magistracy were divided. While Bacon saw it as his duty to arraign recusants, some of his colleagues were less keen. Some indeed were so-called church papists – who went to church while going secretly to mass – and many more justices were more inclined to avoid offending local opinion than to enforce the law. The growing body of regulatory legislation passed by the Elizabeth Parliament would place considerable demands on magistrates: making settlement and bastardy orders; licensing alehouses; assessing rates and repairing gaols. They were important in the development of the Tudor bureaucracy through the meetings of quarter sessions. On the other hand the pressures on them locally and their sense of being Norfolk men first and foremost made the implementation of legislation problematic. As a result Parliament passed an act in 1587 taking from the local quarter sessions the responsibility for trying recusants and handing it over to the assizes.[19] The Queen's judges would administer the law in future.

The pursuit of recusants became more systematic after the Pope's bull *Regnans in Excelsis* released all Catholics from allegiance to her in 1570; for thereafter to be a Catholic was effectively to be guilty of treason. This hardened opinions but one effect was to encourage traffic in priests and seminarians leaving and entering the country secretly by sea in order to sustain the Catholic faithful. The authorities at Wells were given instructions that should any enter who were not known as 'merchants, factors, mariners or sailors' they should be examined as to their associates, whom they visited and who financed them, and made to take the oath of allegiance to the monarch.[20] If they would not they might suffer the fate of Montford Scott who was hanged, drawn and quartered for saying mass hereabouts.[21] Recusancy stubbornly did not appear to be decreasing. As late as the 1580s the squires in one part of north

Norfolk 'were Catholic almost to a man'.[22] Norwich on the other hand was firmly Protestant, even Puritan. Hereabouts the gentry were more divided. Some lacked the resources to pay the fines. The Townshends of Raynham paid up and survived. The poorer people with a few exceptions submitted, unable to pay.

The combination of the pursuit of recusants and the dying off of traditionalist clergy worked its way, but not without argument. Bishop Parkhurst of Norwich was a Puritan but on his death in 1575 his successor, Edmund Freake, was heavily influenced by the recusant faction. Episcopal visitation returns reveal the conduct of both clergy and lay people, not merely as to whether they went to church but whether the ten commandments had been put up on the church wall, what books had been obtained, whether the parson preached and whether he wore the required surplice for services. The visitation of 1597[23] showed that the new curate of Wells, Dickerson, was probably not even ordained; he may well have been one of the many Puritan preachers put in for their views rather than their status. As so often, small things raise big arguments: in some places in East Anglia, particularly in Suffolk, the new clergy refused to wear a surplice, the white over-garment which clergy wear now without comment. Norfolk clergy were, on the whole, less troublesome but this did not include Wells. The parish was warned for the failure of its minister to wear one.[24] Even as late as 1605, as reported to Nathaniel Bacon, a conversation took place between one Owen Griffeth, a merchant selling coal, and another which took place in a Wells alehouse. Perhaps Griffeth's tongue had been loosened by the ale, but he displayed a singular lack of caution about his enthusiasm for the old religion. He said that he had been at mass and would again be at mass, saying that 'the papists do in their mass serve God better or as well as we the protestants do in our service now, and that the seminarians and Jesuits which are executed here, suffer for religion and not for treason'.[25] Things cannot have gone well for him.

The 1597 visitation concerned itself with other matters, such as those who were practising forms of medicine without a licence. The wife of one Bastarde was excommunicated for practising surgery having failed to turn up to the visitation in Fakenham parish church to explain herself. This was more than the mere regulation of medical activities. A widespread concern existed amongst the new Protestants about the use of magical activities, alleged cures achieved by charms, sorcery, soothsaying or witchcraft. Belief in magic, opposed by the old Church in principle, but practised in the form of exorcisms and a variety of other rituals, was more sternly opposed by the upholders of the new religion.[26] (The visitation unearthed the existence of fourteen so-called 'cunning men' and women, practitioners of magical cures, in the diocese who apparently travelled from place to place offering their services.[27])

The status of England as a Protestant state had international ramifications; one of which was the nineteen-year war with Spain. Both countries were continuing to expand their navies, the Spanish in order to defend their trade with the Americas, the English to take advantage of it by attacking the ships loaded with valuable cargoes; but the war was, in part, a religious one: Elizabeth supported the Protestant Dutch whose lands were ruled by Spain.[28] The violent clashes between the troops of Philip II and Dutch populations everywhere from Antwerp, Delft, Utrecht and Amsterdam brought refugees to the safety of Norfolk. (They seem to have integrated quickly but a number of features of the town indicate a pervasive influence.[29])

All of this brought closer the threat of invasion. Then in 1587 Elizabeth had Mary, Queen of Scots executed, she who had been implicated in various Catholic plots. This appears to have been the final straw for Philip, who thereupon sought the advice of his councillors and began to assemble an Armada. The Norfolk coast was reckoned to be the most likely place where the Spaniards would land and fortifications were built at Weybourne and at Cley to protect the land to its north where the cliffs sloped down to the shingle spit. Not for the first time local people demonstrated their independence of mind. The Admirals wrote asking for two ships to repel the invasion; the mayor of Lynn, Thomas Sandyll, replied that his vessels had gone to Iceland or Holland and that the towns along the coast, Blakeney, Cley and Wells, ought to help. He wrote 'We sent also to the town of Wells, which is a member of our port, a town very well furnished with shipping, within which there be many rich men inhabiting; but they have denied altogether to contribute to our charge.'[30] One vessel, the *Mayflower*, was available but they had not the money to equip her. A ship was eventually sent from Cley the following year. In 1597, invasion was, once again, feared: 'trained men . . . [were] to be in readiness at an hour's warning armed with powder, bullet and match to repair to several places of rendezvous appointed . . . to make resistance where attempt of invasion shall be.'[31]

Elizabeth also had problems with Ireland – or its people with her. At any rate, Catholic Ireland, remote as it might seem from Norfolk, engaged governmental attention for similar reasons. 'Norfolk men, Norfolk arms were being demanded in order to help resolve problems in the Queen's other kingdom of Ireland.'[32] The use of press gangs was one means of doing this. On 1st August 1599 Bacon ordered the impressment of nineteen men from Wells, eight of them shipmasters, more than from any other port locally.[33] The men were taken to Chatham for embarkation. A year later, eight men between the ages of 17 and 34 were impressed.[34]

In short, this period known as the Elizabethan settlement was a precarious affair, marked by competing interests and opportunism. Norfolk's local identity had been maintained and defended by the influence of Thomas Duke of Norfolk until his execution in 1572; his land holdings in Norfolk were immense. The vacuum left by his death was filled by competing gentry: Bacon, Coke, Heydon and Sir Arthur Heveningham among a number of others. Some saw advantage in allying themselves to the centralising force of government; others wished to maintain local autonomy exemplified in the now long established role of justices of the peace. Edward Coke was particularly outspoken and active about his concerns about corrupt practices in relation to the recruitment of local militias.[35] Religious

A drawing of Stiffkey Hall by Arthur Rackham.

difference added to the problems as faith had now become a matter of personal conviction rather than, as hitherto, an expression of community life in which the terms of conflict were mostly agreed. It was not only Protestant against Catholic, but Puritan against those who would come to be called Anglicans.

The new men exhibited their status by building themselves grand houses. With the availability of building materials from the now disused monasteries – Binham and Walsingham were pulled down for their stone – the gentry were now able to put up or extend houses suitable to their wealth and status. Stone masons, no longer employed on ecclesiastical buildings, would readily turn their skills to such tasks. Bacon built himself a splendid turreted house by the river at Stiffkey; Warham Hall, now long demolished, was doubtless equally grand. Hill Hall at Holkham was a Tudor manor house, extended several times to accommodate the increasing wealth of its owners, the Cokes. There was an element of competition in their grandeur as in their use of power.

One example of the latter was the use of licences and patents obtained from the Crown ostensibly for public works but which were often obtained without financial scrutiny, resulting in the misuse of funds; another was the oppressive use of powers exercised over local people. Bacon, his Puritan conscience driving him, worked tirelessly to expose abuses. Among his concerns were the activities of the Vice Admiral's court and its under-officers. He wrote complaining to Sir Robert Mansell, the vice-Admiral in Norfolk and Suffolk, about the court's wrongful claim of jurisdiction over wrecks which belonged to the lord of the manor. The court's procedures were particularly abusive in that it was able to arraign people without specifying the charge and to make use of informers to bring evidence. 'Members of those maritime communities which clustered around north Norfolk's creeks and havens must have been especially vulnerable to the informers' activities, since they gained a livelihood as opportunity presented by fishing, trading, smuggling or even piracy; the entire procedure presented unlimited opportunities for blackmail.[36]

Bacon, ever even-handed, was just as concerned about the treatment of local mariners and fishermen when he thought them unjust: doles had been taken from the Iceland fishers contrary to statute 'so as it hath cost the town of Wells £30 or £40 in a year that way only'; he sought a remedy. Other complaints were the empanelling of jurors at quarter sessions from among the mariners and fisherman without exception 'and so draw them from their labours . . . punish[ing] all absences for gain sake'.[37] They had to be at sea when the weather allowed; if this proved inclement, as might be the case for days or even weeks, they needed to be able to sail when conditions improved and might be away for months.

It was a time of great flux for other reasons too. The population had grown rapidly, taxing the fractured resources of communities. Incoming vagrants combined with increasing family size put pressure on many communities, from food supplies to sanitation. The dissolution of the monasteries and the abolition of gilds and chantries – the latter supported schools in many places – left many communities unable to cope; their resources had been confiscated and until Poor Relief in the 1590s and the first Charity Act of 1601 private giving, encouraged by government but patchy in its provision, was the only means of relief. The poor harvests of 1595, 1596 and 1597 were the immediate issues; parishes had no means of raising money to meet the needs of the indigent poor.[38] The act of 1597 provided that churchwardens were to be or to appoint overseers of the poor, under the eye of the justices. Overseers were to administer the collection of the poor rate and distribute it to those assessed to be in need. It was followed by the Poor Relief

Act in 1601 which formalised the administration of poor relief. In the longer term, the rising Puritan class, the so-called 'godly', increasingly regarded charity as something to be practised by organisations rather than individuals and marked more clearly the distinction between the deserving and the undeserving poor; legislation provided that the latter, called vagabonds, be punished not helped.[40]

The population of Wells at that time is difficult to estimate but we have some clues. The Muster Roll for 1565 gives the number of householders in the town as ninety, roughly the same size as each of the Glaven ports and far fewer than the 542 recorded for Lynn.[41] This seems a very low number until one realises that these householders headed up sometimes large families which would include grown-up sons; children worked from a very early age. Extended families might include a dozen people. There would have been a degree of under-recording. The demands of the fishing fleet and of the fields suggest a population of up to 800 souls. It was the third biggest settlement after Binham and Walsingham. Muster Rolls were a means, introduced during the reign of Henry VIII, of assessing the number of able bodied men fit for war service; but they rapidly became a source of information for the collection of taxes.

Amidst the flux, some things continued as normal and some rather well. Church registers, required by the Tudor government in 1538, give us a glimpse of another side to life in the town. (The earliest extant register for Wells dates from 1547.) Written up by the incumbent they were to tell stories of individual lives so that until printed forms constrained what was written, glimpses into the town's life were revealed. Margaret Burwood died on 12th August 1598 aged 95. She was not the only person to live into her tenth decade in the years before mains water, sewerage and modern medicine. She was however remarkable in other ways. 'She was a midwife, gracious for never decaied (died?) any woman under her hand, she was devoute, charitable and to her abilitie a good keeper of hospitalitie.' At a time when death in childbirth was common, her abilities were wonderfully to be valued.

As for the condition of householders, we are told that chimneys had begun to proliferate, a development made more possible by the wider use of brick. Houses thus provided need no longer be smoke-filled; hearths used for cooking now might have flues to carry the smoke away. Lacking local stone, brick proved a great boon even if it was only used for the chimney breast, the rest of the structure being made of wood, wattles and clay. Indoors, flock mattresses were beginning to replace straw, and pewter vessels to replace wooden ones. In the houses of merchants shutters and wooden lattice windows were gradually being replaced by glass.[42] The cheaper broadsheet glass, produced by opening out a bubble of blown glass, was flawed and seeded with small bubbles making it difficult to see through. Crown glass, made from a flat disk produced by spinning molten glass on the end of a 'punty' pole, was of a far higher quality. But panes could only be of small size, joined together by lead strips to make a large enough window. The poorest might instead use oiled paper or parchment to let in some light while of course not enabling anyone to see in or out; but keeping out the rain.[43]

The effects on the fishing

The Reformation had a negative effect on the fishing. The Friday fast when only fish must be eaten was abolished, thus dealing a death blow to ports like Walberswick in Suffolk. It had become one of the tests of protestant orthodoxy that men ate meat on Fridays. Back in 1528, as we have seen, the ports of Norfolk had done more than half our national trade with Iceland.[44] The decline by two thirds in the number of vessels caused resentment amongst impoverished East Anglian fishermen. Robert Hitchcock wrote in 1580 that there were several hundred coastal towns 'now in ruin and void of English inhabitants, to be peopled and inhabited by her majesty's own peculiar subjects: to the great strength of this realm and the terror of the enemy.'[45] Its effects on the defence of the nation were realised only slowly. The monarch was dependent on experienced seamen to man the ships of her navy. Thus in 1563 William Cecil, Elizabeth's chief advisor, caused the reintroduction of the fast on Fridays, but also on Wednesdays and Saturdays, in order to sustain the fishing fleet and keep mariners in their jobs.[46] Parliament was suspicious and it had to be explained that it was for military not religious purposes.

The act would slowly achieve the objectives of its promoters. In 1565 Wells had seven ships for work off Iceland, each between sixty and eighty tons. By 1595 its share of the fishing fleet had grown to ten ships and three barques, larger than all the Glaven ports and only overtaken by Southwold, Yarmouth and Lynn. The work was labour intensive: even a small barque might carry twenty men, while complements of forty manned the largest ships. The long lines were laid for distances of hundreds of yards, even miles, fixed to the seabed at intervals with small anchors, with baited hooks every three yards so.[47] The bait, most often whelks, had themselves to be caught, packed and shipped (though tallow candle-ends were sometimes used). The bulk of the population must have been engaged in the fishing one way or another.

The sea took its human toll. Wells Parish Register includes the names not only of those who died offshore and were buried in the churchyard but also those many who were buried at sea. Malign forces were sometimes thought to be at work: the loss of fourteen men returning from Spain in December 1583 was laid at the door of a Lynn witch, the so-called Mother Gavle, who apparently boiled eggs in cold water. The

Iceland fishery, in particular, was costly in human lives: on 29th June 1590 twenty-four men died working off the island. Every other year penny numbers were lost. Added to that on the 'lamentable voyage' to Portugal in that same year over a dozen men were lost.[48] One sixteenth-century report notes the loss over twenty months of thirty-seven ships from Kings Lynn, Wells and Burnham. Losses continued into the seventeenth century. Storms on the east coast could blow up quickly. One shipmaster reported how he and his crew fared on a disastrous voyage from Wells to the garrison town of Berwick in 1551 when 'there arose such a great tempest and sudden storm of foul weather that it beat . . . the ship so far upon the rocks and the shore that she break on sunder (sic), almost in pieces'.[49] No doubt it was conventional, but the skippers of such doggers who set out on such dangerous voyages were called 'masters under God'.

This sense of events not being under one's own control is a particular characteristic of the age. The sea was believed to be the habitation of monsters – whales had not entirely disappeared from the North Sea; forests might also contain their own denizens – the country was much more heavily wooded than it is today; the natural order was believed to contain spirits, some good some malign. Belief in witchcraft, evidenced in the Mother Gavle story, was sometimes parasitic on religion, sometimes a rival to it. Religion and magic were uneasy bedfellows. Magical rituals intended to avert the consequences of human action or bring about desired ends were attractive; they filled the gap left by the banning of prayers to the saints which had been part of the stock of the mediaeval church.[50] The 'cunning men' were their practitioners. The distinction between prayers animated by faith and the attempt to manipulate events by magical practices, believed to have automatic effect, became blurred.[51]

If some matters were mysterious, others were more easily understood. Prices fluctuated sometimes wildly. It was always a matter of feasting and fasting. The rise in population during these later decades of the sixteenth century increased demand and therefore raised prices. On the other hand, foreign competition and foreign restrictions made life harder. The Danes had doubled the duties on English fishermen in 1530 fishing off Iceland. As we have seen government legislation did not help: in 1603 forty-two fishermen from the town signed a petition, some with a mark, asking that 'at next Parliament some such course may be taken for the relief of the said town and other coast towns as also for the trade of fishing craft as in your good discretions shall seem fit and convenient'.[52] Eventually the trade began to revive. By 1614 the Iceland fleet had almost doubled to 125 vessels, almost all from Norfolk and Suffolk.[53] Perhaps the Wells fishermen's petition had been heard. Certainly imports of Spanish salt, brought via the Netherlands, were substantial. Reciprocal trade with the Icelanders was limited by the poor resources of the country, but one remarkable import recorded several times was of hawks, gyrfalcons mostly, which were highly prized by falconers.[54]

Among the other threats to the fishery was piracy. From the latter part of the sixteenth century Dunkirk had become notorious as being a port served by pirates. Ship-owners of Wells and Burnham claimed that £13,000 worth of damage had been caused to their craft by the Dunkirkers, which seriously reduced the Icelandic traffic.[55] In 1620 the mayor of Lynn claimed that Lynn, with Wells and Burnham, had been sending, on average, 70 ships a year on the fishing voyage to Iceland since 1580, but that the number had dropped to only twenty in the year of writing, due, in his opinion, to the numbers of ships lost to pirates from the Dunkirk region.[56] A petition was sent by the inhabitants of Wells to Sir Arthur Heveningham, Commissioner for Musters in Norfolk, complaining about the loss of a ship from Iceland 'the loss of which . . . one John Housegoe, master and part owner, is utterly undone'. The petition points out that whereas formerly the 'Dunkirks' came in small boats they now came in 'very great ships of 200 tons a piece very well furnished with men and munitions so as the coast is no way able to resist them'.[57] John Motts, master and part owner of the *Gift* of Wells of 45 tons, had his ship taken by Dunkirks on 17th September 1631 off Wells.[58]

Ships were forced to travel in convoys; new ships needed to be built for the purpose of resistance. Bacon was instructed to tell Wells seamen 'to encourage adventure against them'. The incentive was that the Admiral 'is pleased to bestow upon them all enemies' goods that they shall take by that means without yielding any duty to him'.[59] Eventually, after a long delay, the matter was put in hand: by 1657 coastal shipping was guarded by fourteen ships carrying 234 guns and 1,600 men in winter and by sixty-one ships carrying 6,760 men in summer. Wells was one of three bases for the ships; the other two were Yarmouth and Lynn.[60]

As always there were those who wanted a share of the rewards of the fishery: government, merchants; and the church. On the arrival of a ship on the Quay, the Crown's toll of the catch, known as the 'prise', was taken off, usually in the form of money payment rather than numbers of fish; after which those who had lent 'venture' money had to be paid at high rates of interest; after all they would have lost everything if the ship had failed to return.[61] Finally, the 'doles' or shares in the voyage were divided between the mariners. In this process the church took its share. The old system of tithe by which everyone in a community contributed towards the church continued seamlessly after the break with Rome. Fishermen paid their tithe as individuals like everyone else. There was in addition a tax known as Christ's dole derived from the profits of a fishing trip after paying the expenses of the voyage. In the case of large ships the profits were divided into eighty doles, in the case of small boats like cobles, it was forty. A half of a dole, the so-called Christ's dole, was to be paid to the parish priest. The fishermen objected to paying, as they saw it, twice; and also because the tithe was paid to their home parish but the dole was paid to the port where the ship was based. Thus the rector of Wells,

William Toll, received the dole from mariners who lived in nearby parishes. The justice of the peace, Nathanial Bacon, whom they petitioned, was unsympathetic.[62] (Bacon was more energetic on behalf of the townsfolk in forwarding their objections to the extension of the claims of the lord of the manor to exact tolls from ships' cargo to include corn. It admittedly included a bushel of coal and salt from each cargo; they claimed that the custom of charging measurage, as it was called, on corn was unheard of.)[63]

The future nevertheless seemed set fair. In 1638 4,000 fish were sent to London and 600 to Newcastle. The following year the number sent to London was 14,000.[64] The matter which damaged the fishery most lay not with the market or the church or Parliament or even with the pirates, but with the King.

Fish were salted on board after they were caught. Much of the salt was imported from Spain. Charles I who was in dispute with Parliament sought ever more desperate and legally questionable measures to raise money without calling Parliament together. He raised the duties on salt, something which he claimed to be able to do by his own prerogative. Salt was one of the principal items of expenditure in the fishery. Moreover, Charles stopped the fishermen from claiming back the duty on salt, much of which was imported from Biscay, if the salt was subsequently used in the fishery. In just five years the number of vessels halved.[65] Where the Dunkirks failed, their own king succeeded. The outbreak of the Civil War added to the troubles – by the increase in lawlessness and the growth in privateering in particular. Naval protection was eventually provided and while in 1656 thirty three vessels assembled off Wells to make the Iceland trip, mostly from Yarmouth, this figure rose to sixty in 1657, seventy-two in 1658 and by 1659 a naval officer reported that he had convoyed seventy-seven vessels.

Salt was only one of a number of factors; fresh fish was increasingly available to the increasingly important London market from inshore fisheries and salt fish was now obtained from Newfoundland.[66] Shorter trips to the Dogger Bank were undertaken from more southerly ports such as Harwich and Barking; such trips obviated the need for salt because the fish could be landed live. At any rate the decline was as rapid as the increase: by 1675 only twenty-eight ships sailed there. The resumption of the Dutch wars, when the Dutch fleet got as far as the Medway, was surely another cause. In the longer term the salt tax seems to have had its effect; the sailors themselves certainly thought so. An act was passed in 1713 to ameliorate the effects of the tax but the new regulations were judged so complex as to defeat the fishermen's attempt to understand them.[67] It took until 1825 for the hated salt tax to be repealed, far too late for the fishermen of Wells or of any of the other East Anglian ports to benefit. All too soon even the memory of the great days of fishing faded; those who promoted England's fisheries a century later only wrote of the herring.

Herring fishing was dominated by the Dutch; the so-called herring busses, double-ended, two-masted drifters, enjoyed a monopoly of the trade. The Wells fishery continued supplying local needs but the international trade had gone. Until hostilities broke out in earnest between the two countries in 1652 Dutch boats in Yarmouth harbour were the norm.[68] (It was the Scots who finally revived the herring fishery in the nineteenth century but they passed us by, following the fish down the coast from Grimsby directly to Yarmouth.)

Old trade and new

Traffic into and from the harbour was always subject to changing demands and changing opportunities. The sixteenth century saw the creation of new chartered companies, the Eastland, the Muscovy and the short-lived Spanish Company, intended to challenge the monopoly of the Hanse. The Merchant Adventurers of London, which dealt mostly in cloth, had been in existence for more than a century.[69] Between them they bade fair to control all overseas trade with the Continent, attempting to exclude local merchants and ship-owners. That the merchants of the ports around the Wash managed to maintain their independence was largely due to two factors: they traded with smaller ports like Flushing and Veere instead of Antwerp or Amsterdam; and much of their trade was illicit. At any rate, most of the trade recorded was conducted by local vessels. The town may not have had good river access inland as Lynn and Yarmouth did but there is some evidence that overland access made it a convenient port even for remote suppliers.[70] Wells lay at the end of the old pilgrimage route, the Palmers Way from London to Walsingham, which was still in use as a major artery. It was apparently one of the half dozen great roads of mediaeval England.

Local trade served the needs of the fishing industry in the provision of salt but it also continued to supply coal and occasionally iron for local smithies. With each passing decade more utensils were made of iron, from shovels to frying pans, nails and saws; the denuding of the country's woodlands had become a matter of concern; coal was a better alternative. Some could afford coal for their domestic hearths. But the largest user of iron by far was the shipbuilding industry. It was to meet these needs that the Wells fleet grew from fourteen in 1565 (half of which were fishing boats) to nineteen by 1582; the port had become the most important of the Lynn creeks and larger than any of the Glaven ports.[71] The reply to the Marquis of Winchester's enquiry at the earlier date as to the state of the four creeks of Lynn – Dersingham, Heacham, Burnham and Wells – was that they were 'in good state to serve the prynce'.[72] Of these Wells was by far the most significant.

As a result, questions came to be raised about the antique system of customs which regulated trade. It was inefficient and, with the doubling of duties under Mary, merchants had begun seriously to question the sense of honest dealings. Thus, it served the interests of both London and the north-east for wheat, rye, barley and malt to be in good supply at reasonable prices; an act of 1563 thus restricted their export if prices rose above 10 shillings for wheat and 6*s* 8*d* for malt and barley.[73] A second act, eight years later, gave the Crown complete discretion over exports. The aim was to ensure that England could feed herself and was not supplying a scarce resource to her neighbours. But the means of enforcement were never adequate and the incentive to obey the law was lacking. Customs officers were poorly paid and local farmers and merchants sought open markets and the best prices that could be had. The result was the large-scale conduct of illicit trade enabled by the bribing of officials. Thomas Sidney, now owner of the site of Walsingham priory and a justice of the peace, was one of a number of locals who engaged personally in unlicensed exports through the harbour.[76] The leak of information to the Privy Council halted the traffic for a short time; it was reported that the huge sum of £7,000 was owed by local merchants to the Exchequer; Sidney nevertheless remained in charge of the Lynn customs office which served Wells at that time and soon resumed his trafficking of grain with Flanders and Spain.[77] Astonishingly, when these ports were closed to them as a result of war, East Anglian vessels, seeking trade elsewhere, entered the Mediterranean and traded their herring as far as the port of Candia on the island of Crete.[78]

Direct information about the Wells trade is patchy and incomplete, partly for the above reasons but partly because few of the records have survived.[79] Even so, from time to time the veil is drawn back. The 1611 Port books are among the few to survive. They record the arrival of small amounts of coal from Liege via Rotterdam, though they show nothing of the coastwise coal trade with the north-east which was longstanding and substantial. They do however record the export of grain, wheat and barley. Lynn and its creeks, Burnham and Wells, were estimated to have been the greatest grain exporting ports in the country, certainly of eastern England.[80]

Other items indicate the growth of more sophisticated tastes. They include the import of quantities of French and Rhenish wine, of sherry and aquavit. The Bordeaux wine trade had not been affected by the dislocation of the Reformation, doubtless because without it, as was well recognised, the region would be ruined. Prunes, raisins, currants and hops came from the southern Dutch ports of Flushing and Veere (then known as Camphire). Other evidence indicates that shipbuilding, well recorded four centuries later, seems to have been longstanding. The quantity of imported spars, literally in hundreds, together with masts and baulks of timber, tells the story. And masts were useless without rigging as anchors without cables. Pitch, cables and tarred ropes came from Amsterdam and timber from Norway. The Norway trade had begun in earnest in the 1570s, carrying grain outward and timber inward.[81] The merchant Henry Congham from Wells traded with timber, pitch, tar, salt for the Icelandic fishery and even glassware.[82]

Outward trade to Veere included saffron and lead.[83] Lead from the mines of Derbyshire had been exported for centuries largely to be used as a roofing material; saffron was so widely grown in north Norfolk that Walsingham was described as a place where 'groweth very much saffron and very good'.[84] Nathaniel Bacon grew saffron commercially in Stiffkey. Two ships in particular, the *Estrich* of Veere and the *John* of Wells, carried this extremely valuable cargo, the latter to Rotterdam.[85] Saffron was both food flavouring and a dyestuff.

The records for the 1639 inward trade of the town are much more detailed. Again the ships consisted almost entirely of colliers which doubled as grain ships on their outward journey, over 150 of them, sometimes as many as four on one tide, bringing coal from Newcastle or Sunderland. Over 2,800 chauldrons, some 6,000 tons,[86] entered that year.

We also see evidence of the new trade in groceries from London, as well as soap, linen, pots, glasses, woollen goods, household 'stuff' and even chairs. Roof tiles came directly or via the north-east from Rotterdam.[87] The importation of salt, however, had almost dried up; taxation had killed the trade.

Cargoes leaving the port in that year were almost entirely of barley and malt. The coastwise trade had mushroomed: south to London, Ipswich, Dunwich and Colchester, north to Hull and Newcastle. The *Tryall* of Wells arrived on 29th January with twenty-five chalders (sic) of coal, and departed for Newcastle on 9th February with twenty-four lasts of malt and twenty binds – 400 skins – of tanned leather. Some vessels did make the return trip in ballast, their holds filled with sand to be discarded – at some cost – in Newcastle before being loaded with coal. (Where it was dug from in Wells harbour is unknown but it will have amounted to thousands of tons over years.) The *Hopewell* made the round trip on 8th February, 28th March, 12th May, 9th June, 11th July and throughout the year but took malt only once to Newcastle; her other revenue earning trips outward were with malt to Hull, Sunderland and London. As always, skippers had to be opportunistic in ensuring that every trip was revenue earning.

Finally, again tantalisingly, we have only a little idea as to the condition of the Wells harbour at that time. Yarmouth had been the subject of huge investment in what would now be called a civil engineering project in order to make it accessible. Blakeney was reckoned to be a difficult harbour because of the sand shoals offshore. Pilotage was provided for incoming vessels – Yarmouth had three – and Lynn had a system of buoyage which made it accessible through the shallows of the Wash (though the buoys were unlit and there were no lighthouses, making safe landfall by night almost impossible).[88] We do know, however, that the condition of Wells harbour was a matter that was shortly to become a matter of concern and controversy.

5. The New Men

Civil War and Restoration

The English Civil War (1642–48) was followed by the imposition of yet another Reformation. Wells church suffered some desecration. Apart from the removal and destruction of images, prayers for the dead were a particular object of hostility. Thus the opening words of the brass dedicated to Thomas Bradley, who had rebuilt the chancel in 1460, inviting prayers for him, were scratched out.[1] What else was mutilated or removed we have no record of. North Norfolk, unlike Norwich, mostly escaped the depredations of the iconoclasts. However, the Bishop, Joseph Hall, was removed; the prayer book was everywhere banned; funerals were no longer allowed – the dead must be buried virtually without ceremony. Mungo Morray, who was made rector in 1640, dying in 1685, lived through the several changes; he appears to have been a Scot and, since England was at war with Scotland, in 1650 he had to obtain permission to remain in England having given 'security for good behaviour'.[2] Nevertheless, three years later, a Register, so called, one Thomas Wiggen, was appointed having been chosen by the 'cheife of the inhabitants' with authority to register not baptisms but births, as well as marriages and burials. Morray became a mere 'clerk'.[3] What authority remained to him is unclear but a marble tablet over the vestry door of the church recorded that he was a man of many virtues, learned, devoted to his flock and generous to the poor.[4] He was succeeded by James Garlick some time before 1675.[5] John Coke, second surviving son of Sir Edward Coke, the famous Elizabethan jurist who had established himself at Holkham, was an ardent Parliamentarian, 'a member of every parliamentary committee in the county'; the Pastons, on the other hand (one of whose members, Thomas, had inherited Binham Priory), turned Catholic and were deprived.

What the Commonwealth did was to break forever the unity of the church and the monopoly of the Church of England. At the Restoration of the monarchy in 1660, Charles II returned from exile, and the old order of bishops and Queen Elizabeth's prayer book were reimposed by Parliament. Those clergy who objected were ejected from their posts, two thousand of them across the country, sixty in Norfolk. Thus was formed the first significant dissent. Congregationalists, whose view was that the primary unit should be the local church rather than dioceses and their bishops, had first surfaced at the end of Elizabeth's reign in Norwich; their numbers were now much increased. Sometimes called Independents, some of them came eventually to form the Congregational Church in Wells. In 1669 it was reported that there were twelve Anabaptists worshipping in the town.[7]

The Restoration did not end the religious flux begun the century before. The various loyalties remained deeply felt. In 1663, in a house in Holkham, one Thomas Robinson was heard to say that 'the King had promised to maintain the Protestant religion, but was turned Papist. He spoke of being mounted within a fortnight in a troop of horse, and asked the informant to join them.' Clearly he regretted his statement for a day or so later when confronted with reports of his opinions; he denied all knowledge of the conversation.[8] Still, as we have seen before, you clearly had to be careful what you said. On the death of Charles II in 1685, his brother James's Catholic sympathies were soon revealed. Even so, Sir William Coke and Sir John Turner and two other Norfolk MPs voted in Parliament against William of Orange being invited to become king in place of James.[9] William was married to James's daughter, Mary, but her religious sympathies were towards Protestantism. William, who arrived supported by 17,000 Dutch troops, attempted to impose a much more rigorously moral character on the country than his Stuart predecessors had, expecting, as he wrote, that churchwardens would report incidents of fornication, adultery, drunkenness or scandalous behaviour on the part of local people. That no reports of such conduct were made to the Consistory Court from the parish may tell us something of the blameless character of the citizenry of Wells or perhaps of the indulgent attitude of the wardens. That the town had not always been free of troubles is indicated however by a request a few years before for the appointment of a further justice of the peace, William Armiger of North Creake, 'as it is necessary that some gentleman who is near them have a commission to keep them quiet and to determine their differences that arise among them'. Wells, it was contended, was 'a contentious seaport town' in which there were 'daily disorders'.[10]

The ending of the Commonwealth in 1660 also saw the rise of a new kind of man. The era, sometimes known as the long eighteenth century, saw a reaction against Puritanism. There was a new confidence in human powers in which scientific discovery was coupled with colonial exploration, industrialisation and agricultural development. John Coke, already mentioned, had acquired, by marriage, the Manor of Holkham from the family of William Wheatley, Lord of Hill Hall at Holkham.[11] Wheatley was also a lawyer, Chief Clerk of the Court of Common Pleas. His family had inter-married with the Pepys's. The adjacent manor of Neals had previously been bought by Coke's father, Sir Edward, in 1609; its manor house, near to the site of the present Hall, became their family home. He later bought the reversion to the third manor, Boroughall, which came into his hands in 1659.

The younger Coke began land reclamation in 1660 to the west of Holkham Gap with the building of a bank. Previously high tides had brought the waters to just north of Holkham church. Now a process was to begin which reached its first high point four generations later with the building of Holkham Hall, a Palladian mansion built to house a collection of paintings bought on the grand tour. Thomas Coke (1697–1759) who built it was, as well as being an admirer of European culture, an agriculturalist. He probably did more than his famous descendant and namesake to enhance the use of the land belonging to the various halls. Made Earl of Leicester in 1744, it took him thirty years to build the new hall; it was in fact completed five years after his death in 1764. That such a great house should be built in so remote a spot is made more remarkable by how far the materials had come: there is no freestone in Norfolk. The famous white bricks were made locally at Peterstone but the obelisk was made of Bath stone shipped through Wells harbour.[12] As for the marble hall, a clue comes in a bill of lading of 1757 for the ship *The Good Intent* 'now riding at anchor in the Trent, by God's grace bound for Wells'.[13] The items include 56 blocks of alabaster and 16 hogsheads of lime, the former coming from Derbyshire to form the 'marble hall'. Though he died childless, the dynasty of the Cokes (who are still with us today) continued through his nephew by his sister, Wenman Roberts, who changed his name to Coke.

The manor of Wells, which had been in the hands of Sir Cloudesley Shovell, Admiral of the Fleet during the War of the Spanish Succession (1701–1714), came on his death[14] to Sir Charles Turner, merchant of Lynn. Turner was to be responsible for the reclamation of much of the marsh around Wells.

The poor meanwhile were always with us. The Elizabethan Poor law had brought some system into local provision but charity was still encouraged; it was, after all, a godly act. It was enjoined in the New Testament. As reading had been a godly activity so education was one focus of charity, meeting physical need another. Christopher Ringar of Field Dalling in 1678 left £8 per annum to two widows each of them to teach thirty children, the boys to read, the girls to read, knit and sew and also £16 to be laid out in wheat meal to be given monthly to poor persons in Wells who did not receive parish relief. Mungo Morray, rector of the parish (whom we have already met), on his death in 1685 left £18 from an estate of 126 acres in Bale for the poor of Wells, payable £8 on Christmas Day and £10 on Lady Day, 25th March. In 1738 Ann Tidd left £20 a year to the poor of Wells. The rector was one of the trustees.

Landowners and merchants

One major development which occurred after the Restoration related to the harbour. Dues had long been exacted on cargoes brought into the harbour by lords of the manor, the extent of which had at various times been a matter of dispute. Their exaction was a matter of ancient manorial custom. However, there did not seem to be a corresponding duty on the part of the lord to maintain and improve the harbour. Back in 1558 deputies for the Commissioners of Havens and Creeks had been appointed, including Ambrose Fiske, a substantial ship-owner who was one of the churchwardens.[15] By 1639 172 ships were recorded as entering the harbour from east coast harbours and a further twenty from European ports.[16] But the harbour was not in a good state. Thus it was that a number of merchants and mariners in the town petitioned Parliament for authorisation to raise the money to finance the repair of the Quay and for the maintenance of the harbour. They declared the Quay to be 'ruinous' so that if nothing were done the 'whole trade and commerce of the town [would] be lost and overthrown'.[17] Parliament, in those days, was a different creature from that which we are accustomed to. Acts of Parliament had to be promoted by individuals. Thus the services of one of Norfolk's two MPs, Sir Jacob Astley, were obtained. He was persuaded to promote this the first of the Harbour Acts.

In what may seem to be a display of hyperbole the Act, passed in 1663, declared that failure to act would be 'to the damage not only of the adjacent country but of the whole kingdom for the preservation thereof'. The Act authorised for a period of five years from the passing of the Act the levy of harbour dues on every cargo laden or unladen there and specified the uses to which the levies should be put. The sum of six pence was to be charged on every chauldron of coal or cinders, and on every last[18] of grain or ton of other goods or merchandise. The monies raised were to be used for the repairing and preserving of 'the Quay, creeks, channel and landing place'. On the expiration of the five years, by which date it was presumably hoped that the major works would be completed, the sum charged was to be reduced to one penny. This was to be the pattern for the future. Optimistic expectations that the job could be done in short order were again and again frustrated. Like so many civil engineering works the costs would outrun the predictions.

The task of administering the harbour fell to two Collectors and Receivers of Harbour Dues who were to be elected by the merchants of the town and those 'owning a part of any ship' on an annual basis, subject to their appointment being approved by three justices of the peace. Their powers included the inspection of cargoes and detention of goods in order to ensure that they were paid. Remarkably to our health and safety culture, their powers extended to the casting off of ropes or cables of vessels which were hindering the arrival or departure of other vessels. One wonders what it was thought would happen to the vessels! As for the maintenance of the buoys and beacons, a Haven Man was to be appointed who was able to charge ships' masters a penny a ton for performing this duty.[19]

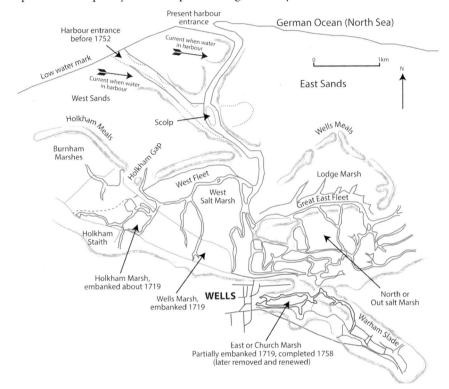

A map, from late 18th century sources, showing the various stages of embankment.

There followed a number of regulations of the Exchequer Commission extending and defining the area of responsibility, first in 1676–77, then in 1732 which defined the harbour as extending from the west end of Burnham Overy Staithe to Morston New Sluice, including all the marshes and shore line south of a line fourteen fathoms deep out to sea.

Wells was to become a port in its own right. Until 1676 the collection of Customs dues at Wells was the responsibility of the Custom House at Lynn, in spite of local requests for a change. In 1603, townsmen of Wells and Burnham had petitioned the Earl of Salisbury to be allowed to collect their own customs. It was inconvenient and expensive to travel to Lynn, they said; customs dues would remain uncollected without 'an immediate officer [who] will better look thereto'.[20] After a long delay Wells ceased to be a 'creek' of Lynn and became an independent port with its own Custom House and Collector.

The Lords of the Manors adjacent to the coast looked to the marshes as potential farmland. Here, the Cokes of Holkham and the Turners of Wells between them drove the process. (At Salthouse, embanking, as it was called, had been attempted as early as 1522 by Sir John Heydon; later at Wiveton and Cley, Sir Henry Calthorpe cut the two old harbours there from the sea in 1637, entirely without consultation.[21]) In 1714 Holkham Staithe still gave access to the sea at Holkham Gap – the northern end of Lady Anne's Road – through Micklefleet Wash. The waters occasionally ran up the Clint, the little stream which is now submerged by Holkham Lake. A small amount of reclamation had taken place to the west of the gap. In 1719 a further embankment, approximately east–west, was built cutting off the Staithe at Holkham from the sea and then running south along the parish boundary between Holkham and Wells, providing the Coke estate with some 560 acres of farmland. Turner extended this western embankment eastwards as far as the town, enclosing a further 108 acres. In the following year, he built an eastern embankment from the ridge on which Wells stands across the low lying land south of the Old Channel, so called, cutting off Church Marsh from the sea. This, according to report,[22] affected the silting up of the Pool which previously could accommodate 'two or three tiers of vessels [which] would lie afloat and swing about'.

The issue of the silting up of the harbour had long occupied the minds of mariners and merchants alike. The problem is that the water rushes in when the tide flows during the space of three hours and takes up to eight hours to empty the harbour on the ebb; the effect is that particulate matter, sand and silt, which is carried into the harbour is deposited there at high tide when the water is temporarily still; the slower ebb tide then fails to scour it leaving much of it behind. What would counteract that would be the presence of a constantly flowing river which Wells lacks. It is therefore of more than passing interest that in 1573 it is recorded that part of the waters of the river Stiffkey 'runneth again to the sea through Wells haven and through Burnham haven', though how this could happen is not clear.[23] If true it means that at that time there would have been a freshwater flow, at least in wet weather, from three sources: Church Marsh, the River Stiffkey and Warham Slade. By 1721 two of these sources had been stopped, and the third would be a matter of prolonged controversy.

Probably in 1738[24] it was proposed by a Mr Freestone, a merchant of the town, that a sluice be built at the entry to one of the subsidiary creeks (now known as Sluice Creek), so that the flow of water through its narrows would be faster and have a more powerful scouring effect. In 1758 however, Sir John Turner MP, who had succeeded to the baronetcy via his father, younger brother of Sir Charles, built a further embankment to join the Nass Point bank[25] thus completely cutting off Warham Slade to the east from the sea and creating, in the process, a new area of potentially rich farmland.

Freestone's sluice, not very well built, rapidly deteriorated; its successor built in 1765 fared no better, having apparently been destroyed by worms, and there lacked funds to repair it. In fact the harbour was in debt. Parliament, it was declared (probably by the local merchants and ship-owners), needed to act. Acts of Parliament in those years were much more informative than they are now, as we have seen; they give us clues as to both the particular concerns and also the state of the harbour and its activities at that time. The new Act, obtained in 1769,[26] recites the fact that since the first Act over a hundred years earlier 'the duties made payable . . . have not been sufficient for the effectual reparation and improvement of the harbour which, notwithstanding a great sum of money raised by a voluntary subscription of the merchants and ship owners belonging to the said town, are encumbered with a considerable debt'; it notes the harbour's continued importance 'to the trade of the kingdom in general' and that it 'must in a short time fall into decay unless some further and more effectual provision is made'. It therefore proposed that action be taken first to pay off the debt. Now for the first time Commissioners were named who were clearly the creditors: Sir John Turner, Wenman Coke, Henry Lee Warner of Walsingham, Sir George Chad of Thursford, Charles Boyles, the Revd James Robinson the incumbent of Wells, twelve named merchants, a brewer, and ten named ships' masters and owners.

The act then declares that once the debt was discharged, the merchants and ship-owners of the town, as before, should constitute the electorate for the nomination of ten 'of the most substantial inhabitants or merchants of the town' who would be joined by Sir John Turner, Wenham Coke, Henry Lee Warner, and George Chad, local landowners, to act as Commissioners to be re-elected every three years.

To prevent the recurrence of debt, new higher duties were fixed. Trade at the time evidently included coals, wheat, rye, barley, malt and salt, the first and last of these presumably being imports. Wells mariners were to pay six pence and masters of ships not belonging to the town were to pay a shilling per chauldron or last. It is noticeable that nothing is said about fishing boats. Other evidence suggests that the fishery was no longer commercially important though undoubtedly there were still local fishing boats. The Dutch herring busses dominated the fishery.

The Commissioners were also empowered to borrow against the security of the dues up to a maximum of £1,500; they could make bye-laws; as with the previous

An extract from the map published by William Faden in 1797.

Act, they were to appoint Collectors to receive the dues; they were to appoint a man to take care of the buoys and beacons and to give instructions as to where vessels should lie or be moored; their powers extended also to the control of fires on board, the discharge of ballast 'or any other sort of rubbish, and over any who would do anything to prejudice or annoy the same', subject to a forty shilling fine.[27] Clearly the harbour was often crowded with vessels, all built of wood, lying alongside each other; in those days there were buildings quite close to the harbour's edge. The fear of fire, as the Act makes clear, was 'that not only the ships and vessels but also [that] the said town would be in great danger of being destroyed'. For that reason, the lighting of fires on vessels moored at the Quay was prohibited, a fine of ten shillings to be paid for breach of the rule.

The Commissioners set to work. However, it rapidly became clear that the silting was continuing and a series of legal actions followed in which Thomas Coke, nephew of the old earl, the now ageing Sir John Turner and the new Commissioners were major opponents.

The question was whether the silting up of the harbour was a natural and unstoppable process or whether it was the result of human agency in reducing the area of water run-off by land reclamation. As always the participants, even including the Commissioners, were a disparate group: local merchants among them were concerned to keep the harbour open; the landowners, on the other hand, had an interest in expanding their lands by reclamation. Each side employed their own experts to support their views. It was argued on the one hand that the Warham Slade would provide water for the scouring of the harbour long after high tide; on the other that its bank enclosed only sixty-six acres, a small area compared with what had previously been enclosed, and that the silting up of the harbour was inevitable. After three trials and several appeals to the High Court, Turner's bank was removed in 1784.[28] Turner had died in 1780 intestate and insolvent. His executors needed the dispute to be settled in order that they could sell the estate to pay Turner's debts, and it was they who brought the matter to court. They were finally defeated at a hearing before the court of King's Bench and sold out to T. W. Coke. Having lost the case, the sale price was reduced by some two thousand pounds.

The effects of the removal of the bank were that there was some improvement in the flow. However, some thirty-five years later in 1808 Coke renewed the action. He sought the Commissioners' permission to renew the bank, promising however to build a tidal reservoir which, it was agreed, would hold five thousand tons of water which would be released 'several times a fortnight' to return a powerful body of backwater to assist in cleansing the harbour. This would be more efficient than the waters of the Slade which produced nothing like this amount. Coke went on to build his bank, somewhat to the south of the earlier one; he began but never completed the reservoir; it soon silted up. North Point Bank, as it is now called, was the result.[29]

Malt and grain

During the century Wells was to become one of the more important ports engaged in the manufacture and transport of malt. As we have seen, the production and export of malt in the town goes back to the fourteenth century.[30] As well as trade, farms would both malt their own barley and brew their own beer; great houses would do the same, as would inns and beer houses. The Bowling Green inn had its own malthouse as late as 1789. However, until the use of hops as both flavouring and more importantly as preservative, unhopped ales could not be transported any distance and local consumption was the norm. Hopped liquors, beers, on the other hand could be both stored and transported. The rise of commercial breweries and the building of large maltings (and the decline of home and farm brewing) date from this time. Hops had long been known about but it was the growth of London, a huge market for beer, which fostered their increased use. The other major

A 16th century malt house – Croft Yard.

constituent apart from water was malted barley: the barley was dried, steeped in water and then allowed to germinate on a large floor, after which it was kiln-dried to halt the process of germination. Steeping lasted about three days and the germination process which followed took about a fortnight. This caused the starch in the grain to become sugar by enzyme action. The malted product was then ground up into what was called 'grist', boiled up with hops to dissolve the sugars and then fermented with yeast to make beer. Because malt was less bulky than the beer which it made, it made every sense to transport it.

Malt was used both for beer and for spirits. In the latter case the 'beer', made by malting, boiling and fermenting without hops, was distilled. Early in the century Wells became a centre for such malting, sending its products abroad, mostly to Holland, as also for local consumption and coastwise transport to London. Barley, too often neglected by comparison with wheat, the so-called queen of cereals, and which had long been a major corn grown in these regions,[31] would become a major export.

The rapid growth of malting for export was during the eighteenth century. In the years from 1727 to 1750 volumes of malt production in the town more than doubled.[32] They contributed nearly a third to the total national exports, a figure that beggars belief. Not all of this production can actually have come through the port of Wells; as a Custom port it will have had added to its totals the trade through Burnham Overy and Brancaster. Also, a large proportion of the malt which left Wells Quay will have come from surrounding small towns and villages which had their own maltings, including Fakenham, Dereham, Swaffham, Ryburgh, Burnham and Brancaster. The great malt house at Brancaster, reputed to be the largest in the country, was not built until 1798 but it replaced an earlier building; that at Overy was reckoned to be 'capacious'; both had three malting floors.[33] Nevertheless, tonnages leaving the coast from Wells and its nearby creeks, almost as great as those of Great Yarmouth, made of the town a place of national importance. The maltings in Wells, with their kilns topped by the characteristic cowls, their many vents allowing a free flow of air for germination, were a dominant presence in the town. All operations in the maltings were worked by hand, with only the mechanical assistance of pulleys to haul the sacks or baskets. One man could cope with about fifteen quarters of steeping capacity, an annual production of about 750 quarters. Including those employed on ancillary tasks such as cleaning the grain, bagging, stoking the furnace, carting and loading, more than a hundred men must have been employed at the task at the height of its success,[34] many in Wells but also in the village maltings inland.

At the end of harvest, many of the labourers who had worked in the fields during the summer and autumn would come to the maltings for work. Before that, it was too hot for malting to take place. No malting could be done when it was frosty either as the germinating grain would spoil. It was a very part-time and insecure occupation. Temperature was so crucial that the many air vents had to be opened and closed in order to regulate it. The whole process was dependent on judging the point at which germination should be stopped and the malt loaded into the kiln. The work was thus a combination of waiting and vigorous activity. All of this may explain the otherwise curious fact that few men were described as maltsters in censuses at a time when malt exports from the port were at high and increasing levels.

For the purpose of distilling, the appropriate malt was of a poorer quality, so-called 'long malt' which was exported to Holland. However, as the industry grew it became a target for taxation and government intervention made life sometimes difficult for the maltsters. The process of steeping increased its volume by as much as 20% which was the point of taxation; in those days it was not technically possible to assess the specific gravity and therefore to tax the potential alcohol content of the resulting beer. Arguments raged over how long steeping should last and, in addition, whether at times of poor harvests at home malt could be exported. There was an export bounty which made even poor quality barley worth malting so it was a very advantageous trade. Thus, in 1767 John Hill, merchant and maltster of Wells complained that his malt was 'of no use in England or Ireland but will be entirely spoiled and probably eaten up by Vermin unless they can be permitted to export it, it being proper only for Dutch distillers'.[35]

The Dutch trade was not to survive. Even in peacetime cargo vessels had to run the risk of attack by privateers, which meant that they tended to be armed.[36] Then to the perennial disputes with government, was added the advent of war, first over American Independence and then with the French. By 1780 England was at war with the American colonies, with Holland, with France and with Spain. Thereafter, 'the Dutch for want of their usual supply from Great Britain, have established a correspondence with Hamburgh, Dantzig and other countries for Barley and . . . they do now make it into Malt in Holland and . . . the total loss of this very valuable Branch of Trade is to be feared'.[37] The fear was justified and the Dutch trade faltered and then died.

In addition, privateers now encouraged by the French, were making severe inroads into east coast shipping. It was a cheap form of military action. The French government authorised or permitted privately owned vessels to plunder enemy shipping at will, allowing them to keep all or most of the proceeds. Of many incidents one was that of the taking of the *Eagle* and the *Jupiter* on 2nd April 1797 by the *Intrepide* out of Dunkirk; naval ships then as always were on patrol but were often unsuccessful.[38]

Coastal shipments of barley continued at high levels until 1786; after that there are few records but it appears that the industry collapsed.[39] The next set of figures, that for shipments coastwise, mostly to London, in the first quarter of the nineteenth century, is minute by comparison.[40] What happened to the surplus barley production and to the work of the maltings is hard to guess. War was the major cause of decline which affected other ports like Yarmouth equally.

The harbour also had its problems. These were less about the silting up of the harbour than the alteration in the alignment of the outer channel. It had moved eastwards so that it was now much less safe than it had been when a ship could sail directly in on a flood tide which ran roughly in the direction of the channel. Now that the tide set across the channel, without a good wind ships could easily be carried onto the sands and lost.[41]

It is of course conceivable that Wells was engaged in the overland shipments to Burton on Trent, by canal to Liverpool and the north west, which were undoubtedly on the increase (in spite of the fact that the journey to the latter took seven weeks[42]) but the evidence is of considerably reduced levels of production which must have affected the prosperity of the town. The war would bring hard times; social disruption would follow.

Other grains were also grown of which wheat, as being the only cereal suitable for the baking of bread because of its gluten content, was the most important. There had always been mills locally, mostly driven by wind, some by water and some even by horses. Mills are mentioned in the Domesday Book. In 1604 William Dowse was 'slayne with the stroke of the armes of a wyndmill sail'; a map in 1780 shows five windmills on Mill Road, two on the land to the north and two plus a horse mill near the corner of where Mill road turns at right angles to the coast. In 1796 three windmills and a horse mill were auctioned at the Fleece Inn. Two post mills can be identified standing side by side at Mill Farm, on the north side of Mill Road, one of which was probably demolished in the early 1800s. A tower mill was built on Mill Road about 1827 to replace the demolished mill; it had a four-storey tower, and a bake office and the horse mill operated from the same site. A mill stood on Black's Lane at the top of Market Lane (the site of a murder in 1817!). Yet another, the Wells smock mill, was built by Augustus Dewing. It stood at the other end of the ridge on which Wells is built, on what is now

The last windmill in Wells in the 19th century, in Northfields Lane.

Northfields Lane. Smock mills were a type of windmill that consisted of a sloping, horizontally weather boarded tower, usually with six or eight sides; this had ten. It had a bakery adjacent capable of 'baking upwards of forty stones of bread at a batch'.[43] There were thus seven mills at one time in the nineteenth century. The Market Lane mill was removed in 1850 and the post mill on Mill Road in 1866. The smock mill on Northfields Lane survived until after the turn of the century, following the building of the new steam driven roller mill in 1893.

Transport

The increase in the levels of trade over the century need some comment. Historically, ships carrying coal from the north-east had rarely carried more than thirty tons. Sea transport was dependent on wind and weather (and would remain so until the advent of steam). The same was true to some degree of inland travel. The old Roman road from Norwich to London was 110 miles long and took five nights to travel by waggon 'if God permit'.[44] The sandy soil hereabouts drained well so that Nathaniel Kent regarded Norfolk roads as better than 'almost any other county' but this may not have been saying much. Geese and turkeys were driven to London on foot from August to October when the mud became too deep. Herds of cattle were driven from Norfolk to Smithfield market which cannot have improved the quality of the roads.[45] Nevertheless, the eighteenth century, the century of the so-called Industrial Revolution was to require if not a matching revolution in the development of transport, a rapid series of developments. The changes were many and various: larger ships now carried more than four times the tonnage of coal than a century before. Their capacity to carry grain to the miners of the north-east, to London and to the continent reflected that.

Hull had become important in attracting wool imports for the West Riding weaving industry and Norfolk wool, suitable for the manufacture of worsted, passed through Wells 'in considerable quantities.'[46] Perhaps it was then that the Golden Fleece, still on the Quay, acquired its name and its plaster reliefs depicting scenes relating to the wool industry.

With the rise in coastal traffic the dangers became more evident. This was not only the result of wild weather; there was no proper system of shore lights to guide vessels along the coast until the nineteenth century. The light at Cromer was first lit in 1719, but was only a coal fire till 1792; Happisburgh's light was only established by colliers in 1789; Orford and Southwold not until the next century. The lightship at the Dudgeon shoal was put on station in 1736, only the second of such vessels to be deployed.[47] Before then 'the sea was so full of wreck on these coasts that those at sea are forced to look sharp for clear of it.' In 1692 a hundred and forty of a fleet of light coasters were wrecked on the north Norfolk coast, together with fifty ships outward bound for the Wash, a total destruction in one night of two hundred ships and over a thousand lives.[48] Another factor was the abandonment by the 1780s of the old custom of laying up ships for the winter months. Colliers were notorious for their poor condition, 'cruel to the point of depravity', whose crews, sleeping in the focs'le, 'were occasionally frozen to death and continually contracted consumption.'[49]

Conditions would gradually improve but until the coming of the railway the only way to carry heavy cargoes any distance was by sea. Another limitation affecting exports was that the larger ships could only carry what could be brought to the harbour from inland (an issue which was to exercise the minds of merchants a generation or so later).

Roads, since 1555, had been a parish responsibility. Only in 1691 was power given to levy a rate for their upkeep. The traditional packhorse, able to negotiate poor roads, had a very limited carrying capacity. Heavy waggons which began to supersede them during the century caused huge damage to dirt roadways in wet weather. At best they proceeded at about walking pace. The first response was to limit the size of waggons. Turnpike trusts, controlled by justices of the peace, then began to be formed. They provided better road financing but they were not a panacea; they improved the quality of roads partly by restricting their use; they made roads no longer a common utility but a private facility available only to those who could pay. For that reason they were opposed in many places, their gates torn down. The Wells Turnpike was not built until 1826, but local initiative did not wait: driven by commercial need, it had already, forty years or so before, created a carrier network, based on inn yards, which took goods between Wells, Fakenham and Norwich.[50] The carriers themselves rarely travelled more than thirty miles; what they did was to provide a feeder network to Norwich and thence to London and other provincial cities.

Waggons equally crucially brought grain to the harbour from outlying farms and maltings and delivered coal to the shipyards, to forges, to the maltings and to great houses. Hundreds of tons, particularly of barley and malt, were to be brought into the town by the middle of the century. The havoc wrought by broken waggon wheels when waggons fell into ruts can just about be imagined. It resulted in improvements to their design. Variable front axles enabled them to be steered; rudimentary springs and brakes made them better able to cope with the still poor roads.[51]

Passenger travel had become quicker by the changing of horses at regular intervals, the so-called stage coach. Stage coaches were first run in March 1785 running from the Standard Inn to Norwich. At three pence a mile, the journey was as costly as a week's wages for a working man,[52] but they were not intended for him; they were a response to the desire and need for merchants and manufacturers to develop and maintain an efficient and deepening contact network. Subsequently they ran from the Fleece and then later from the Ostrich Inn near Church Plain. Travelling times were reduced again and again.

Gentrification

The rise of trade had brought money into the town and hence a growth of   the merchant classes. Trade was not without risk: bankruptcy became common.[53] Perhaps some of the merchants overreached themselves. At any rate some of the inhabitants took advantage of the greater availability of household articles, once the preserve of the rich. They and their wives dressed first in the new fashions in wool coming from Norwich, which reached its zenith in the 1750s, and then latterly in cotton. The Norwich worsted textile industry 'had no match in Britain or the Continent'[54] in the middle of the century and more and more garments were being bought from tailors rather than made at home. The removal of restrictive legislation in 1773 allowed the growth in the production of lighter cotton goods, from Lancashire and the Derbyshire dales; the weaving industry in Norwich began its slow decline. Norwich's loss was Wells' gain as people began to dress better and live a more genteel lifestyle.

In part this was stimulated by the self-aggrandising of the gentry. The Cokes of Hill Hall had a large number of servants, in excess of fifty, some of whom they dressed in livery. The women dressed in home-spun garments made by themselves, but the men were supplied by local tailors. Richard Hackett, a tailor of Wells, in 1737 supplied eight livery mourning suits for male servants on the death of the wife of King George II.[55] Undoubtedly Hackett's business was also with people of the town. The same would be true of Joseph Baker who supplied gloves for the servants at Hill Hall. Dressmakers in the town were readily to be found. Meanwhile, the increasing wants for furniture and drapery which could not be supplied by the town came from London by ship to the harbour; a regular service ran from the Thames to Wells.[56] Doctors were few and far between as well as being expensive; apothecaries were more numerous. Mr Haylett[57] of Wells attended both master and servants at Holkham; he doubled as a vet. Food, apart from what was grown in the kitchen garden or came from the dairy, was bought in. A butcher in Wells supplied the meat. Wells had no market by this time so the market at Burnham was patronised. Gradually, Wells grocers began to stock tea and coffee, spices and even, by 1749, bottled capers and olives. Isaac Nickals of Staithe Street made clocks. By 1800 we can find tailors such as Thomas Tingey and Richard Clarke, drapers such as Miss Mary Alderson, and milliners such as Miss Jickling. Wells had a wine merchant, Mr William Foster. Messrs Bloom and Haycock ran general stores, selling everything from oats and wine to coal. There was even a book club.[58]

The families of the merchants of Wells attempted to imitate the Cokes, the Bedingfields, the l'Estranges and their kindred in their dress and in their furnishings, if not in their making the Grand Tour (which the young Coke undertook from 1712 to 1718). Those who served them participated in their lifestyle at one remove; but such a world was a long way from that of fishermen and farm labourers.

The town would change its appearance over the century. One factor was the gradual development of window glass. Glass, still expensive, was improving in quality and larger windows could be made. Crown glass could now be made into panes more than a foot square. The government responded by the 1696 introduction of a window tax of two shillings annually to be collected by Commissioners drawn from the ranks of JPs. Some bricked their windows up – as can still be seen in the town – but the tax was repealed only in 1851. But the other contrary effect was the introduction of shop windows. One could see out; but one could also see in. Shops on High Street and Staithe Street whose windows had previously been no different from those of other dwellings began as the century progressed to have larger windows, still consisting of a number of panes, but large enough for passers-by to see what was for sale. Thus Staithe Street, whose wide thoroughfare was fringed by a number of large houses, some with long gardens stretching up the hill, began to assume its current look as shops were built in front of former front doors. Some can still be seen. At home the development of the sash window made it easier to keep a house wind and weather tight, a little revolution in domestic lives. At eleven pence a foot, mid-century crown glass was nearly twice the price of broadsheet glass;[59] it seems it was worth it.

Smuggling

Smuggling had been a maritime industry even before customs duties were imposed by King John in 1203. Contraband might be concealed amongst cargoes entering large ports or brought into small creeks or open beaches without any quays at all. Valuable commodities – in the early days it was wool – could be sold abroad to huge advantage if no duty was charged.

In the eighteenth century smuggling became more a matter of record partly because of the increased quantities involved. It was said that in some places more was traded illegally than went legitimately through port records (though in the absence of successful prosecutions figures are inevitably hard to come by). Nevertheless, the trade was known to involve rich and poor alike, the aristocracy, the gentry, the clergy and the labouring classes.[60] Robert Walpole, sometime Prime Minister and local landowner, had been frequently visited by James Swanton, smuggler from Wells, who provided him with fine linen and wines free from customs duties. Even the navy became implicated. In 1722, twelve tubs of brandy were found on board one of Her Majesty's ships, HMS *Hawke* at Harwich.[61] The import of brandy, rum, gin, tobacco, tea, linen, silk and whatever was in demand became a huge industry involving literally hundreds of men.

By the late eighteenth century[62] smuggling gangs around the country had become larger and better organised, able to buy fast boats which bade to outrun the Customs boats; the gangs were violent and well armed. Once ashore they could sell their wares at considerable profit but still for something like a quarter of their cost if bought legitimately. There was no police force in the country at the time and, while local constables in each parish could deal with minor matters, this kind of large scale crime became the responsibility not only of Customs and Excise officers but also of the regiments of Dragoons who were billeted in large towns in their support. Serious armed confrontations became increasingly common.

Wars are costly, impacting upon tax rates. The American Revolutionary War which led to the declaration of independence in 1776 was driven partly by a resistance to British taxation 'without representation' but also by republican and egalitarian ideals. Supported by France and Spain for political reasons, the French themselves were shortly to adopt radical opinions in a Revolution which was to lead to war across Europe.

Taxation in England at the time was largely derived from trade. Excise duties, at that time collected by a separate government department, were imposed on a range of domestic and imported goods, including malt, which was therefore taxed twice. In 1787–88 the contribution of the malt and beer industries to the Exchequer was £4.5 million out of total excise revenue of £6.5 million.

Excise men were socially unpopular and the risks of successful prosecution of smugglers were low. In the May of 1779 Robert Bliss was appointed as Excise Superintendent at the port of Wells. He was to lead the forces of law in a series of clashes with smugglers running the inland distribution networks for locally landed contraband. Such landings were an almost daily occurrence. Smugglers were able to recruit 'troops' from local villages, such as Holme and Thornham, of up to 200 men according to one of their leaders, William Franklyn. To enter such villages without adequate support from Dragoons was to risk being lynched. Bliss's first action was to raid six licensed establishments in Wells simultaneously. He confiscated in all a hundred gallons of spirits from the Fleece, the Red Lion, the Standard, the Tuns, the Bowling Green and the Fighting Cocks.[63] He continued with such raids in the months to come, all along the coast from Wells to Hunstanton, supported by locally billeted detachments of Dragoons. Auction sales of seized contraband goods became a regular feature of Wells life. Bliss even raided Old Hunstanton church during the service on Christmas Eve, retrieving a large hoard of barrels from the church tower.[64] Franklyn's revenge was to lure Bliss to the village of Thornham where his small troop was surrounded by a mob and he was almost bludgeoned to death and was saved only by one of his own men who took hold of the reins of Bliss's horse and galloped off thus escaping by the skin of their teeth. Too badly injured and psychologically scarred to continue, Bliss left Norfolk and was eventually dismissed the service without compensation.

Franklyn's supplier was the master of the cutter the *Lively*, William Kemball, who was equally given to violence. In September 1784, confronted by Dragoons on horseback as he unloaded barrels of cognac onto the beach at Burnham Flats, he shot and killed a Customs officer and a Dragoon, wounding several others. As with Franklyn earlier, no jury could be found to convict him at his trial for murder at Thetford Assizes.[65] Subsequently charged with smuggling by the Court of Exchequer, Kemball jumped bail and was never seen again. That he and an associate were able to pay the bail fee of £299 per man shows how profitable smuggling was.[66] Resuming his profession shortly thereafter, he dealt with one Customs cutter by offering its crew 30 tubs of cognac, which offer was duly accepted.

The ending of the War of American Independence in the same year brought the Royal Navy into contention with its combination of brig-sloops and warships, but the French Revolution and subsequent declaration of war against Britain in February 1793 once again gave smugglers their opportunity.

6. Revolution Deferred

The nineteenth century began with a country divided, a government fearful and at war. For Wells, as for much of the country, it was a time of uncertainty and poverty which brought its own social unrest. In the event England avoided the turmoils which affected most of Europe but at the time it must have seemed a close run thing.

Subversion and Dissent

The coming of the French Revolution in 1789 was part of a larger process by which new ideas were ventilated in relation to the established social order and to traditional beliefs and practices. Many people, including the citizens of Norwich, a well-known centre of Dissent, welcomed it. One Norwich Baptist minister, the Revd Mark Wilks, asserted that 'Jesus Christ was a revolutionist', adding that the Revolution was of God.[1] The Norwich Revolution Society was formed in 1789. As news of the grim character of the revolution permeated English society, the government, never liberal in its sympathies, moved from nervousness to repression, banning meetings of more than forty-five people, setting up a Committee of Secrecy and legislating to suppress dissent. After the secretary, Isaac Saint, was arrested for seditious libel the society was disbanded only to be succeeded by the more subtly named Norwich Patriotic Society, one of whose objects nevertheless was the widening of the suffrage. It apparently had members 'in every town and almost every village in Norfolk'.[2]

The pressure for change and its expression through direct action were given impetus after the poor harvest and hard winter of 1794–95. The Home Secretary, the Duke of Portland, required magistrates to submit returns of grain held by them. One of the needs was to supply the cities, particularly London. Bread had more than doubled in price from sixpence to thirteen and a half pence. It was this which set off the bread riots which took place in Wells that winter. They extended over several weeks. The precipitating factor was the discovery that a shipload of wheat was to be sent to the London market; the riot that ensued was met with the intervention of the militia armed with bayonets. A large gathering mostly of women sought physically to prevent the loading of vessels. As the days went by matters apparently grew worse; farmers in the neighbourhood together with some local landowners attempted to repress the rioters, while sailors joined the mob threatening the troops. The Lord Lieutenant of the county, Lord Townshend, ordered the horse artillery, the Pembroke Militia, from Holt which was eventually able to restore the peace.[3] But this was not the end of the matter: flour intended for transhipment held on nearby Sharrington Common was the subject of further conflict between local people and the militia, though Townshend reported that Wells itself was quiet following the military intervention. He noted in a further letter to Portland that 'Mr. Hoste [a local clergyman and magistrate] is arrived from Holkham with news that Thomas Coke and other magistrates have settled allowances in Wells for the poor, who have been much neglected there'. He hoped 'that the Admiralty would suppress and correct sailors who join in the disturbances in the sea port towns'.[4]

As the fear of invasion by the French grew, recruitment began in earnest. The loyalty of the sailors, which was certainly in question, was encouraged so that they might 'serve on the Norfolk coast'; T. W. Coke gave them five guineas each for their trouble.[5] In 1803 Townshend called on all districts to raise volunteers of fifty men each. Wells did so and by 1st June it had raised its first corps. By 15th August it had raised a second. Holkham meanwhile by 14th September had raised a corps of sixty men. In the same year several of Wells' ship-owners offered their ships, twenty-two of them, to be converted into warships by equipping them with cannon.[6] Eighty men were recruited in the town as 'Sea Fencibles' to see off any invading force by boat. In the event, no invasion was attempted and it turned out that Napoleon's proposed invasion site was in Kent. But Norfolk had become, for a while, a militarised community with one in five men under arms.

There remained a mood, expressed radically in thought and violent action in France, which found its expression elsewhere in what people believed. Freethinking characterised the response of many like Thomas Paine of Thetford, author of *The Rights of Man*, who supported the protesters, arguing against the hereditary principle and rejecting the claims of revealed religion.

Religious expression found itself more and more various. The Established church had become one of several churches and was no longer the sole expression of English religion. In Wells the Independents, also known as Congregationalists, had built their first chapel in 1817; it would be enlarged with galleries in 1826. The Society of Friends, or Quakers, had built theirs close to the Workhouse in 1783. The Methodists had themselves divided. The Wesleyan Methodist chapel was built in 1808 by Tinkers Corner. John Wesley had visited the town in 1781 possibly to a house in Cocks Yard owned by a Miss Franklin. (The yard became successively known as Ranters Yard and then Chapel Yard.) These Methodists had become respectable; less so their Primitive brethren. Primitive Methodism was part of an upsurge of religious

The Primitive Methodist chapel in Wells.

enthusiasm and social concern which affected Norfolk in the years after the battle of Waterloo. Energised locally by the Yarmouth coal heaver turned evangelist Robert Key it swept through the villages so that scarcely a village locally is without its, now sadly closed, Primitive Methodist chapel. The 'Prims' as they were known became closely allied with the Agricultural Trade Union movement and hence with unrest.[7] They initially met in the open air and prided themselves on what they called Camp meetings. They began meeting in cottages but eventually put up modest chapels. The Wells chapel was built in Cocks Yard. A new chapel was built in 1891 in Theatre Road; it is now the Methodist church of the town.

The Agricultural Revolution

Agriculture was becoming a cockpit of change. The population of England increased by nearly 80% in the eighteenth century, from five million in 1701 to over eight million in 1801 (and was to double again from 1801 to 1851). Arguably the various improvements in husbandry were one of the causes. So-called rational approaches to farming held that it was a human duty to increase productivity and to do otherwise was culpable. Nature was there for the taking. Thus was combined a huge increase in the amount of land under cultivation, a 70% increase between 1769 and 1859, and a number of developments in agricultural practices.

Increased production was associated with the work of another generation of Townshends, the famous 'Turnip' Townshend (1674–1738) who owned land around Wells and who was responsible for promoting the Norfolk Four Course system of crop rotation. He in turn learned a good deal from the Dutch, our near neighbours. Among the improvements was the use of clover and of turnips as an animal feed crop, which meant that more fresh meat was available for consumption in winter; animals could be kept in larger numbers rather than having to be slaughtered in the autumn. 'Cattle and sheep could not be supported without them', wrote Nathaniel Kent the agriculturalist in 1775. The introduction of clover as part of rotation was the means by which nitrogen was put back into the soil, saving the need to let land be allowed to go fallow for a year. So-called artificial grasses like lucerne and sainfoin made for better pasture and hay for winter. Arthur Young, first secretary of the Board of Agriculture, who toured Norfolk in 1768, described the spirit of improvement which had seized the inhabitants and wrought an amazing effect: 'instead of wild and uncultivated wastes, inhabited by scarcely anything but sheep, the country is cut into enclosures, cultivated in a most husband-like manner, richly manured, well peopled and yielding a hundred times the produce it did in its former state'.[8]

Young's early enthusiasm for enclosures was not universally shared. Nor was he correct about the allegedly parlous state of the land prior to enclosure. The system of cooperation between landlord and tenants by which corn and sheep alternated had been in existence since before the sixteenth century; the problem, outlined earlier, was that it relied upon precise cooperation between landlord and tenant in agreeing where sheep would be fed in summer before the harvest – on fallow land and the heath – and this cooperation had begun to break down; but the failure was human not agricultural. Small scale enclosure of strips by tenants and landlords alike denied access by sheep to so-called half year land, such as existed in Wells.[9] Enclosure made so-called 'shackage', the feeding of sheep on the fields after harvest, more difficult too.[10] The human cost of excluding villagers from the common was the creation of a class of dependent landless labourers who would become hungry, restless and resentful. That truth was something which Young was himself to realise, unhappily to no good purpose. Those who had been supportive of his Board of Agriculture no longer wanted to listen when he changed his tune.[11] It was true that crop rotation and the advent of the turnip made a difference to the productivity of the land, but few were concerned with the social cost or with the virtues of the previous system which relied upon collaboration rather than private initiative.

The emphasis on 'improvement' according to rational principles showed itself in farm buildings. No longer did labourers live in the farmhouse and eat around the kitchen table. Coke built solid farmhouses for his tenants and cottages for his labourers. As for the farm buildings they took on the characteristics of the 'model farm' with a central courtyard surrounded on one side by the farmhouse, opposite

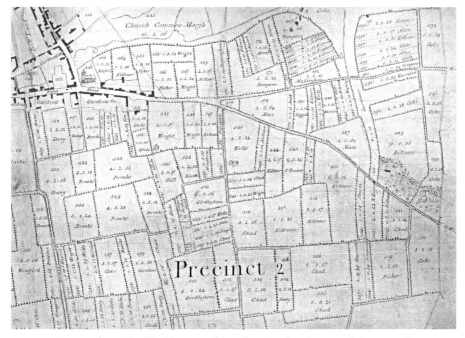

*A map from the Holkham archive showing land ownership around
the church in 1793*

which were barns, dairy and henhouse. Manure was collected in a pit or stack in
the centre of the yard.[12] Less grand versions of Coke's model farm were built in the
town. Subsequently, farmhouses were moved away from the smells and noise of
the yard, allowing specialist buildings to be put up on an E shaped plan. (In Wells
Manor Farm may have been a later version of this process.)

Another practice, applied more widely and systematically, was marling, the
spreading of a lime-rich loam, dug from pits, which made the soil friable and less
acid – which marshes tended to be. It was dug locally but also brought in by sea. It
was sometimes made a condition of tenants' leases that they should marl the soil
at an agreed number of barrow loads per acre. (There are a dozen marl pits still
visible within five or so miles of the town.) New breeds of cattle and sheep were
introduced with better meat-producing qualities. (In the case of sheep this was
sometimes at the expense of the quality of the wool.) The seed drill, invented by
Jethro Tull in 1701, allowed seed to be planted in rows, enabling effective weeding
with a hoe. Horses had replaced oxen to pull ploughs which, themselves, began to
be made of metal rather than wood. The first steel plough was invented in 1830.

All of these developments and more were to be taken up and promoted.

95

Thomas William Coke, about whom we have already heard a little, was their major champion. He was the son of Wenham Coke, and as such Lord of several manors at Holkham, and also in Wells; he was to become, like his great uncle, Earl of Leicester. Until his second marriage in 1821 at the age of sixty-nine, he conducted what were effectively annual agricultural shows, also known as sheep shearings.[13] They were first reported in the press in 1798. Originally the event was simply the shearing of sheep in the great barn on the estate, but Coke began to invite his numerous contacts to visit the estate when he would arrange a tour on horseback for his guests; they would then admire his livestock and the new machinery laid out for them to see. The tour was followed by a meal for upwards of 200 people when speeches would be given and the opportunity provided for animals to be sold by auction. The Prince Regent attended. Coke himself was more of a publicist than an innovator but he improved his grassland so that he was able to increase his flocks of sheep from 700 to 2,400. He became a promoter of better sheep breeds. He also, whenever he could, bought land locally. One of his means of doing so was to secure its enclosure.

Enclosure of open arable fields and of commons had been a gradual process, proceeding differently in different parts of the country. Norfolk remained comparatively unenclosed until the eighteenth century. The 'assarting' of waste – clearing and draining woodland and marshes – and making of it arable land or pasture was one means by which the common was reduced; another was 'engrossment' by which tenants exchanged land so that they could combine adjacent strips into one plot, which could then be enclosed. In both cases common rights were reduced. Common land was, in theory, open to all, though the rights to it belonged to those who owned land not to their tenants who farmed it or labourers who worked on it. They would receive no compensation when common land was enclosed. Hitherto, the common had been effectively open to all to gain firewood, catch rabbits or pasture a cow. Two wide droves, west and east, connected Wells Common, known as the Heath, which lay to the south of the town, with the marshes. (The west drove, some forty yards wide, ran from the west marsh – now farmland – southwards to the heath; the east drove, much narrower, followed the eastern parish boundary more or less.) Sheep and cattle were driven from the one to the other, depending on tides.[14] (Sheep bridges had been constructed across the creeks as far north as East Fleet.) The desire of farmers to obtain exclusive use of their land, understandable though it was, was resisted by many, not just the poor. Petitions against enclosure drew many signatures locally. Nevertheless, large landowners, led by T. W. Coke, eventually obtained a private Act of Parliament for the enclosure of the land in their parish. By his efforts and expenditure an Act of

1811 brought about the appointment of a Commissioner who was to first map the parish and then allocate every acre, rod and perch of it to some landowner, great or small and in the process to deprive others who were held to have no rights.

The Commissioner, John Dugmore of Swaffham, not only recorded the land ownership of the parish but also changed it.[15] Some roads were to be stopped up and new ones created. Every plot of land in the parish was allocated to whoever appeared to Dugmore to have the best claim. Appeal against his judgement lay to Norfolk Assizes which, of course, was beyond the means of small landowners. He sat week by week in the town for nearly two years, listening to every claim and making his judgement, his decisions to be recorded, perch by perch and acre by acre, in every field and every street. Some matters were easy to decide. When land was not indisputably owned by one person it was different. The Heath, which had been available to common landowners to pasture their animals, was divided up into small plots, to be allocated in compensation for the loss of common rights; but many of these plots were too small to be farmed, and too expensive to fence. As a result Coke had, by 1820, bought most of the small landowners out. He usually offered sums above the market price but the effect was to render many townsfolk landless.[16] They would become a mobile workforce, made idle whenever the weather kept them off the fields or the landowner did not need them. It was easier to employ them in the summer and pay them off in winter, leaving them to their own devices. The widely expressed view was that peasant people, assumed to be lazy, should be put to work as and when required.

Deprived of pasture and legitimate sources of meat, some sought out food on the marshes; some poached. The early fowlers had no guns, so they used snares and nets to entrap the fowl. The development of punt guns altered things and brent, pink foot, bean and greylag geese were shot both for the pot and for sale. Wells was to become a Mecca for gentlemen wildfowlers a hundred years later; but these men were making their living.[17]

The dispossessed

The Cokes were great believers in providing for their tenant farmers. They were less solicitous about the needs of the landless poor.[18] To those who no longer had access to the common were added the many men returning from service in the Napoleonic wars. The Overseers of the Poor, appointed as they were each year by magistrates, in practice, from nominations by the parish vestry, faced a difficult task. Collection was not easy: arrears were often incurred and the collection did not always meet need. In 1601 the Wells Overseers collected £18 0s 10d against an expenditure of £23 3s 2d. Twenty-seven monthly recipients were named together with six children. Occasional payments included £4 for an apprenticeship.[19] Because the system was based on the parish it was important that poor people were only assisted by their own parish. Jane Downey, a vagrant singlewoman of Wells, was one of hundreds returned to their home parishes. She was sent back to Wells from St Peter Mancroft in Norwich.[20] Apart from vagrants there was the wider question of who should relieve the poor: the issue of settlement. Under the Poor Relief Act 1662 a person could gain legal settlement in a parish by parentage, by marriage, by birth, occupation of property worth more than £40 a year and 40 days residence without removal. Additionally, those serving an apprenticeship, being hired in service for a year, holding parish office and paying parish rates gained the right of settlement. This discouraged people from moving in search of work; it also encouraged landowners to pull down empty cottages to prevent their being occupied by potential paupers, and farmers from taking on labourers for an entire year.[21]

Various factors, especially population growth, made a more substantial provision necessary. In 1723 the Workhouse Act empowered the building of local workhouses. Wells Workhouse on Church Street, probably built in the 1770s, was one of the largest buildings in the town; it was one of over 2,000 constructed across the country. The census of 1793 records the residents as numbering forty-one probably including staff.

Even so the system was showing signs of strain. The parish was too small and inflexible a unit to cope with growing need. Food prices had been driven high by the blockade of English ports. With the ending of the war in 1815, cheap imports of wheat from the continent caused the price of bread to fall dramatically, an apparent blessing to consumers, but a nightmare to farmers. In some places land was abandoned by insolvent tenants who could not sell their grain. Riots and acts of destruction ensued in the countryside as labourers, now relying on wages, were thrown out of work; at Littleport in the Isle of Ely, two rioters were killed and seventy-five arrested. More locally, covert action, which took the form of arson, animal maiming and machine breaking, became common. Property owned by the Wells overseer of the poor was set fire to.[22] The poor harvests which followed in 1816, and then in 1822 and 1829 drove prices up. The latter was particularly bad, and the winter that followed was harsh. This was noticed by some of the wealthier citizens of the town who made a distribution of coal and food to the distressed the following January.[23]

The so-called 'Swing' Riots of 1830 began that autumn. Local farm labourers got together, making demands which were accompanied by threatening notes

Sir

Your name is down amongst the Black hearts in the Black Book and this is to advise you and the like of you, who are Parson Justasses, to make your Wills

Ye have been the Blackguard Enemies of the People on all occasions, Ye have not yet done as ye ought

Swing

A typical anonymous letter from the the time of the Swing riots.

signed 'Swing' addressed to local farmers.[24] They wanted higher wages and more secure employment; they wanted bread. There were twenty-eight fires in Norfolk that autumn; the following year there were fifty-two. (It cannot have been a coincidence that the Lucifer match was invented that year.) One observer wrote wryly to the press that the fires ignited by the rioters might keep some people warm that Christmas and that others owed their Christmas dinners to the increased wages which farmers had been made to pay; it was signed 'Swing'.[25] The troubles continued for some time; animal maiming was particularly distressing and Coke convened meetings of landowners in order to coordinate a response. Covert action rumbled on for more than a dozen years.

One of the elements of dissension was the tithe. Until 1836, the payment of a tenth of everything produced, whether from the land or by manufacturing process, went to tithe holders. Until the Reformation the recipients of tithe had been the Church, whether monasteries or parishes. The system dated back to the tenth century. But that part of the tithe which had gone to the monasteries now went to their successors, who were secular landowners. Thus the gentry and the clergy between them continued to receive this biblical tax from villagers at a time when village labourers were experiencing unprecedented difficulties. In the autumn of 1830 'tithe owning clergymen found themselves besieged in their rectories and vestries, waylaid and surrounded as they moved around their parishes, and confronted and jostled at tithe audit meetings. In many cases peace was only restored when a promise of some kind of abatement had been extracted'.[26]

The church, in the persons of the minister and the churchwardens, often found themselves the administrators of charity; payments were made out of income from land purchased by the trustees, a position for whose exercise they were sometimes criticised. In the case of Ann Tidd's charity, the position was otherwise: the land on which the sums payable were charged was in private hands – Sir George Chad and, on his death, Joseph Haycock. It appeared that neither had paid more than £5 instead of the £20 due. The Commissioners appointed to inquire into the administration of charities were not happy. 'Some dissatisfaction has, with reason been expressed with regard to the dispensing of this charity', they note laconically. It was in fact the rector, Valentine Hill, and his churchwardens who came up smelling of roses having discovered this matter, and responsibility for the charity was assigned to them as a result.[27] Hill and his co-trustees were less effective in administering William Elliott's charity for the distribution of bread from income from stock dividends. It was thought that they should determine 'upon a mode of appropriating the funds in some manner more beneficial to the poor than that which hitherto has been adopted'.

There were also two seventeenth-century charities previously mentioned: Mungo Morray's gift of £18 per annum for the poor and that of Christopher Ringer for two widows to teach thirty children each and for wheat flour to be divided amongst about 150 poor folk. The school was apparently still running in 1834 and the flour being distributed; the two charities were running together. Clearly it was desirable that such charities should be properly administered but private charity was no longer an adequate solution to the problem. Self help societies offered one solution; government intervention seemed necessary as another.

The Poor Law Amendment Act of 1834 was in part a response to the unrest. It empowered the creation of something which had begun to develop in any case, the union of parishes, each of which was to have its Union Workhouse. The poor were no longer to be supported by what was called outdoor relief, living in their own rented homes; instead they would work for their upkeep in the Union workhouse. Their condition was supposed to be one of 'shame' for their alleged 'fraud, indolence or improvidence'; workhouse provision was to be worse than that of the lowest paid labourer.[28] The Walsingham Union workhouse which was to meet the needs of fifty parishes was built in 1836, in Great Snoring, to replace the old workhouse in Wells on Church Street. The latter was then sold at a meeting of the ratepayers in July 1838. The new workhouse was originally to have been built at Thursford but Sir George Chad successfully persuaded the Commissioners not to put it in the village

The entrance to Thursford Castle, the workhouse at Walsingham.

where he lived. Like most workhouses it was actually remote from any village centre, on the very edge of the parish. Workhouses were never as full as their planners expected them to be. Local farmers were glad of extra hands at harvest. Moreover, they proved not to be as awful in every respect as intended; the lawmakers had no conception of how abject was the actual condition of some labourers. The amount and quality of food, according to union accounts, were very reasonable: 'in the early days of the new Poor Law the material standard of living of able-bodied paupers in Norfolk was much better than that of the independent farm labourer'.[29] Workhouses were clean and relatively warm. They were also to be a cheaper form of relief than hitherto, and they were; it was hoped that they might 'in the longer term convert the disloyal bad poor into good useful members of local society'.[30] Such were the good intentions of the gentry.

On the other hand, they were demeaning and hostile environments. Some of those cast into them had never before left their village; the sexes were separated as were members of the same family; they found themselves living with strangers; all were required to dress in the marked uniform clothing supplied to them; discipline was rigid. Some commentators feared that the workhouse 'would break up their homes and family connexions rendering them incapable of ever rising from the condition of parochial paupers and prisoners'.[31] Initially they provoked a violent response. A labourers' strike in nearby Great Bircham drew men from other villages and there was considerable violence so that the Dragoons had to be called in and the ringleaders arrested.[32] A proposed solution to the surplus of labour was the encouragement of emigration. Men were encouraged to go north or abroad to the colonies, the largest number being from the Docking, Aylsham, Erpingham and Walsingham Unions. Coke only stopped his financial assistance for emigration when he discovered that it was the good labourers who were leaving his estate.[33] In retrospect, it can be seen that working families, falling on hard times, were caught between two inconsistent demands: between the parochialism which demanded that they should be the responsibility of their home parish and not become a burden on others on the one hand; and on the other the desire of some farmers and landowners, gentry and clergy that they should not 'vegetate and be supported' where they were attached 'by accident of birth' but offer their services wherever they were needed, whatever the cost in social disruption or family breakup.[34]

Two portraits of the town

The 'Inclosure award', as it was called, of 1813, gives an unrivalled picture of Wells in the early nineteenth century, simply because it is so comprehensive. In describing every piece of land, every yard, every coalhouse, every malting, every cottage, every great house, every field, it is a picture in words.[35] To begin with it shows the many malt houses along the Quay, possibly as many as a dozen, each with its kilns rising above the houses. It shows the several butchers crowded on the Quay. It shows the granaries on the Glebe and Haycocks Yard. The majority of the population lived in the many yards running up from Burnham Road, as it was then called, along the Quay; they lived in cramped and squalid conditions, cottages being sometimes as little as thirty feet by ten feet including their yards. We are reminded by the existence of coal yards of the importance of the harbour in bringing coal from Yorkshire and the Tyne to supply maltings, smithies, forges, hearths and cooking ranges. The great houses such as Marsh House near the church and Westward House where Peter Hudson the mill owner lived were up and over the ridge on which Wells stands; the windmills stood along the ridge of high ground from east to west; Ilex House commanded a view over the western marshes. Closer to the Custom House on the Quay, where the shipyards were, was Tudor Cottage and down the hill towards the church was the Ostrich, now as then a private house but for while a public house. (All of these buildings can still be seen.) The presence of stables reminds us that horses were the main means of motive power. Some men rode, some drove behind them in carriages, some hitched them to ploughs. The countryside was not alien to the town. Farmhouses and their yards lay all along Burnt Street and off Bases Lane, for south of Theatre Road was all fields. Only a thin strip of buildings ran up Staithe Street to 'Little London', the area around the Methodist chapel that is now the Library, and then between High Street and the Buttlands down the hill to the church about which were public houses, shops and a playhouse.

The Award shows us how much of the town was owned by absentees. There was Sir George Chad who lived in Thursford Hall; Henry Girdlestone, a Wells man but now a vicar in Wiltshire; Robert and Elizabeth Jeary who lived in Kings Lynn; Benjamin Kittner who had houses in Walsingham and Norwich. T. W. Coke of Holkham owned land all over the town as well as the estate to the west; Thomas Wright who owned a number of properties lived in Marsh House. We know too where Matthew Emms the clay pipe maker lived on Church Street; his ostrich design on the bowl of his pipes was well known. John Fryer, famed shipmaster of the *Bounty*, had a house in Newgates Lane. Fryer had retired from the navy in 1812 to his place of birth, having survived being put into an open boat by members of the crew who had mutinied. Together with William Bligh, his captain

John Fryer, Sailing Master of HMS Bounty. *His original gravestone can be seen in the church porch and a modern stone marks his place of burial.*

and seventeen crew members they had sailed no less than 3,618 miles in an open boat making landfall on Timor in the Dutch East Indies. Having reached safety Fryer gave evidence on Bligh's behalf at the latter's court martial. He eventually returned to Wells and died in 1817.[36]

In many respects Wells had not changed very much over the previous hundred years from the fishing town it had been from of old. (The question was asked, in Parliament no less, whether it had changed since the Reformation!) Of course it had; but it remained a pretty noisome place in need of drastic attention. So it was described in evidence to Parliament in the June of 1844 by petitioners seeking legislation to facilitate the necessary improvements.[37] Their proposals, some of them dramatic, give us an unrivalled insight into what it was like to walk the streets and conduct business in the town in the early years of the nineteenth century.

Having no proper sewers, the town smelt; there were pigsties in the High Street, in spite of attempts via the old Court Leet to have them removed. Water ran down the middle of the street which was no more than a mud track, as indeed were all the roads in the town. So uneven and full of pot holes was it that waggons were apt to collide with buildings, smashing shop windows, even breaking their wheels, broken on the large stones which littered the highway, in the process. So it was reported.[38] Walking down the street was a hazard. Posts had been erected on either side of the street to prevent carts and carriages from hitting the buildings, but these could not be seen at night. Pedestrians were in danger of stumbling into them. The town was dark. Nowhere, it was said, was it possible for two waggons to pass each other. Though it contained many shops in those days High Street was often blocked with empty waggons awaiting the arrival of ships. Carriages

The maltings on the Glebe , behind the cottage.

were often forced to drive through the Crown yard in order to get to the south of the town.

Staithe Street, similarly unmetalled, was only nine feet six inches wide at its narrowest. Captain Ryley, a Trinity House officer living in the town, found himself on one occasion unable to get home and had to have his horse and gig led to his house. On another, he needed the services of burly coal porters to lift the same gig over a waggon which had become stuck.

As for access to the Quay, the only way to get there from the east was to circumnavigate the town to the south along Church Street and Burnt Street, making one's way to the bottom of Two Furlong Hill, through the streets to the Glebe and thence to the Quay. On arrival, waggon drivers would find the Quay itself narrow, lined with various shops and workshops with only a small section of eighty-six feet suitable to accommodate large vessels. The time taken to load and unload cargoes was thereby increased so that extra charges were incurred by importers and exporters alike.

Apart from the main streets, the town consisted of a large number of even narrower yards, hemmed in by tall maltings and granaries; there were coal yards and forges whose fires often provided the only illumination at night. Set among

Maltings in Staithe Street about 1972.

these were the poor tenanted cottages, some of which were described as ruinous. Those who visited from elsewhere or had dealings with other places were almost unanimous is describing it as the worst of places in which to live and trade. Captain Ryley had however a good word for its people. 'I will tell you', he said 'that there is an enterprise in the people of Wells which is not to be found generally. Now in the colliery trade they have sent the vessels to sea when other people have refused to

Another view of the 19th century malthouse in Staithe Street

The tithe map of 1846.

do it.' In spite of all his tribulations, Ryley described the town as 'the eye of Norfolk', with a harbour which avoided many of the dangers of Lynn and 'surrounded with a rich agricultural country at the back of it'.[39]

Seen from the sea the town's aspect was dominated by the tall masts of ships lying at the Quay, by the maltings which lay close by and, inland on the skyline, by the various windmills. There were some new buildings, though not all of them put up to good purpose: there had been a deal of speculative building of cottages some of which lay empty. This was also the time when the Buttlands was being built up; the residents would be able to enjoy the view while not having to own its greensward. (The new glass technology allowed the inhabitants to see out of their houses and enjoy the view.) Not all of them were occupied on completion. Of the 776 ratepayers identified in 1844, fewer than 200 paid rates. The rest were excused on the grounds of poverty.

The petitioners do not tell the whole story. Infant mortality rates were shocking. On the other hand, those who survived to reach their first birthday stood a good chance of reaching the age of seventy. Ninety-year-olds were not completely unknown in the burial register of the eighteenth century: Anne Twight died in 1762 aged ninety-two; nine other people died over seventy in that year. John Walden died apparently aged 102 on 30th November 1820.[40]

Epidemic disease was another matter. In 1727, there were 238 burials most of which were of people who had died of cholera. (The disease was believed to have been brought in to the port by sailors.) The smallpox epidemic of 1758 had killed a hundred people in the town, most of them children. Fortunately, inoculation had been introduced half way through the outbreak which limited the number of deaths, a very early example of its use. When the disease returned in 1769, the community was better prepared and its effects were not nearly so severe: thirty died out of nearly 500 who caught it; over 280 people were inoculated, none of whom died. The rector, James Robinson recorded both epidemics in the burials register of the church. In 1796, four years after his death, sixteen people died of the disease.[41] Then in the 1820s and 30s the town was hit by a whole series of epidemics. In 1828 measles took nineteen small children in a couple of months. In the years 1832–34 forty men and women died of scarlet fever, fifteen of small pox and seven of cholera.

Disease was not the only cause of premature death. The lack of regulation of either working practices or household safety meant that people were injured and died in the ordinary conduct of their lives. In 1820 over a period of months six children died in their homes by fire, including one little girl who had gone next door to boil a kettle for her blind neighbour.[42]

No doubt a combination of factors fuelled the energy for change. A desire to see trade improved was undoubtedly at the forefront of this. There was a degree of civic pride: comparisons were made with Holt, a town whose streets had been 'macadamised' and whose lay-out was now much more spacious. Hence perhaps the proposal by James Chapman, never implemented, that the houses on one side of High Street all be taken down. It was an unpleasant place to move about; shopping was a trial. No doubt too the much vaunted Victorian philanthropy played its part. It would do so increasingly but slowly.

Overland communications continued to improve. Those who ran coaches gave them names both to identify them and to give them prestige. The *Hero*, which went from the Crown in the 1840s, travelled to London via Swaffham and Newmarket three times a week, leaving at six in the morning. Carriers took parcels to London, Dereham, Lynn, Norwich, Barney, Binham and Bircham. Journey times continued to be reduced. In 1817 London could be reached from Wells in less than twenty-four hours; by 1835 a coach leaving Wells at 5.30 a.m. was timed to reach Charing Cross by 8.00 p.m. whereas by sea either to London or Hull vessels went only once a fortnight.[43]

The new turnpike road from Wells to Fakenham opened in 1826. Empowered by an Act of Parliament, the trustees raised funds for what is now called the 'dry road', named, it is generally thought, because its macadammed surface made it useable

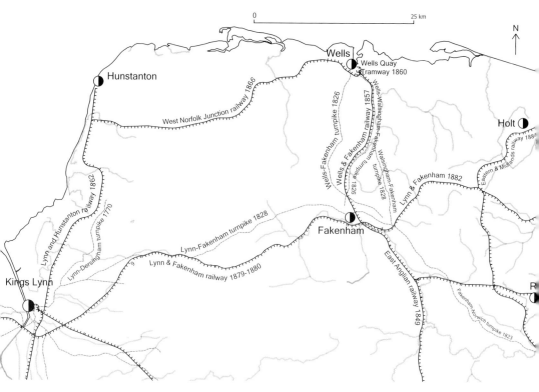

The principal turnmpikes and railways in north west Norfolk.

in all weathers. John Macadam, the Scottish engineer, had made this possible both by his determining the right degree of camber to ensure good drainage and also by use of pauper labour, men, women and children, to break stones into regular sizes for the creation of a compacted, even surface to the road. In the aftermath of the wars, such labour was readily available.[44] The sum borrowed for the building of the road was recouped by the trustees annually auctioning off the right to exact tolls at each of its several entry gates. The house that still stands at the top of the hill just outside the town, now called Ashburton, marks the gate which was to prevent vehicles avoiding the Wells toll by joining the road via Market Lane. Other gates allowed entry from Warham, Holkham, Kettlestone, Fakenham and Walsingham. The network of inland waterways built in the latter part of the eighteenth century allowed barges to reach the Midlands and even the north-west, by coastal travel to the Wash and then up the rivers which ran into it.

7. Prosperity

As far as business was concerned a number of the leading citizens looked back to the year 1831 as the *annus horribilis* of the town. The local press reported the day that year when 'every merchant in this respectable port has recently experienced the sad reverse of fortune to such a degree as to be either declared insolvent or voluntarily to discontinue business. There is not now a merchant in business in the place and we have just learned that Mr. John Parker, a respectable shipbuilder has determined to discontinue his extensive concern.' Parker apparently paid off his twenty-four employees and trade in Wells was 'completely at a standstill'.[1] James Chapman, maltster and trader, had been made bankrupt as had George and John Crofts; Joseph Southgate had been briefly jailed for debt: all were merchants in the town. Valentine Hill, the rector had been jailed twice. Edmund Powditch, owner of the Vine – shortly to become the Globe – was bankrupted the same year. There may have been a degree of journalistic exaggeration in the report – Parker was still building ships in 1842 – but it gives an indication of the fragility of the harbour and its overwhelming importance to the well-being of the town.

In truth, the physical condition of the harbour was not the only problem. Finance was another. The advent of banks, widely regarded as a boon, meant that merchants were encouraged to borrow beyond their means, overtrading as they called it. Chapman had been encouraged by the agent of the branch of the Bank of England in Norwich, a Mr Welton, to borrow excessively. Joseph Southgate had spent money on building ten cottages most of which lay empty (Welton was apparently dismissed and local merchants turned to Gurneys who had a bank in Fakenham, run more cautiously.) The finances of the town depended excessively on a very few people. Robert Hudson who lived in Warham but farmed in Wells had a highways rating assessment of one eighth of the total.

Another factor, which mariners everywhere had to work with but was particularly difficult in Wells, was the unpredictability of the wind. Southerly winds were best for carrying vessels out of the harbour but could make travel south to London impossible. On the other hand a good northerly which would blow them to the capital made it difficult to get out of the harbour in the first place. Prevailing winds in 1831–32 resulted in a large number of what were called 'detentions', when ships could not get out of the harbour; 'the object of many a voyage [was] lost' in those years.[2] Cargoes intended for London ended up on the Humber. The prevailing westerly would answer their problems but, as often since, there are seasons when it scarcely blows.

Harbour legislation

The resolution of the issues relating to the embankment of the marshes in the previous century had satisfied some but not all. Nor was the issue dead. Mariners and landowners remained divided in their views; nearly 700 acres of flood water had been lost in the eighteenth century; and another 66 acres when Warham Slade was re-embanked. These areas, which had been covered to a depth of several feet at spring tides, had caused a substantial scouring effect as the tide ebbed, admittedly much of it north of the Point, the loss of which, it was to be claimed, was the root of the problem.

The aftermath of the Napoleonic wars saw a revival in shipping. The transport of grain coastwise, almost entirely to London, now replaced the export traffic (though London was itself a huge market for grain some of which may well have crossed the channel). Whereas the town did not feature in records of coastwise traffic in the 1780s, by the 1820s it had become the ninth biggest grain port in the[3] country, sending out on average nearly 60,000 quarters of barley per annum The shallowness of the channel nevertheless remained a problem. Ships were becoming larger (more than doubling in size), and those with a deeper draught could not reach the Quay but had to be partly unloaded at the Pool, the cargoes being transferred to lighters. This caused delay and additional expense. In 1804 two Norwich surveyors had proposed to drain the entire east marsh and to bring the water from the River Stiffkey into Wells, thus providing the continuous supply of fresh water needed to scour the harbour; a huge proposal, it came to nothing.

The first known efforts by the Commissioners themselves were in 1818 when they took action by closing off East Fleet where it entered the main channel and the creeks that fed it at their eastern end in an attempt to direct all the water from the marsh down Sluice Creek and hence out to sea via the Quay. (This was judged thirty years later to have had a long term effect on the depth and ease of navigation of the inner channel, though it was also thought to have accelerated the silting up of the East Marsh.[4]) Then in 1828 Benjamin Leak, a surveyor from Holt, proposed to straighten and confine the channel north of the Point by a bank on the western side and another on the east to Wells Meals; but given the huge movements of sand generated by wind and tide the technology did not exist to keep the banks in place. His proposal was turned down. Leak had also proposed to block off the eastern exits from the East Marsh by a continuous bank from Wells Meals to Nass Point so that none of the run off would escape eastwards. The commissioners apparently, at some time, partially achieved this by building banks across the eastern ends of the Great East Fleet and of Stonemeals Creek.

It seems plain that it was the bankruptcies of 1831 that galvanised the local mercantile community into more positive action. The first major step was the obtaining of an Act of Parliament which enabled them to raise the necessary finance to improve the harbour.[5] The act, passed in 1835, sets out their several concerns. They needed to improve the harbour; they needed finance in order to achieve this; the major source of income was from dues paid by incoming vessels. They were, in this endeavour, in competition with other ports, most particularly with Blakeney which in 1817 had acted to revive its own fortunes by the passing of an Act which allowed them to cut a new channel from the Pit to the harbour and thus to open it up to larger vessels. The Wells merchants were evidently concerned to prevent the diversion of traffic into Blakeney. The new duties charged on vessels using Wells harbour to be one shilling per ton for imports and eight pence per ton for exports; but, for as long as Blakeney by statute provided a discount for its own vessels, boats belonging to the port of Wells were to pay half of those rates. (In practice there seems to have been a 'foreign rate', an English rate, a local rate and a rate charged on Blakeney vessels which was three quarters of the foreign rate.[6]) Their borrowing powers were increased nearly fourfold to £5,000.

The Commissioners named in the Act included all the major players: T. W. Coke, shortly to be Earl of Leicester, and Francis Blaikie, his agent; Thomas Garwood, local solicitor; James Chapman, George Crofts, the rector Valentine Hill; Joseph Haycock, the inevitable Joseph Southgate and seventeen others, including local brewers, ship owners and three more clergymen. They alone were to choose their successors to fill up any vacancies as they occurred. Their new powers included those to 'alter, deepen, widen, restrict, divert, embank, cleanse, scour, enlarge, diminish, straighten or improve any of the present channels, creeks etc.' This would be quite a challenge when men worked at low tide with shovels, barrows and carts within the channel.

As for the organisation of the traffic of vessels, the Harbour Master, now for the first time so called, was given enlarged powers 'under the orders and directions of the . . . Commissioners' over the mooring, anchoring and moving of vessels in the harbour and to enforce his directions if necessary by direct action even to cutting moorings in order to move vessels if recalcitrant ships' masters refused to do his bidding. His powers extended to the ballasting and unloading of ballast from vessels and to the removal of wrecks and any other obstructions to free navigation. Abandoned vessels were a feature of every harbour, a danger to vessels entering and leaving the harbour but expensive to remove. The Commissioners' power to pass bye-laws about these and other matters was now supported by a power of enforcement in the courts. Most of the penalties were money fines, some of them substantial enough to deter even well-placed merchants. However, the penalty for 'wilfully or maliciously' damaging or breaking down what were called the 'works of the harbour' or any ship, anchor or buoy, was clearly taken much more seriously: the maximum penalty was transportation for a term of seven years to Australia.

As to responsibility for buoyage, no buoys or beacons were to be fixed without the approval of the Corporation of Trinity House. Trinity House had itself in 1834 established a depot from where they could survey and mark the dangerous sandbanks to the north of the harbour. They also supervised local pilots. (Established in 1514, Trinity House was originally a gild, one of the few to survive albeit in a very different shape from its origins.)

It appears that the Commissioners began the building of a stone sea wall along the front of the Quay; what else they did is not clear. However, regardless of their effectiveness in this respect, the prosperity of the town depended upon solving not one but multiple problems. The channel needed to be kept open and made more accessible; the Quay needed to be improved so that larger vessels could be accommodated in greater numbers; and the town itself needed to become a more accessible port for cargoes entering and leaving. The solution of one of these alone would not help.

One problem needed no legislation, only local initiative. Five of the Commissioners banded together and in 1840 they purchased a steam tug, the *Economy*,[7] which was able to tow sailing vessels out to sea and, when necessary, to tow incoming vessels into the harbour. Days could be saved by vessels no longer being harbour-bound or moored in Holkham bay unable to get up to the Quay. She also acted as a salvage vessel.

The adoption of a more comprehensive solution was supported by 'the bulk of the respectable people of the town', including the Earl of Leicester, who signed the memorial, as it was called, seeking the will of Parliament to pass not one but twin acts, one relating to the harbour, the other to the town. The bills were presented to Parliament in February 1844. Thomas Garwood, the solicitor, who was also agent to Lord Leicester, provided the necessary legal expertise. There was opposition. A town meeting was called on the Crown Green – presumably the Buttlands – that

May. It was evidently an ill-tempered occasion. The rector was persuaded to chair it much against his will and, when the uproar proved impossible to control, it was adjourned to one of the rooms of the Crown. It was argued that the enormous expense could not be contemplated. A petition against the proposed legislation was headed by John Middleton of Holkham and Sir Charles Chad but signed by people of all classes, some with a mark. It set out their objections to the scheme, which were heard before a select committee of the House of Lords on 16th July. For the town, Chapman, Southgate, Robert Keppel and Hudson appeared together with Captain Ryley and a surveyor, Nathaniel Beardsmore, to be examined and cross-

The east end, with the Granary, some time between the wars.

examined by counsel for the opponents. They would be questioned as to the need for an Act of Parliament, as to the practicality and affordability of the proposals, and the suitability of those who wanted to implement it to undertake the task. Clearly the evidence of the state of the town persuaded their Lordships: the Wells Lighting and Improvement Act and the Wells Harbour and Quay Acts were passed on 29th July 1844.[8]

The first and less contentious issue was the Quay. There were a number of private wharfs but there was a clear need to extend the public quay, which was a mere 86 feet in length at the bottom of Staithe Street. It was proposed that the stone wall be extended by a massive 685 feet to the east and by 483 feet to the west. The new Quay would run eastwards as far as Jolly Sailors Yard and west to the Stone. Some twenty-eight properties were to be demolished from Sun Yard in the west to the East End using the new power of compulsory purchase given by the Act. They included the row of shops along the north side of Burnham Road between Sun Yard and Knotts Yard (the area of the present car park), a dwelling house, a carpenters shop, two cobblers, an oyster shop, and a hairdresser's. East of the bottom of Staithe Street a number of coalhouses, granaries, wharfs and yards and some cottages were also to be removed.[9] For five years after the passing of the Act the Harbour Commissioners could purchase the properties identified in the Act up to twenty acres.[10] The cost was estimated at £7,000.

To achieve these ends the Commissioners were also given yet further borrowing powers – £9,600 in addition to sums already approved up to a total at any one time of £14,600 against the security of harbour dues and the Commissioners' modest landholdings. This was almost to treble the borrowing powers given in the 1835 Act. They were empowered to buy other land for slipways for the repairing of ships, for providing wharfs, jetties and places for the landing of passengers and livestock. They were empowered to build or make use of means of dredging the harbour mechanically. (The stone Quay was begun but it appears never to have extended eastwards much beyond the Granary; some of the buildings on the Quay survived until the 1950s.)

The 1844 Act also required the commissioners to provide an efficient and well appointed lifeboat and crew with heavy penalties for every day such vessel might be unavailable. The tug *Economy* was to prove useful in towing the lifeboat out to vessels in distress.

Improving the town

The second issue, the state of the town, had taken up most of the time of the House of Lords committee. As we have already seen the claim was made that the town was not fit for the purpose of being a trading port. In his evidence to the Lords, Thomas Keppel, rector of Warham and a harbour commissioner, pointed out that there was no advantage in providing more space on the harbour wall for more and larger vessels if their cargoes could not be got through the town.[11] It was, as already described, insanitary, noisome, with narrow streets and ruinous buildings, so that some people seemed to be moving out of the town including even some of the mariners. Understandably the idea of knocking down the houses on one side of the two main streets generated alarm. There was also the question of cost. The improvements to the harbour could be paid for by revenue earning vessels; the highway rates on the other hand had a very narrow base; all those paying less than £3 a year rent were excused, a higher proportion apparently than in neighbouring towns.[12]

The Improvement Act stated that 'it would conduce to the advantage and comfort' of the people of the town if it 'were better lighted, drained, sewered, widened, paved' and otherwise improved. The streets were to be lighted with gas, paved and widened and various nuisances removed including ruinous buildings and, most important, those occasioned by sewage.

The first solution related to the question of access. In order to make the Quay accessible, a new road was to be built running south-easterly from Tinkers' Corner at the top of an improved Standard Yard Road, as it was then called, across Church Marsh to join the Warham Road; then called New Road it is now Polka Road. Vehicles wishing to gain access to the Quay could do so without entering from the town.

The wider issues of the habitability of the town were dealt with by a series of other measures. Commissioners, to be known as the Improvement Commissioners, were to be appointed in order to implement them. They were the local justices of the peace of the North Greenhoe hundred together with the Hon. the Revd James Keppel, the Revd Valentine Hill, George Crofts, James Chapman, Abraham Dunn, William Ransom, Hugh Rump, Jeremiah Robert Rump, Joseph Southgate, James Tyzack, Henry Tyrrell and James Young. They were to stand for two years after which they had to retire on a four- year rotation, and stand for election by the ratepayers of the town.[13]

As with the Harbour Commissioners they were given wide-ranging compulsory purchase powers. This new power cut a swathe through all other rights, whether manorial, leasehold, in possession or expectation. Land tenure at that time was still very complicated (life tenancies, entails and copyholds were only some of the different entitlements) so that, even with good will, securing the sale of land could be well nigh impossible. All of these were, for a five-year period, capable of being swept away. This would enable not only the building of the new road but the building of sewers, the 'macadamising' of the streets of the town , the provision of street lamps, the pulling down of dangerous buildings and much else.

Of the Commissioners appointed Southgate, Chapman, Rump and Tyrrell, local businessmen, were to give the lead. (Keppel and Hudson did not live in the town.) To set about improving the streets, they employed a Mr Warren to put in hand the 'macadamising' process and the laying of sewers beneath them. The new roads with their stone foundations were finished with compacted chalk, the most abundant stone available locally, which enabled the roads to be levelled but which became greasy in the wet and dusty in dry spells. Their maintenance was put in hand by the appointment of a surveyor of roads and streets, cesspools and all other works at a rate of twelve shillings a week, one William Allison. A water cart was eventually employed in 1865 to lay the dust. (Later, Belgian granite would be imported by sea for road stone and a steam roller hired to compact and level it. The making of dust-free road surfaces made with a tar mixed with furnace slag, the famous tarmac, did not come until the early twentieth century; Staithe Street was first so treated in 1913.)

Mention has been made of the various epidemics. The conclusion had been reached that disease was much of it water-borne and not caused by 'foul air' as hitherto believed. Sanitation for many people meant a hole dug in the yard, latterly covered over by a privy with its seat with a hole in it, to be emptied out once a year and, in the meantime, for the excrement to be covered with earth or ashes. In addition culverts and so-called common sewers of uncertain age carried away rainwater and household waste. Many streets were badly drained and excrement was liable to overflow in wet weather, running down streets and yards, together with all manner of rubbish to leak into the many wells from which people drew their water supply or to run into the Quay. There were upwards of 180 wells in the town at that time.[14]

The new powers allowed the construction of a system of sewers and permitted the commissioners to repair and cleanse any existing 'common sewers, drains and culverts' and to require 'the owners and occupiers of houses etc. to . . . make communication of private drains with the common sewers in the streets'. The slow task of creating a public system for removing waste had begun: they gave notice to those who allowed the effluent from drains to run across public roads to abate the nuisance; they required the removal of 'muck bins'.[15] Night soil from earth privies was to be removed between the hours of eleven at night and four in the morning, and measures taken to contain it. Scavengers were appointed who would, apart from watering the streets, collect dirt, ashes and rubbish from them and from houses and yards, and remove the various substances to a place 'as shall be appointed'. Among the many substances for them to deal with was night soil from cesspits, which had to be removed with long handled ladles; the places appointed were the fields around the town.

The gas works were built on Mill Road in 1845 both for street and domestic lighting. It was not until 1892 that householders could cook with gas. There were 78 public lights lit free of charge from 1st September to 30th April from one hour after sunset until 11 o'clock (except upon six nights at each full moon), the income being generated from those who had gas lighting in their houses, each one metered.[16]

The costs of all these works, which were initially reckoned to be of the order of £7,000, were to be paid for by borrowing. Gurneys bank lent them £6,000; they also issued bonds which were taken up by a Miss Hamond of Swaffham, by Francis

Southgate and by Daniel Burlington; others would follow. They then levied a rate of 1s 6d in the pound based on the 1838 valuation of all property in the town, charging their occupiers, all except those who, out of poverty, could not pay. And they employed Robert Faircloth to collect the rates. (As we shall see, the system of rate collection was to prove ineffective and the funds raised insufficient.)

The wide ranging powers extended not only to the streets, but to ruinous and dangerous buildings which could be pulled down. The compulsory purchase power was subject to valuation agreed by a County Jury if the owner did not agree. The Commissioners had all sorts of other powers: over dogs suspected of rabies or blacksmiths who failed to shut the light from their forges from the streets at night; over drunkenness, riotous or indecent behaviour; over street musicians; over soliciting by prostitutes; over those driving vehicles to the public danger; parking on the street, street trading; selling indecent or obscene books or prints; ringing doorbells without lawful excuse; making slides upon ice or snow; shaking or beating carpets, rugs or mats before nine in the morning; even placing a flower pot on an upstairs window ledge without securing it from falling. The health and safety culture had arrived early; the Act's promoters had thought of pretty well everything.[17]

Included in the powers was that over anyone found 'undressing in the quay or open place called The Stone or [who] shall bathe or wash himself in the sea channel . . . after ten o'clock in the morning without the aid and assistance of a proper machine or tent in which to dress or undress himself'. The seaside holiday had arrived. Sea water was claimed to have medicinal properties by Georgian doctors and the first bathing machines arrived in Lowestoft in 1768. In 1803 Princess Caroline stayed at Southend. The potential of Wells to attract visitors had been noticed. 'Three to four thousand visitors would come to the town if improvements were made . . . for the purpose of lodging' it was stated in evidence to Parliament in 1844 – another straw in the wind.

One major difference between the two acts was that the newly appointed Improvement Commissioners were to be elected whereas the Harbour Commissioners, named in the 1835 Act, were to continue and to remain self selecting (as they are up to the present). This was to be the subject of adverse comment within a very few years.

The Harbours Commission

Local acts were expensive, piecemeal and dependent upon local initiative. In relation to the ports they were an ineffective means of protecting the country's

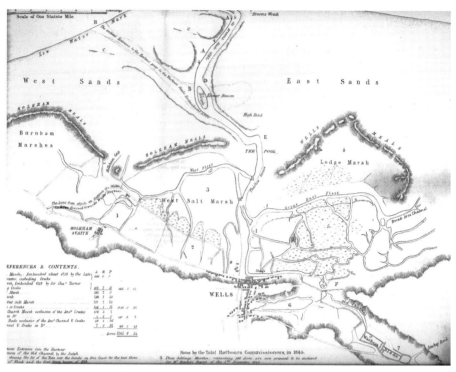

A 1780 map of the approaches to Wells reproduced inthe Tidal Harbours Commissioners' Report of 1846.

maritime resource, wasteful of resources which were often misapplied by 'self-elected irresponsible Commissioners' who lacked the appropriate expertise – rarely a sailor among them: this was the view of the Tidal Harbours Commission appointed that same year and which reported to Parliament two years later. It reported on every significant harbour in the country. Wells merited an entry. The opinions expressed by the Examining Commissioner Joseph Hume, MP for Montrose, a port city of Scotland, were not complimentary: the enclosure of lands against which 'the inhabitants struggled for nearly a half a century' was, it said 'to the great detriment of the harbour'; the Commissioners, 'many of whom do not even possess property in the town,[18] have the power of nominating others to fill up vacancies'. The Report was not complimentary about the ubiquitous Joseph Southgate who, wearing yet more hats, was 'secretary, collector and treasurer, paymaster and superintendant of the steam tug and who has the whole management of the works and finances' without any checks by even a clerk or an engineer.[19] It spoke of gross mismanagement against which neither merchants nor inhabitants had any redress.

In particular huge sums had been spent on the building of the Quay but that 'although the harbour has so much deteriorated no portion of the harbour dues, or of the money borrowed, has been applied to dredge or deepen it'. He was not as sanguine as the reporter of White's *Directory* of the previous year who had reported that the new stone Quay was almost complete and that 'the Harbour has been much improved of late years . . . vessels of 150 to 200 tons can get up at high water'.[20] One wonders where he got his information.

Hume believed that the time was past for local interests to determine the future of the harbour; he opposed any further embanking and draining of the marsh and recommended the creation of a national body, a Harbour Conservancy Board, to administer harbours.[21] Southgate appears to have been a somewhat unreliable witness. (In cross-examination in 1844 his claims were frequently contradicted by counsel.) In any case, whatever the probity of Southgate's conduct, it was plain that the lack of accountability and of any professional advice was not good practice.

The Commission considered reports made at various times over the previous sixty and more years including that commissioned by the Earl from a London surveyor named James Rendel on the practicality and desirability of completing the enclosure of the marshes to the west of the channel. Rendel proposed the building of an embanked roadway from the west end of the Quay to the Point, straightening the main channel which would improve the flow, he said. It would, he contended, prevent vessels from being blown onto the marsh when there were strong westerly winds. It would, of course, also reduce the amount of water available to scour the outer channel and would provide the Earl with five hundred acres of additional farmland.

In his report, Hume contended that sluices did no good, that they actually hastened the accumulation of soil on the marshes; he disagreed with Rendel that the straightened channel consequent upon the creation of an embanked roadway would increase the scour; less water would be available. He advocated instead that 'the main channel be dredged throughout and every fleet opened to the freest possible action of the tidal water'.[22]

His recommendations for a national regulatory body came to nothing and, in spite of his fears, the Earl decided upon building the embankment, which was completed in 1859, following Admiralty approval.[23] The West Fleet, which drained Holkham marshes behind the dunes as far as the embankment of 1780, was thus finally cut off from the sea. Abraham's Bosom, whose name presumably derived from its having been a refuge for vessels coming in driven by northerly gales, became a pond.

Hume's fears may not have been realised; the several creeks which entered from the west including the largest of them, West Fleet, entered the channel well north of the harbour. The straightening of the channel, and its dredging, which Hume recommended, undoubtedly improved the flow from the Quay northwards to the Point. On the other hand, without a source of fresh water to carry out the silt only mechanical action seemed likely to keep the port open. Shortly afterwards, in 1862, a high tide broke through the sand hills to the north and flooded the newly drained marsh.[24] The Earl responded by having the dunes planted with conifers, Corsican pines, in order to stabilise them, thus creating a recreational area for which the beach and town have become well known.

Shipbuilding

The importance of the harbour lay not only in its maritime traffic but in the building of ships. This seems to have been carried on for centuries but it had, by the end of the eighteenth century, begun to assume a degree of commercial importance.[25] Wells was one of a number of north Norfolk harbours in which boats were built (Sheringham, Cley, Blakeney and Morston) but Wells appears to have been the most important. (Small boats were built at Cromer and Burnham Overy.) The vessels were all built in the open and the transition from wood to iron was never made, but locally built ships became a source of employment: sawyers, shipwrights, carpenters, caulkers, blacksmiths, sail makers, mast and blockmakers and riggers. On shore there were a number of ropemakers, though rope was also imported. There was a ropewalk along the backs of the houses on the west side of the Buttlands, another in the east end, and a third running along the west wall of the Rectory garden. Rope was twisted from twine into strands and the strands twisted – the opposite way – into ropes, made at that time from hemp, by being stretched between two distant points. T. S. Fox's yard was 744 feet long and had in addition rope, hemp and tar houses, as well as wheel houses for turning the rope.[26] There were three sail makers in the town.

There were, apparently, four shipyards at one time, two to the east end and two to the west, though by the nineteenth century only two figure in the sources. A yard for building small open boats existed on Freeman Street. The first reference to the larger yards is an advertisement in the *Norfolk Chronicle* for 2nd January 1796: Nicholas Everitt's shipyard was up for sale.[27] The land was owned by T. W. Coke so presumably it was the lease which was sold to a Great Yarmouth man, Richard Parker, whose family went on to build more than a dozen ships until 1842. It was Richard's younger son John, whom we have already met, who took over the yard probably in the 1820s. The other east end yard came into the hands of

John Lubbock, originally of Hemsby, some time before 1819; he both built and bought and sold vessels beginning with the 90 ton *Isis*; he passed the lease to the indefatigable Joseph Southgate in 1843.[28]

Lubbock's and Parker's yards were located to the east of Jolly Sailors Yard. The Custom House appears to have been the centre of the Quay at that time; the customs officials needed to be able to oversee the loading and discharging of cargoes. The ships were large, up to 150 tons, and occasionally greater;[29] because the channel was narrow and launching required water space they probably would have been launched at an angle. Each had a saw pit where tree trunks were sawn into planks, a building with a steaming box so that planks could be bent around the frames, and a blacksmith's forge. Nicholas Everitt's yard was so described. Apart from the slipway there were gridirons, a framework of heavy timbers bedded into the shore, on which ships in need of repair could be berthed and worked on at low tide.

The ships built were mostly cargo vessels, bringing in the coal and taking out corn. Usually they were built to order but sometimes a yard would build on speculation. The design was agreed between the yard owner, the shipwright and the customer. The shipwright would then supervise the building. Half models would be made from which patterns were made for the frames. Good timber could be had from Holkham though some was imported from Scandinavia and even North America. 178 ships were known to have been built altogether in Wells at that period, an average of two ships per year, though there were boom years and slack years: in 1838 seven boats were built, in 1836 and 1842 only one each. As we have seen 1831 was a particularly bad year. This variation between extreme demands and slack times, as always, affected the conditions of life of working men severely; winter was, in any case, the worst time. Pay for a skilled man was double that of a farm labourer, about a £1 a week; labour was still a commodity to be utilised only when required. In 1839 there were seven blacksmith's shops and two tin-men, most if not all of which would have done work for the shipyards.

Almost everything on a ship from the bolts and spikes to fasten the hull, the iron brackets for internal strengthening, to navigation lamps made with copper or brass, would have been made locally. Only gradually were these components supplied more cheaply from the 'metal bashing' factories of London or the West Midlands.

They built schooners, brigs, brigantines, sloops and barques; even small fishing smacks. The different kinds of vessel were the result of history and tradition but also a matter of purpose. The rig of a vessel depended to some degree on its size and thence the number of masts. Broadly, a sloop was a single masted fore-and-aft rigged vessel with a foresail and mainsail; ketches were fore and aft rigged with a foresail, main and a smaller mizzen mast; schooners were fore and aft-rigged with two or more masts of equal height; a brig had two masts and was square rigged; a brigantine was square rigged on its foremast, fore and aft on its mainmast; barques had three or more masts, the after or mizzen mast only was fore and aft-rigged; ships, properly so called, mainly had three masts and were square rigged; then there were snows and barquentines . . . Almost every combination was tried.

Fore and aft sails were used because they enabled vessels to sail more efficiently towards the wind; but larger vessels which would undertake long voyages were still most often square rigged; the sail tended to lift the vessel and speed its passage through the water. Requiring a larger crew, they became less popular as time passed. Brigs would become brigantines. The other major issue was the draught, the depth of water required by the hull. Virtually all vessels had to be able to take the ground safely. Shallow draughted vessels had an advantage. One specialist hull was that of the billy boy, which might have one or two masts but was very flat bottomed and double ended. None were built in Wells; they came mostly from the Humber, but several were registered here. They were slow, ungainly vessels and several were lost locally in gales.[30]

By 1845 there were sixty-seven vessels registered in the port, with a total tonnage of 2,885 tons. The number of coasting vessels outward was 222; and inward with cargoes 330. Customs dues received amounted to £500. There were thirty-two fishing boats; mostly, it seems, fishing for oysters and mussels.[31]

The yards seemed a sound investment for local businessmen. Whereas Lubbock and Parker seem to have been shipwrights, their successors, men like John Bloom and subsequently Joseph Southgate, Henry Tyrrell senior and Robert Leaman, were first and foremost businessmen. Southgate derived his position on the Harbour Commission and in the town from his being a local merchant who traded in coal and timber, corn, wine and spirits. When he turned his attention to ship-owning and ship-building in 1843, taking over Lubbock's Yard, he kept Lubbock on as foreman shipwright; Lubbock was still working there in 1851 by which time he was aged 74. Southgate built more than a dozen ships culminating in a 210-ton schooner launched in June 1857. He appears to have given up when he lost money on the railway. Henry Tyrrell, the prosperous grocer and draper with a shop in the High Street, had sent his son of the same name on a seven-year apprenticeship as a shipwright. Presumably the elder Tyrrell thought that this was a coming industry. The young Henry was just twenty-five when he took over the yard in 1845, launching his first ship, the 77-ton schooner *Sarah*, that year.[32] In 1847 he built the prestigious *Countess of Leicester* in which his father bought shares; she was intended for the deep sea trade and in 1850 sailed to Leghorn and back. Robert Leaman, a well-to-do farmer from Whitwell, who bought up a number of properties in the town, followed Tyrrell in 1863, probably having a number of vessels built, but by this time the trade had begun seriously to decline.

Shipowning carried a certain prestige and ownership of many ships was divided into up to sixty-four shares; Randle Brereton who also owned a malting, had thirty-two shares in the *Blakeney and Hull Packet*, a Wells-built boat; Francis Southgate, the postmaster, had shares in the *Amarath*, a Sunderland-built brig registered in Wells. Everyone from clergy to coal merchants, drapers, printers and master mariners took shares in boats during those heady days of the 1850s.[33] Some subsequently mortgaged their shares when times became hard for them.

Mid-century

The census of the town in 1851 gives some clues as to the general effects of the initiatives taken six years earlier, though many of them were the result of long term trends. Among other things it shows the rise of shopping. The process begun a hundred years before had accelerated. Hitherto, apart from open markets, people mostly made or employed others to make what they needed; food was either grown or traded locally. Manufactures were a novelty. Other places where business was done were the public houses and, of course, the Quay itself.

Increasingly commodities arrived from elsewhere, some of them by sea but also brought by the increasing number of small carriers. In 1851 those supplying the domestic requirements of the town, shopkeepers, shoemakers, milliners, dressmakers etc. made up nearly a quarter of the working population,[34] though many people had multiple occupations. Martha Rust was a maltster; she was also a wine and spirit merchant. William Tyzack ran a business in the High Street which combined ironmongering and hairdressing. Food was sourced locally: there were nine butchers; grocery and drapery seemed to go together. Many articles were made and repaired on the premises by shoemakers, carpenters and so on. Hatters, milliners and glovers continued to thrive. Wells had got its first bank in 1830 owned by Gurneys; the East of England Bank established a branch in Staithe Street in 1854.[35] Meanwhile, manufactures from elsewhere were increasingly available, 'London goods', as they were often called. Window displays could now entice the casual shopper. The improvement of glass mirrors meant that people could now see properly what they looked like. Vanity, essentially competitive in its nature, became an engine of commerce.[36] As for the shops they would be mostly staffed by the proprietor and his family but Henry Tyrrell's grocery and drapery business also took on apprentices. The market was revived by a local auctioneer in 1888 for the sale of cattle, sheep and poultry in the yard of the Ostrich Inn.

Shipbuilding and related trades provided work for only 5.2% of the working population. There was an iron foundry, mills, maltings, a brickyard and three rope walks. Metal working continued to be in demand. Twelve blacksmiths were recorded in 1851.[37]

Those who manned the ships, masters, mates and mariners numbered more than ninety, far more than the twenty-two fishermen of the town. Mariners could expect very low wages, £2 or £3 a month, much less than agricultural labourers, but their chances of promotion, if they avoided injury or early death, were much greater. A man might rise to the post of mate or even master when to his £5 or £6 a month could be added commission on the freight. The impression is that seafarers were a distinct group, few of whom had any connection with work on the land.[38]

Farm labourers were still a major element of the workforce, over two hundred men. They tended to live close to the seven farms on the outskirts of the town. Their work was seasonal and they almost certainly worked in the maltings after the harvest and when it was cool enough for malting to take place. After the railway came, some East Anglian men were known to have followed the barley to Burton on Trent for the malting season, particularly after the Agricultural Depression set in.[39] Methods of malting had not changed in over a hundred years: though the season was from late September to April, during only three of those months was the best malt made. The weather, particularly the temperature, still determined the rate of germination and if there was a likelihood of frost operations had to be suspended[40] which meant that men would be laid off.

Without an ability to find work in winter their life would have been hard. The workhouse beckoned. Those listed as paupers, some seventy-eight of them, were many of them elderly, some into their 80s, some without any support; others were supported by families themselves in precarious employment. We are reminded of the terrors of old age before the advent of state pensions. A small number were in receipt of Parish Relief. Then there were those on small fixed incomes. In January 1861 conditions for agricultural labourers and fishermen worsened so much as a result of severe weather that there was a public meeting to raise a subscription to meet their needs.[41] Few women were engaged in paid employment. Those who did paid work were often found in domestic service and dress making. One source of employment for women and children was their use in agricultural gangs, weeding, stone picking, bird scaring and setting potatoes (which could not be done by a drill). Apart from the dubious conditions of such work, there was little likelihood of children being at school after the age of 10.

There was also in 1851 a small cadre of professionals. Apart from the Harbour

Master and the Customs Officer there were three surgeons (father and son, both called Hugh Rump, and a third, Patrick Vincent, who acted as Registrar of Births Marriages and Deaths). There were two solicitors, Thomas Garwood and Robert Loynes, both of whom were active in public affairs. Leading citizens included the merchants and shopkeepers Joseph Southgate and Henry Tyrrell. The rector and patron of the living, the Revd John Hopper, not only chaired the Parish Vestry but presided over the distribution of charitable funds and was called upon to arbitrate in claims for salvage and, on one occasion, even bailed out a failing shipbuilder. Amongst colourful examples of the new professionals was Tolver Silvers who ran a private school from 1844 to 1859, was Clerk to the Harbour Commissioners, Assessor of Taxes and Collector of the Improvement Rate. He was a leading member of the Oddfellows and the Independent Chapel and was the Wells correspondent for the *Norfolk News*.[42]

The Oddfellows Hall in Club Lane in the 1890s.

The merchants and professionals were much connected both commercially and as families. Thomas Garwood was married to Robert Hudson's sister; John Southgate had married Sarah Rump in 1823; Thomas Rust, maltster, had married Martha Parker in 1824. The same names recur, though there will be new arrivals like Robert Leaman and, later, George Smith.

Most of the cargo which left the harbour was carried in locally owned boats. The volumes, and the number of vessels, were considerable. The overall tonnage peaked in 1864. Coal from Newcastle; grain and malt to London; grain to Wakefield; salted herring and fruit to and from the Mediterranean; Italy, South America, the Baltic: Wells traded with the world.[43]

In all things the influence of the Earl of Leicester was felt. The death of the first Earl in 1842 left his son to carry on in a very similar way: he would be the chief local investor in the Wells & Fakenham Railway; he owned much of the land in and around the town including that on which the shipyards stood; he offered his patronage to local projects and good works such as the local branch of the Oddfellows.

125

The Oddfellows were one of the most successful of the self help societies which arose in the seventeenth century. By 1730, such friendly societies, as they were called, were formalised and in 1793 legislation was passed controlling their activities. Their primary purpose was that of mutual support for members who fell ill or were injured at work; they were even known to pay for a proper burial. They provided a source of welfare that was decided upon by the representatives of the contributors, rather than, as was the case with the old charities, by trustees who were not answerable to the recipients. The Wells branch of the Manchester Unity of Oddfellows, the Loyal Leicester Lodge, was founded in 1844. It became very popular; in 1906 it had 382 members. Its original hall was built in 1856 in Knotts Yard; subsequently the branch removed to the Crown Hotel yard and in 1885 a new hall was built in Clubbs Lane. Its annual parade with banners flying and band playing was a colourful spectacle which drew crowds from all parts of the town's community. There was also, for a while, a branch of the Independent Order of Rechabites, a friendly society associated with the temperance movement. How long it lasted is not known.

The 1851 census also recorded for the first time attendance of the populace at acts of worship, morning, afternoon and evening on 30th March, which, that year, was Mothering Sunday. For those who had assumed that England was, to all intents and purposes, a country allegiant to the Church of England, and, for that matter, a Christian country, the results came as a shock. Not only was attendance at nonconformist chapels nationally almost as great as attendance at the Church of England, but almost half the population were not in church anywhere. The Church had long been associated with the property owning classes: in Wells the merchant classes, represented by such as Joseph Southgate and the Rumps, were members of the Church. Methodism had become more 'respectable' over the years. Working men, particularly those who worked on the land, tended towards the Primitive Methodist chapel; the fisherman and sailors, it was said, went nowhere other than to funerals. In the event the town proved itself more religious than the country as a whole. According to the figures, 71.5% of Wells people including children were in church on the census day compared with 60.8% nationally; 2,574 attendances were recorded out of the population of over 3,600.[44] The best attended church was the Wesleyan Methodist chapel with 960 attenders at its three services and Sunday school. The Church of England with two services and no Sunday school had 567 attendances. As to how many people went twice (or three times) various guesses were made.[45] The Congregationalists and Primitive Methodists recorded just over 500 attendances at their two services each.[46] The Society of Friends had no meeting that day, but an average of twelve souls. Religion still played an important role, though divided on class lines, and provided a focus of social solidarity and networking amongst the merchant classes. It was sometimes (but not always) accompanied by a degree of moral seriousness both in the conduct of business and in the relief of need.

The town at play took many forms. Public houses were a major resort for many men and a few women. Fist fighting was a popular pastime. Undoubtedly, outdoor occasional entertainments had long been provided at fairs since time immemorial. Cockfighting, which had been practised in public house yards earlier in the century, seems to have declined in popularity and was made illegal in 1849.[47] The Shrove Tuesday Fair was still in existence.

The arrival of a theatre in Wells was a great event. An announcement was made in April 1793 of the formation of a 'respectable' company of comedians by William Scraggs and David Fisher, both of Norwich; it was an appeal to the 'nobility and gentry' who, it was hoped, would not be offended by their touring show. This they were to bring to 'the principal towns' in the counties of Norfolk and Suffolk, which included Wells.[48] They performed first in premises on Honeymoon Row near the church and Fisher, wishing no doubt to cash in on the popularity of his shows in Wells, built his own theatre in 1812. Costing somewhat less than £200 it was apparently planned to accord maximum accommodation with minimum outlay. Like Fisher's other theatres across the region it had a six week season every other year, plays being given for not more than four nights weekly. On other evenings bespoke performances were given in the houses of local gentry. Performances included Shakespeare, Sheridan and Goldsmith, pantomime, ballet and even opera. The 'astonishing' Fishers numbered as many as eighteen members acting in the circuit. A fundraising concert, attended by the gentry of the town and country for the new school, took place in December 1836. The theatre closed in 1844 and was converted into tenements, being finally demolished in 1965. The opening of another venue, the Assembly Rooms behind the Globe Hotel, was due to the initiative of one Robert Spicer who bought the inn in 1858. By 1862 he had built the Assembly and Concert Rooms as they were officially named, which became the town's centre of theatre, music hall and other entertainment as well as the venue for meetings. Visiting artists staying at the hotel included a pianist from Birmingham, a ventriloquist from Reepham, and a comic vocalist from West Bromwich.[49] Spicer appears to have handed over the running of the Assembly Rooms by 1878 and by 1885 they had migrated to the Oddfellows Hall in Clubbs Lane.

Another portrait, or rather series of portraits, is provided by the various Directories published during the period. Pigot's 1822–23 Directory was among the earliest. William White of Sheffield produced one every ten or so years, covering a number of counties of which Norfolk was one. White's Directory of 1845 shows

Wells becoming more diverse. Of particular interest is the range of professions. In 1845 there were thirty-seven inns and beer houses. The latter were not off-licences but rather less respectable places of resort which had been, in times past, where smugglers might meet and where outsiders would be easily noticed. They were thought to be dangerous places of dissent at the beginning of the century. The number of both declined over time. On the other hand the presence of perfumers and hairdressers, tailors and drapers, watchmakers and booksellers tells of a new kind of demand. Fire and life insurance companies, banks and private schools likewise tell of the continued growth of the middle class.[50]

The coastwise trade

Trade after the Napoleonic wars grew steadily ; remarkably so since until 1845 Wells lacked the onshore infrastructure possessed by Lynn and Yarmouth by which goods could be sent inland. Its survival and indeed expansion may have been due to the fact that it specialised: coal in, grain out. The demand for grain had been growing for some time. In 1819 it was already sending over 35,000 quarters of barley coastwise, the third largest volume of east coast ports; a figure which was to be more than doubled by 1824.[51] Malt left the port in much smaller quantities, though volumes began to increase as London brewers recognised the possibilities of Norfolk malt. It was a happy combination of circumstances which came to the aid of Norfolk maltsters and which caused its industry to grow again, albeit from a low level. Traditionally many inns had brewhouses and did their own malting; local brewers supplied the retail trade; excess production went increasingly to London. Norfolk had become known for its pre-eminence in the development of agriculture, its barley of the highest quality. Added to that, the promotion of the turnip as a food crop for animals proved a blessing for the maltsters because turnips, grown as part of the newly promoted crop rotation, proved an excellent partner for barley. As a result production was well in excess of local demands.[52] The cramped streets of London, whose demand for beer was insatiable, were no place for large maltings, filled as they often were with the acrid smoke of a million chimneys. The London breweries turned initially to the maltsters of Hertfordshire but then to Norfolk and to Wells where the higher qualities of malt enabled them to extract higher amounts of fermentable material per quarter.[53] In the face of a declining market nationally and reduced profitability this was important. (The use of sugar in the mash tun was permitted only in 1847.) Truman's, the London brewers, placed a huge regular order with the malting at Burnham Overy.

The volumes of malt leaving the harbour were not much more than a sixth of eighteenth-century levels but the increase in shipments was significant: the twenty years from 1818 were to see a fifteen-fold increase in shipments of malt to London.[54] Barley shipments remained at much higher levels only exceeded in England by Lynn and Yarmouth and by Montrose and Dundee in Scotland. Greater investment in grain ships seemed a very good proposition. Even so after a steady rise in harbour dues they had peaked in 1841 and had begun to decline.[55] This appears to have been another reason for the pressure to rebuild the Quay. In the following years dues increased again to £939 in 1869.[56]

The growth in commercial malt production was due to a number of factors: one was the continuing growth of London; a second was the decline of farm and local brewing and the rise of commercial breweries.[57] Because Wells was able to supply them it was well positioned to benefit from this change in patterns of production. Larger floor maltings were being bought or built. Stephen Leeds built the Staithe Street maltings probably in the 1850s and subsequently leased them to James Everitt, a farmer turned maltster from North Creake. Robert Leaman bought Randle Brereton's fifty-quarter malting; he proceeded to acquire a number of others over a two-year period beginning in 1863 and even built several maltings himself, one in conjunction with James Everitt. Everitt apparently built a second malting only yards from the new railway.[58] Leaman's purchase was the beginning of a swathe of purchases: five pubs, granaries, brewhouses, wharves, coalhouses, several malthouses, a brick works and a town house.[59] He was a man of strong views who claimed to have revived the town's commerce but wrote that for his pains he received nothing but hostility. For this reason, after a mere three years, he wrote to the press that he would be leaving the town. He did not however sell up his investments. His death in 1878 coincided with the arrival of another man whose family were to be major players in maltings in Wells, George Frederick Smith; Smith's family business, F. & G. Smith, was in Great Ryburgh and moved to the town. He leased the Staithe Street maltings from Stephen Leeds that year,[60] and so began the process of accumulation of the whole maltings estate of the town.

The coastal trade brought other commodities as well. The *Blakeney and Hull Packet* was on a regular run in the 1850s from Wells to Hull, delivering grain and returning with parcels of groceries, Baltic timber and linseed cake, as well as carrying the mails.[61] Mails to the continent largely went from Harwich and Dover; places like Wells were used only for coastal services, a system which went back to the seventeenth century.[62] Ships carried coal now from Goole as well as Newcastle. Cities, growing in size, continued to suck in supplies, London most especially. The Royal Navy, whose role was increasing, required effective victualling. Bulk cargoes could still be carried more cheaply and in greater quantity by water than by road. The railway would change all that.

Top: *A barque lying at the quay: the Granary under construction.* Centre: *The tug* Marie *with a vessel under tow.* Bottom: *The* Marie *towing again, but now refitted with a single funnel. The ever-moving narrow channel, usable only around high tide for vessels of any size, made a tug advisable for sailing vessels.*

Top: *A malting floor at Great Ryburgh illustrates what the interior of a Wells maltings would have looked like.* Centre: *The schooner* Minstrel, *built in the town and then owned by John Savory, miller and malster.* Bottom: *The* Marie *tows out a steam coaster; even with your own power a tug was advisable.*

Wells' reputation as a smugglers' port is still current. Since smugglers do not advertise their activities the only evidence of their presence has been the bringing of prosecutions. What evidence there is indicates that the 1840s opened an era of free trade which made smuggling less profitable. Two tons of tobacco and 650 gallons of brandy and geneva had been seized off Brancaster and brought to Wells in 1832; but beach landings were now more difficult and public attitudes had become less sympathetic.[63] Tobacco and spirits remained the only goods from which good profits could be made. Ships' crews, both fishermen and traders, were known by the Coastguard to have brought these items in, sometimes in large quantities. Whenever there was cross-channel traffic there was the likelihood of smuggling. There were no longer, however, any pitched battles on the beach between smugglers and revenue officers in Norfolk, or anywhere else for that matter.

Coastal vessels ready for cargo at the quayside in the first decade of the 20th century. A steam coaster, a billy-boy and another steam vessel are alongside.

8. A Narrower World

An aerial view of the town in 1925 reveals the many roofs of maltings, rail wagons at the quayside and a vessel at her berth to load cargo.

For hundreds of years the sea had been a gateway connecting Wells with the wider world; for some of that time it was the major highway. The town had been a major producer and distributor of foodstuffs. Ironically, that same sea increasingly had come to define the town as remote and dependent on other places. The sea was ceasing to be a highway; it would eventually become a barrier. The town had become unable to match either the scale of manufacturing production or the good communications to which other places had access. The harbour had merged with Cley in 1853 until 1855 when Wells custom house took over responsibility for ship registrations. Receipts from harbour dues peaked in 1869; by 1872 tonnages had fallen significantly and by 1894 they were at a quarter of their highest levels. In 1844 there were twelve pilots for incoming and outgoing vessels. By 1890 there were only three. Harbour dues, averaged over ten years to 1869, were £780; by 1879 they had fallen to £469; by 1904 to £240 and by 1914 to £140.[1] It was not unknown for cargoes to be transferred from storm-bound vessels in the harbour to the railway to ensure prompt delivery.[2]

The fall in income meant that there was little money to spend on the harbour which had now silted up badly and had become tortuous between the Quay and the Pool. By 1876, the blocked exits from the East Marsh had eroded or been swept away entirely. Unable to spend money on professional advice, the services of Sir John Coode, the distinguished London engineer, were obtained, apparently without charge. (Coode had done work on Portland Harbour and the East London docks.) He recommended the building of a training wall to straighten the channel. Required expenditure was £1,165 for just essential works and a further £5,000 if the training wall were built. Bondholders were initially reluctant to fund this but were eventually persuaded by the issue of new bonds and the threat that if nothing were done they would lose their investment entirely. What was called a near miraculous cure was achieved by digging out a bank of hard clay in the channel without the need for a training wall in 1884. It was reported that 'a vessel lying in the Quay, as soon as it can float, can now proceed to sea.'[3]

By the 1850s the demand for new ships by local owners had declined. Investors had diverted the money towards the building of the new railway. The last cargo schooner built in Wells was the 94-ton *Roseola* in 1869. By 1890 Frederick Whitaker was working solo as a boat builder and shipwright at the old shipyard at the East End. A few small boats were built in the early years of the twentieth century, mostly leisure craft.

As to the vessels which came into the harbour, they were still mostly sailing ships. Steam propulsion, initially using paddles, was expensive – wind was free – and bunkering coal took up a lot of space. Only high value cargoes could be carried. Tugs justified their expense because of the time they saved in getting sailing vessels in and out of the harbour. The development of the screw propeller in the 1840s quickly caught on; even so steamships were a rarity until the 1880s.

The coming of the railway

The railway was hailed as the transformer of hopes in the nineteenth century, bringing increased trade, extending social horizons and opportunities, even

Top: *Wells railway station operated until 1964.* Centre: *The full name Wells-next-the-Sea was too generous for the station and signal box at the junction; it was shortened to Wells on Sea.* Bottom: *The station and Dewing and Kersley's mill in the background, 1956.*

introducing a standard time to the nation: if trains were to run to time clocks had to be synchronised. The line to Wells was awaited with high expectation but, as so often with large civil engineering projects, it did not prove to be the bonanza that had been forecast. Of the local businessmen who invested in the new venture, and took their money out of shipbuilding, many lost money, Joseph Southgate being one of the hardest hit. The shares issued by railway companies ultimately turned out to be worthless.

The first railway to arrive was the extension of the Wymondham to East Dereham line which came to Fakenham in 1849 and to Wells in 1857. It was at the outset owned by the Wells and Fakenham railway, its services operated reluctantly[4] by the Eastern Counties Railway. A branch leading to the harbour was planned from the outset; until it was opened in 1859 coal delivered by boat had to be loaded onto horse-drawn waggons on the Quay and taken to the railhead to be transferred manually to railway waggons. The line ran to the East End of the Quay from whence horses were used to haul waggons along the tramway to the west end of the stone quay; steam locomotives were only allowed thus far from the station yard before being shunted into a siding. The Wells branch suffered other teething troubles which led to the ending of the short history of the company when it was amalgamated with the Great Eastern Railway in 1862 without any profit to its local investors and shareholders.[5] Gradually, a regular passenger service developed and excursions for day trippers were tried; Regatta Day in August proved very popular; but while visitors might come from Norwich, Wisbech or East Dereham, Wells was further from London than any of the other East Anglian resorts like Cromer, Yarmouth or Hunstanton

Wells railway station on its last day of operation.

The railway station in a later mode as a second hand bookshop.

and lacked the immediate visual amenities of those places. It had no grand view of the sea and no promenade. It lacked the kind of accommodation which would allow London families to take a property for the summer while the husband would come up for the weekend.[6]

For some businesses, the railway was a godsend. James Everitt, whose maltings had been acquired in the 1850s, began to supply the Bass brewery in Burton on Trent. Everitt did not merely supply; he acted as agent for the brewery in purchasing barley for its use. Malt could now be dispatched quickly and cheaply to the centres of urban growth.[7] Everitt was from a local farming family and, as a young man in the 1820s, he had been involved in the family brewery business with its string of twenty-five public houses.[8] Likewise, the 1879 accounts for F. & G. Smith show their transport costs as being almost entirely for rail freight.[9] One can understand why: in the early days of the railway, malt cost 1*s* 4*d* a quarter to transport from Norwich to London against 2*s* 5*d* by sea.[10] These prices were not to remain so advantageous and Smith continued to use the port for the delivery of coal and the sending of malt to London. As evidence of their confidence in the town, young George, son of the founder, moved, on his marriage, to Wells; the firm bought 'Mayshiel' for his residence at the top of Staithe Street, within easy walking distance of the maltings on the Quay.

Three maltings had been added to the town's stock, two by Everitt in the 1860s and one by Smith's in the 1890s.[11] In 1904 Smith's bought up four maltings formerly owned by Robert Leaman together with a landing wharf.[12] Though the

137

commissioners had bought up some properties on the Quay using the powers of the 1844 Act, they had never completed it as proposed and the Quay to the east of the Granary was owned by the Smiths. They therefore themselves undertook the strengthening of the Quay to accommodate their supply vessels, apparently deepening it at the same time.[13]

In 1880, they had also acquired a new tugboat, the *Marie*, to replace the ageing *Olive Branch*, a successor to the *Economy*, to tow vessels in and out of the harbour. (Smiths sold the *Marie* in 1916; she was then requisitioned by the navy and was sunk by a mine.) By the latter part of the century there were probably twelve maltings along the length of the Quay.

A second railway was driven into the town from the west. Parliamentary approval for the Heacham to Wells line from Kings Lynn came in 1864. Completed in 1878, it was nominally the work of the West Norfolk Junction railway, but was sold to the Great Eastern Railway in 1890. Trains to London via Heacham, Kings Lynn and Cambridge took about five hours, running several times daily. Holkham Hall, which was a great user of coal, some 1000 tons a year, had it supplied to Peterstone sidings.

After 1870 local farmers found their wheat prices undercut by cheap wheat from the Canadian prairies. The effect on farm rents was severe; less affected was barley production. Even with competition from the railway by which barley was shipped from Kings Lynn and Yarmouth, Wells retained some of its trade, even though it was not carried by locally owned and built ships. The coal for the maltings had come traditionally from the Humber or the Tyne; it came now also from Swansea. Coal was apt to impart a taste to the malt, whereas anthracite, a high carbon coal found in Wales, was virtually smokeless. From 1886 until 1904 the schooner *Fay* from Runcorn brought regular deliveries twice a year, taking in return malt for Dublin, presumably for the Guinness brewery. The *Fay* was only one of at least eight Welsh built vessels plying this trade.[14] The port finally lost its independence in 1881 when it reverted to being a 'creek' of the port of Lynn. Its splendid Custom House was sold and remains in private hands.

All of this is reflected in the population of the town. From 2,400 in 1793, by 1821 the numbers rose to 2,950 and by 1851 to 3,675. By 1871 numbers had fallen to 3,044, by 1881 to 2,645 and by 1901 to 2,494 almost the level of a hundred years before.[15]

A shortage of fish

Fishing remained a significant though unpredictable aspect of the economy of the town. Fishermen had other jobs in winter. The advent of trawling in the early nineteenth century, albeit from sailing vessels, was at first very productive but at the expense of the traditional inshore line fishermen. It was feared that the fishery was in terminal decline. T. H. Huxley's Commission of 1863 claimed to have refuted these concerns. In his view all regulation should cease; unrestricted fishing should be permitted: the sea was boundless.[16] Yet it was not obviously so. Hugh Rump was one of several people who noted the disappearance of certain species over the previous twenty years from Wells. They included haddock, cod, skate, turbot, gurnard, whiting, flounders, dabs and plaice, all of which were line-caught using lugworms as bait.[17] Rump wrote to the new Commission charged with investigating the state of the Norfolk fishery, which was headed by Frank Buckland, a surgeon turned natural historian. Richard Smith, coxswain of the lifeboat, reported that there were 'no edible crabs or lobsters; there were "hook fish" in winter, cockles, clams, not many shrimps, few whelks, few razor shells; there was no trawling, except with a steam boat; they discontinued trawling because it did not pay, although eight years ago there used to be three or four smacks'.[18] Buckland himself described the huge waste of immature sole, whelks and oysters due to poor systems of capture; 'the oysters have all disappeared', he wrote. Net sizes were one problem. Nevertheless he advised no legislation controlling fishing in Wells.

The arguments continued. Ernest Holt's report of 1891, which recommended regulation of plaice fishing, expressed concern; it was countered by McIntosh's 1899 book *The Resources of the Sea*. McIntosh was a member of the Royal Commission on Trawling and its effects on line fishermen. Line fishing was affected by trawling but it was thought that trawling by sailing boat was comparatively ineffective out at sea. The fishing smacks which towed trawls were hampered by reliance on wind and tide; their impact on fish stocks was minimal compared with that of steam-engined trawlers which were to reduce the North Sea fisheries to below commercial levels within three generations. Buckland had recommended various close seasons and minimum sizes for certain fish and crustacea. 'Vast as are the resources of the sea', he wrote, 'yet it is possible that modern appliances and want of scientific cultivation for fishing may draw too much upon the general stock in certain localities'.[19] As it turned out he was understating the problem; as one species was extirpated, the fishermen seeking a living turned to another.

In spite of Buckland there were oysters to be had. There were, apparently, seven principal beds in the Lynn area by 1875 from which thirty Lynn boats dredged up some 700,000 oysters during the season. Wells had its oyster smacks too. Once again overfishing destroyed the stocks and by 1904 the last smack, the *Little Polly*, owned by Charles Wordingham and crewed by Billy Sizeland, ceased working. Smacks also used to catch sole, brill and thornbacks, but trawling had ceased working by 1875. (It was to return briefly after the Second World War.)

The arguments still continued about sustainable levels of fishing and what was actually going on out to sea. One difficulty was that, in the absence of a historical record, each generation assumed that what it first knew was the norm whereas it now appears that the depletion of the oceans has been going on apace for centuries, not decades. The conclusion has only slowly been reached that the ocean needs to be farmed, not treated as a wilderness for hunter gatherers to predate at will.[20]

Lifeboats

Wrecks had long been a source of revenue for those who would risk their lives to board them at low tide and coal was a valuable prize from wrecks even into the nineteenth century. Salvage was assumed to be a legitimate source of income. Smacks of various kinds competed for what was no more than a trade in the products of wrecks, vying with each other to reach stricken vessels before others. Sometimes their crews were heroes; from time to time they were rightly regarded as sharks, stripping vessels of everything from cargoes, anchors, cables, even brass door hinges. Some of the early lifeboats were actually opposed, even hated, by the so-called salvagers.[21] Only gradually did attitudes change so that the welfare of the sailors became more important than wrecking. The boats were ill-designed, inefficient and poorly used. When therefore in 1830 the Norfolk Shipwreck Association established a station with a boathouse at the west end of the Quay, it is not surprising that it is not recorded as having made any rescues. As we have seen, the 1844 Act required the Commissioners to make provision for an efficient lifeboat with penalties for failure to do so and the lifeboat's existence is early recorded; it was evidently in action in 1851 though there are no records of any rescues undertaken. Thus when in 1868 James and David Stacey took their crab boat the *Pet* and rescued the crew of the sloop *Rose* in June,[22] this was part of the old tradition of voluntary salvaging which was only gradually superseded by the infant RNLI.

The many improvements to the harbour rendered it much safer, but there were always going to be conditions which would overwhelm vessels at sea. There was also the possibility of human error as sailors misjudged either the conditions or their own abilities. So it was in 1869 that the Royal National Lifeboat Institution stationed a boat at Wells for the first time and erected a house for it at the west end of Wells stone quay. (The building, now the Harbour Office, still stands.) The boat was a 33-feet-long self-righting boat propelled by 10 oars set in double banks. Called the *Penny Readings and Eliza Adams*, its name indicated the source of the sum of £500 which it had cost. The readings had been undertaken mostly in Norfolk and Suffolk; the lady concerned was the wife of a surgeon of Bungay, E. B. Adams Esq., who had organised the collection of funds. From the boat house it was drawn by

The Wells lifeboat Baltic, *on service from 1895 to 1913.*

horses to the road a mile west and out to sea at Holkham gap or launched into the harbour at high tide. In the early days the crew received five shillings each or seven shillings and six pence after dark.

The value of the *Eliza Adams* became quickly apparent. Numerous lives were saved in those early years, as William Harman's account vividly shows. Harman was a local fisherman who witnessed many of the rescues and even took part himself; he wrote his memoirs of those days in later years. He describes the dangers of being carried onto the sands east of the harbour (and of the relative safety of steering for

On 25th October 2005, lifeboat crew and townsfolk gathered at the memorial to those who were drowned when the Eliza Adams *capsized.*

Holkham Bay).[23] It rapidly became clear that the lifeboat needed to be housed nearer the sea. On a number of occasions she was towed out to sea by the steam tugs, twice in one day by the same tug (the *Olive Branch*) on 18th August 1872. (The *Olive Branch* had replaced the *Economy,* which had done thirty years service, two or three years before.) She rescued seven people from a yacht and then nine from a 230-ton brig, the *Criterion,* whose crew she landed at Blakeney. She was brought back to Wells by road, hauled by horses. In 1878 she was again assisted by a steam tug to save the crew of four from a four-ton fishing sloop, the *Sally*. On 29th October 1880 five ships were blown ashore at Wells. Having already made one rescue of the crew of the brig *Violet* and having failed to reach another, the *Sharon's Rose,* she went out again to another ship, the *Ocean Queen*.[24] The water was too shallow to reach her so the lifeboat attempted to return to port. On her way home she and her exhausted crew were caught in heavy seas and capsized. Eleven of her crew drowned. It is thought that her mast struck the sand and she could not be righted in time. Some years later a memorial to her crew was erected near the old lifeboat house.

The lifeboat Royal Silver Jubilee on the day of her dedication and hand–over to the Wells station.

In 1893 the secretary reported the impossibility of the lifeboat crew rowing the one and a quarter miles to the Point against a northerly gale. The Point could at that time be reached only by going more than four miles by road. Thus, in 1895 a new lifeboat house and slipway were built at the Point at a cost of £550. The first motorised lifeboat, the *Royal Silver Jubilee,* was acquired in 1936, remaining on service until the end of the Second World War.

Control of local affairs

The reform and reorganisation of local government was a several stage process: County Councils had been created in 1888 taking over the administrative responsibilities of Justices of the Peace; in 1894 with the passing of the Local Government Act of that year the Wells Urban District Council came into being. The Church Vestry, on whom a variety of responsibilities had devolved, from the registration of births, marriages and deaths to the administration of the poor law and the maintenance of roads, was relieved of all but its ecclesiastical responsibilities (and in 1927 was replaced by a parochial church council.) The word 'parish' was now to mean two things. Civil parishes were made quite separate politically from ecclesiastical parishes, though in many country districts the boundaries remained the same and clergy continued, in many cases, to exercise influence unofficially in local communities.

Education likewise was becoming a governmental function; it had become clearer that literacy was needed for the new industry and commerce. Until 1870 elementary schools were mostly provided by the Church, which had begun to take a more systematic interest at the turn of the century. The older endowed schools of various kinds, grammar schools, public schools – so-called because entry was not restricted to the clergy – were few and far between. A school was endowed in 1678 in Wells[25] though it is not known how long it lasted. In the eighteenth century a number of academies had been set up to meet the aspirations of the new middle classes and to provide for industry and commerce. Provision in villages might depend on the local initiative of women often teaching in their own homes, often called Dame Schools.

The broadening of church interest in mass education was marked by the formation in 1811 of the National Society, whose aim was to provide a school in every parish with trained teachers. Not everyone agreed with this idea: it was often opposed by local landowners who wanted children to be available as labourers in the fields. On the contrary, wrote one local clergyman '[i]t was never intended that we should continue in the place and sphere in which we were born'. What would help was 'a little education'.[26] The old workhouse on Burnt Street had become a so-called National School, but its premises were inadequate and it closed soon after. Moreover there were many for whom Church control of education was held to be undesirable. Other Christians, along with liberal Anglicans and some Roman Catholics and Jews, preferred a less denominational approach and in 1814 founded the British and Foreign School Society.[27] Its schools, to be called British Schools, drew on the pioneering work of the Quaker Joseph Lancaster. They taught Scripture and general Christian principles in a non-denominational form. A British school was built in 1838 in Wells following a fund-raising effort supported by the Countess of Leicester and Thomas Keppel, vicar of Warham, among others but fiercely opposed by the Revd John Hopper, the patron and subsequently vicar of the parish. Hopper wrote to Keppel complaining vigorously about the liberal lack of principle which the latter was showing. All manner of fund-raising events were held under the patronage of the Duke of Sussex, sixth son of George III, as well as a great many of the aristocracy.

Other private schools continued in the town, several of which took boarders. White's *Directory* of 1845 records four Academies, two in High Street, one in Staithe Street, and one on the Buttlands run by the wife of the clerk to the magistrates. There were three Girls Free Schools, one on Burnt Street, one on the Quay and one in the East End.

The purpose of the 1870 Education Act was to fill in the gaps left by voluntary provision; to 'cover the country with good schools'. It was plain that governmental involvement would increase. Thus in 1875 the British School was transferred to a School Board and the buildings enlarged. Additional classrooms were built in 1899.

Health and wealth

The issue of health did not go away. 'The emphasis of long practice, the natural bent of public opinion and the Parliamentary mind was on the Poor Law and Poor Law methods, on deterrence rather than prevention, on relieving destitution rather than preventing disease, on organising workhouses rather than clearing slums.'[28] The high principles implied by the 1844 Act were controversial and subsequent events were to show that the building of a comprehensive sewerage system would have to wait for many years. Gradually the Improvement Commissioners replaced the old brick sewers by glazed pipes, but it took time. The west end open sewer was only replaced by 93 yards of glazed pipe in 1895. It would henceforth run along Freeman Street and out to a sluice some distance down the run; the sewers from Staithe Street, Star Yard and Standard Yard and all on the north side of the town discharged directly into the Quay, as did eight smaller drains along the water front. On the south side of the town, a similar system drained surface water and waste down High Street to the Ostrich Inn at the north end of Church Plain and from there to the ditch which ran across Church Marsh east and then north into the harbour.[29] The extended powers of the Commissioners granted in 1877 included the improvement of drains and sewers, requiring all new houses built to have drains and privy accommodation; they had powers over the water supply, over the condition of lodging houses and to act in the case of epidemics of infectious disease.

There were, of course, different methods by which health issues could be tackled. Government, which had long resisted the idea of central direction of health matters, stirred by the latest smallpox and cholera epidemics, began to act in a more coherent way. Under the Public Health Act of 1875 the Improvement Commissioners were obliged to set up the Wells Sanitation District and appoint a Medical Officer of Health, one Frederick Eyres Taylor. The reports of such officers over the years were to identify more precisely the causes of ill-health and of the recurring epidemics and to provide ammunition for those who sought more comprehensive solutions. Taylor's successor Frederick Long was to report in 1897 that 'the general sanitary condition of the town is now good' with almost every dwelling attached to a sanitary pipe. However, apart from the soil from privies and cesspits which was spread on the fields, household waste, waste from toilets, offal from the various butchers, still all went into the Quay. There, the mussel lays were 'washed by sewage matter'. Long was sanguine about the fact that 'sewage matter of itself will not generate typhoid'; his successor Gordon Calthrop on the contrary concluded that 'it cannot be very long before the market will be practically closed to all oysters, mussels and other molluscs which do not come from waters certified to be free from sewage contamination'.[30] In September 1908 having traced an outbreak of typhoid to the proximity of the mussel beds to the town drains into the harbour, he banned their sale. Matters came to a head in the autumn of 1914 when there were epidemics of typhoid, diphtheria and scarlet fever which were traced to a combination of contaminated milk from farms and the now infamous mussel beds. The solution proposed was to move the beds upstream. His recommendation of the building of a sewage treatment works as a better alternative was ignored.

Some people in the town, on the contrary, lived remarkably well. By the end of the century, Smith's had become a major employer in the town; malting was a significant user of labour. The labour troubles which it experienced in 1892, and which were reported in the local press, show a workforce of fifty in his nine maltings in the town, a number which would not have included porters and casual labourers. The report describes the physical nature of the work: the need to carry heavy sacks from waggons to the various chambers; the hot working conditions of the malting floors; the irregular hours which they were obliged to work; and the fact that malting

Dewing and Kersley's mill.

could only be done for less than six months of the year.[31] Men would routinely carry twelve-stone wicker baskets of coal across the quay into the fire-hold.[32] George Smith meanwhile lived a life of comparative ease unconcerned with the conditions of the labour force.

The family 'seem to have been primarily concerned with their own comfortable lives and the level of the dividends which are most carefully recorded.[33] Even so they proceeded to mop up four more maltings in Wells in 1903. By 1913 they were to be one of the twelve leading sales-maltsters in the country by production capacity.[34]

Testimony to confidence in the future of Wells as a centre for malting and the transport of corn, of various kinds, was the building of the now iconic Granary on the quay in the following year by F. & G. Smith at a cost of £3,280. At the other end of the harbour tramway was the mill built by Dewing and Kersley in 1893.[35] Driven by

A steam lorry outside Dewing and Kersley's mill

steam power, the interior was lit by electric light, 'the first installation of that illuminant in the town of Wells'. Dewing was a Wells man, who took an interest in local government and was a champion of the railway; he had been a churchwarden, freemason, harbour commissioner and county councillor.[36] Kersley came from Gloucestershire via New Zealand where he had run a similar mill. The last windmill, the smock mill on

146

Northfield Lane, continued to work for another year alongside the new mill, but was now redundant and was demolished in 1905.

The church

In spite of its withdrawal from the forefront of local affairs the influence of the parish church remained strong. Thus when in 1879 the church caught fire, it was a matter not only of sorrow, but it generated a resolve to rebuild. The fire, which broke out on the night of 3rd–4th August, destroyed the whole of the fabric of the church leaving just crumbling walls and the tower. The cause of the fire was lightning which struck the church during a storm. The rector, Robert Leeder, died seven weeks later aged 82. The two events may not have been unrelated. Ironically, the chancel had been restored only thirteen years previously, its east window filled with stained glass scenes of the Passion topped by a representation of the Ascension in the upper quatrefoil, an ornate chancel screen and an illuminated reredos with seven panels.[37] The restored panels were mediaeval, having been covered with whitewash at the Reformation. All this was destroyed by the flames.

St Nicholas church, before the fire.

The parish church immediately after the fire in 1879.

Superficially similar to the destroyed building, the new design was the work of the diocesan architect, Herbert Green. He retained the ground plan, largely following the same 'Gothic' style and where possible using the same stones. The tower, though it had survived, had been gutted by the fire and the clock and bells destroyed. The cost of the restoration was about £10,000. Though Gothic architecture was hugely popular even for new buildings, there were various theories as to where correctness lay. It may have been a result of this that the windows, notoriously the east window, were made to a design very different from the original, conforming to an approved version of the Perpendicular style. The buildings were also much lighter because the stained glass which had controlled the light, so that it was easier to see the actions of the liturgy, was replaced with clear glass; now, in the morning light, the priest would be hard to see. The church was re-opened in April 1883.

Shortly afterwards, local surgeon Hugh Rump left £2,000 to the church in his will, a huge sum at the time, as can be deduced from the fact that the money was sufficient to purchase a two manual organ, a ring of eight bells and a set of oak pews, all of which remain in use to this day.

9. A Small Town

Sailing ships continued to use the harbour, albeit in smaller numbers, into the twentieth century. In 1895 only twenty-five vessels were recorded of which five were from foreign ports. (The medical officer boarded all foreign vessels before they entered the harbour to check on the health of the crew.) By 1902 the number had risen to thirty-one, forty-four in 1903; foreign vessels were in penny numbers. This was not to change until 1914 when war broke out.[1] Ships were more often made of steel, though still mostly square rigged. Steam driven vessels became more common as shortly would motor vessels.

Williams' blacksmiths, Chapel Yard, about 1900.

It is sometimes said that the Great War which began in 1914 was a watershed in the life of the country; in truth it probably accelerated changes that were already in train. The workforce of the town was gradually showing signs of change. In 1911 there were still over a hundred and forty men working on the land, but far fewer than sixty years before; there were fifty-four fishermen, rather more. The intensification of the maltings industry meant that forty-five men identified themselves as maltsters of one sort or another, whereas very few had done so hitherto. There were grooms and ostlers for the many horses, much used to provide for the gentry, even a horse slaughterer; a number of blacksmiths was still necessary; but there were also lorries and cars. There were tradesmen, carpenters and bricklayers. Women figured as dressmakers, shop assistants and domestic servants. There were fewer engaged in the more specialist trades; no hatters or glovers any longer. More items were bought in rather than made in the town. Many women identified themselves as doing housework whereas in earlier days they were described as having no occupation; there were a number of charwomen. Perceptions were changing. The flour mills employed fewer than a dozen. Over forty men worked on the railway. The town also needed a couple of telegraph messengers and half a dozen postmen. There were an appreciable number who described themselves as being of private means. Children were at school in some numbers until the age of 14, a very few even older, totalling 400;[2] twenty years before the number had been 600. At the other end of the scale, men (sic) were described as 'retired', no longer as paupers. Of course, it was still a town of shopkeepers. As for origins, no one had been born across the channel; over half were born in the town itself; the rest from within ten miles other than one or two Scots, fifty or so Londoners and a smaller number, including the vicar, the Revd George Ingle, who had been born in India.

Health, housing and local government

The reorganisation of the town's governance at the end of the previous century had brought together the several major local concerns of the community. The new Wells Urban District Council emerged painlessly from the Improvement Commissioners – its membership was pretty much identical. It came armed with the same powers and some additional ones. Thus it had the power to build new houses, to clear away slum dwellings and ensure that existing houses were fit for habitation; it had responsibility for sewerage, refuse collection, the treatment of infectious diseases, provision of hospitals, clinics, nursing, mortuaries, cemeteries; the inspection of slaughterhouses, bakeries, etc., of articles of food exposed or prepared for sale and the prevention of various nuisances: all lay within its purview. It had power to provide a library and to appoint two managers for the local school; it retained its responsibility for the management of highways, their paving and lighting; over parks and cemeteries; the provision of allotments; the provision of gas, electricity and water; and a range of other powers over animals, children's employment, factories, fire protection and various licensing responsibilities. It was, in retrospect, the high point of local democracy.

Wells was, compared with many of the new authorities, very small and powers given to larger councils, for instance over pensions and health insurance, were not within its remit. Nevertheless the question for the coming years was how the town was going to deal with its new powers. The machinery of such government required imagination and vision in order to make it work.

Proposals for a hospital had been put forward in 1890 by a Norwich printer, Mr B. E. Fletcher; the Earl of Leicester offered £20,000 as an endowment for its continuation. In the event it was only in 1910 that, at the instigation of a local doctor, E. F. W. Sturdee, a Scot by birth, the hospital was built, paid for by public subscription. He was to be its honorary surgeon from its opening until 1945.

A major challenge to the council came after the elections of May 1913 when among those elected was Sam Peel. Peel was to become an honoured citizen of the town, but at that time he was a newcomer, from Cambridgeshire via Wymondham, and as a newly elected councillor was initially an unwelcome one. He had arrived in 1910, a convalescent, with his wife and family, intending to stay with his parents who had retired to Wells. He took a job as a printer. Gradually, he began to take an interest in the conditions in the town. The decline of the port had left many men without work; drunkenness was rife; no houses had been built for fifty years; many rented properties were of poor standard; some were insanitary in spite of the efforts of the medical officer of health. Plainly housing conditions, far from improving, had actually deteriorated. So shocked was Peel's wife at some of the sights that she described the town as 'the last place the Lord made'.[3]

On election, his first act was to demand that meetings of the Council should be in public; hitherto, like the Improvement Commissioners previously, it excluded the press from its meetings and met in private. He then requested that the Health Inspector should visit houses in the town which he believed to be insanitary. The report when it came indicated the parlous state of many houses, insufficiently drained, filthy and insanitary. In one case six houses shared one toilet and excreta oozed through the walls;[4] washhouses were shared by several houses. Peel proposed the setting up of a housing committee to establish a scheme to build new houses of a regulation

*Alderman
Sam Peel.*

standard. The meetings of the council over the next two years became notorious in the press, packed as they were by hostile members of the public, ratepayers and a few supporters.

The conviction, held by many on the council and among ratepayers generally, that all was well with the condition of the housing stock, was not easily dislodged. In spite of the setting up of the committee nothing happened. The following January, referring to the incidence of sickness among the poorer members of the

151

population, Peel declared, 'No wonder the services of the doctor were needed. It is a crying shame that human beings should be permitted to be housed in places such as many a person would not place horses and pigs . . . It is time that something was done for the labouring classes of today.'[5] Peel's oratory and his persistence paid off. In spite of the chairman's warnings that it would take years to effect change, twenty-eight houses were erected in Northfield Avenue in 1915 notwithstanding claims that it was inappropriate to undertake such works in wartime as well as various attempts by landlords to derail the process. On one occasion the surveyor was plied with drinks so that he could not present his report and councillors left the platform in protest at the report. Abuse was hurled at Peel in and outside council meetings.[6] It was to no avail; the houses were built. Lord Leicester, who had sold the land to the council, laid a stone to commemorate the event. By 1963 there would be 347 houses, representing 37% of the housing in the town.

Peel was an indefatigable and fearless campaigner. In his same first year as a councillor he attacked the old local rating system, by which the tenant rather than the landlord paid the rate. Poor tenants were excused payment and as a result by 1913 the Council was £6,300 in debt. In order to raise the issue in the public mind he organised a rate strike,[7] campaigning for the necessary financing needed by the Council so that it could not only pay its way but also pay for the repair of the gas works. He and fifty-eight other refusers were taken to Walsingham Magistrates Court; after much resistance the tide was finally turned when George Smith, the maltster, said that he would pay his full rate. The Council passed and then rescinded the resolution asking for a local government inquiry into the need to put the council on the same rating basis as the rest of the county. Finally, the clerk to the council, Herbert Loynes, was able to put the case at an inquiry in 1916. 'The doings of Wells had become notorious in that part of Norfolk owing to the conditions under which the town was governed', he was reported as saying.[8] He was opposed by the Ratepayers Association. He pointed out that the process of deciding who should be excused paying the rate was ineffective and unpopular even with councillors, who could only with difficulty be got to attend the meetings. The Provisional Order under the Public Heath Act 1875 placing the town's finances on a proper footing was eventually passed in 1917.[9] As for the gas works, Peel had found them to be ill-managed and much of the equipment dangerous. On his election he had been appointed chairman of the Gas Works Committee. The tasks before him were several: the finances of the works had to be put on a proper footing, gas leakage reduced and the manufacturing process itself renewed. In May 1914, approval was given for the erection of telephone poles at sixpence a pole. Because the exchange was manually operated, calls would initially only be made during the daytime.

A sudden war

The remarkable fact about these changes is that they took place against the background of what came to be known as the Great War. Expected to last no longer than until the Christmas of 1914, it was to last for over four years which was to shock the nation.

The major story of Wells at war can best be told by the memorial to the seventy-six men who died during it which is found on the south wall of the Institute. No war previously had cost so many young lives across the world.[10] War consisting of set-piece battles and mobile armies was replaced by trench warfare attended by almost unbelievable noise, destruction and carnage. Submarine attacks on merchant shipping were a new phenomenon. At home there was more fear than actual danger. Zeppelins were another unwelcome novelty heading overhead towards the port at Kings Lynn. Relying upon visual navigation they appeared to be following railway lines; in consequence the signal lamps on the railways were fitted with hoods, a very early version of the blackout. Yarmouth was bombarded by German naval guns on one occasion and there was talk of invasion; an armoured train, based in North Walsham, was deployed along the coast; it was often to be seen on the West Norfolk line between Wells and Heacham.[11] In hindsight, compared with later events the experience of enemy action was modest indeed. On the other hand, men were allowed home on leave much more readily than when a second world war was being fought right across the globe. It was the stories told by those who came home on leave from Flanders that were to trickle through which began to make its horrors known. The land battles in Flanders and the Dardanelles were the most notorious, but many men fought at sea too and Wells contributed its share. Fifty-seven of the names on the memorial have a known connection with the town. George Smith, son of the maltster, died on the Somme; Frank Southgate, the artist, who was aged 43 at the time, was lost also. Brothers Alfred and Harry Bone both distinguished themselves, Alfred by maintaining wire communications under heavy fire for four days; he received a posthumous DCM in addition to his MM and bar. Harry died of gas poisoning only a couple of days after receiving his DCM for conspicuous gallantry under fire.

The effects of the war at home were many and various. One immediate effect on the malting industry was the increase of 200% in the duty on beer, from 7s 9d to 23s a barrel. The maximum gravity of beer was fixed at 1036 degrees; opening hours of public houses were cut and discussions even took place about the nationalisation of the entire liquor industry. In October 1916 the government took control of the buying, selling and distribution of all cereals. Maximum prices were fixed for barley. In February 1917 all malting was halted; the capacity of the industry was twice the amount apportioned for wartime beer production and the malting season would have produced far more than was needed.[12] One solution was to export malt. Initially prohibited, licences were eventually issued and malt was sent by coastal barge to France and even as far as Italy.

The land

In the years before and after the Great War there were over a million and a half men working in agriculture. Norfolk was overwhelmingly an agricultural county and Wells was still as much an agricultural community as it was a commercial port. Farm labourers suffered more than their employers when the Agricultural Depression occurred in the 1870s; they were after all both land workers and maltsters. The hostility between farmer and labourer was peculiarly bitter, the strikes of 1891–92 resulting in permanent estrangement even between members of the same chapel.[13] Norfolk became one of the centres of Agricultural Trades Unionism; three of its MPs at different times, Joseph Arch, George Edwards, and Bert Hazell were trade unionists. The country needed reliable food supplies during wartime and wages were fixed in 1917. After the war they were deregulated, resulting in farmers lowering wages by four shillings a week. The Great Strike of 1923 followed. Peel, who had left the union to form the National Union of Landworkers because he did not believe in strike action, attempted to mediate (as did Pollock the Bishop of Norwich) but without success. When strikers were brought before Walsingham magistrates' court (on whose bench Peel sat) for intimidating farm workers, even his lenient fines were greeted with rotten fruit, orange peel and clods of earth as he left the court. George Edwards, who was a Primitive Methodist lay preacher as well as a trade union organiser, attempted to hold back the mob.[14]

In spite of this Edwards was opposed to Peel's line in principle; they saw things very differently. Unlike Peel, Edwards had spent a winter in the workhouse as a five-year-old, separated from his mother, his father having been branded as a thief for taking five turnips home to feed his family; his first job was scaring birds at the age of six.[15] As a young man he had cycled for hundreds of miles around the Norfolk lanes recruiting men to the union. The farm labourers' union, the National Union of Agricultural and Allied Workers, believed in direct action. An April 1923 meeting in the town at which Edwards, now in his seventies, spoke was attended by several hundred men. He did not share Peel's view of a golden age when there had been respect between farmer and labourer. The union wanted a wages board, a guaranteed working week and guaranteed county wages.[16] In that April of 1923, ten thousand men went on strike. The compromise that ended with a lower wage but a maximum fifty-hour week left over 1,200 labourers who never got their jobs back. The Agricultural Wages Board was set up by the Labour government in 1924. It was abolished in 2010.

Between wars

The end of the war brought a return to prosperity in the maltings but it was short-lived. The period between 1920 and 1929 saw a halving in beer production and the closure of many maltings. F. & G. Smith concluded that the fall in demand was permanent and closed the Burnham Overy maltings and the mill at Ryburgh in 1923 and, in 1929, the Wells maltings.[17] The directors were advised that each of the three branches, Wells, Dereham and Ryburgh, had much to recommend them, but only two were needed to meet the current demand for malt. The decision was made to axe Wells because of a threatened legal action over the noise produced by the plant. E. B. Loynes, solicitor and son of Robert, objected to the new Crossley steam engine which powered the machinery being started at 4.00 a.m. particularly on Sundays! It was, on the contrary, said the chairman, 'imperative' that the engine start at that time. Within weeks the decision was made to close all the Wells maltings whose efficient working would be 'crippled . . . and entail further capital outlay' by the effects of the legal action.[18] In truth Smiths had lost interest; they were primarily interested in preserving share value; ideas of diversifying into fruit and vegetable canning were rejected and share capital was reduced by returning proceeds to shareholders, which the family then invested in government stocks. Personal tragedy also played its part: George Smith died in 1917 aged 56; his son G. F. E. Smith died in France in the following year; Herbert Smith died in 1921. Ladas, George's younger son, who was chairman at the time of the closure of Wells, committed suicide in the garden shed of 'Mayshiel' shortly afterwards.[19]

Malting seems to have ceased at this point and the buildings were left empty, their machinery cannibalised for other plant. Some of the buildings were taken over by Swaffham-based Vynne and Everett who leased and then bought a number of the buildings, probably for grain storage. Others simply fell into ruin. Favor Parker, feed merchants of Stoke Ferry, bought No 1 malting in 1939 and No 2 was bought in 1941 by Eastern Counties Farmers Cooperative whose Yarmouth plant had been bombed. Malting revived that year when Pauls of Ipswich, some of whose maltings had been commandeered for the war effort, bought Wells No 18, the biggest in the town, for the knockdown price of £2,100.[20]

The town was, for a while, to make non-alcoholic mineral waters. Joseph Bullen established a factory on Standard Road in 1903. Having decided to move to Park

Road, in 1951,[21] he found himself unable to afford to run the new factory and sold out to Robert Claxton whose firm continued until 1974, when it closed and the land was sold for housing. Dawson's Mineral Water Factory, owned at one time by Smiths, was in Sun Yard.

The twenties were to see the rise of motor transport. First driven by steam and then by petrol, the new lorries brought the various communities closer together. Dewing and Kersley's lorries could be seen carrying grain and flour; Tom Grange's carrier business flourished. A rash of garages appeared in different parts of the town.[22] Samuel Abel ran a fleet of buses from his garage on the Quay, next to Croft Yard.

The cargoes that came into the harbour were brought by the ungainly Dutch vessels the *Cite de Londres* and her sister ship the *Hilderthorpe*, bringing cattle cake to feed farm animals. Other steam vessels brought wheat for Dewing and Kersley's mill. Thames barges joined them, the largest being the steel-hulled Everards, all named after members of the owner's family. These spritsail barges graced the channel with their dark red sails, bringing in coal and taking out sugar beet and corn.[23] Beet had become a major source of sugar since the first war. The first factory, at Cantley near Norwich, had opened in 1912. The beet passing through Wells came by road or rail, and was shipped mostly northwards to Selby via the Wash and the Yorkshire Ouse. It lay in huge piles all along the quayside. Tom Grange, who had bought the old Glebe malting, used his lorries

Tug Boat Yard between the wars.

to bring beet in to the town from the farms where it was loaded by chute onto the boats. A few steam and afterwards motor vessels visited the harbour. They brought coal and corn which were lifted out of the ships' holds in sacks, and carried on the backs of men across a narrow plank on the quayside or lifted onto the quay with a grab. Collers had a coal yard on the east end of the Quay, one of several, which were required for bunkering steam vessels but which also supplied the gas works, local factories and homes. The whelkers, double-ended vessels, with auxiliary engines but with a red lug sail, would appear in sight warning those onshore to cycle off to the whelk sheds on the east end to get ready to boil the catch.[24]

Fish was among the many commodities delivered to people's doors. Coal likewise was brought round the streets by horse and cart. Lighter goods like bread would be delivered by handcart. Milk came by pony and trap delivered from churns. An organ grinder was another common visitor replete with his monkey dressed with a pillbox hat. Horses still needed to be shod and the forge at the bottom of Market Lane spilled sparks from the anvil and steam as the hot shoes were pressed onto the horse's hooves before being secured with nails.[25] All would soon be gone.

Harvest on the local farms was still a communal activity involving whole families, scything the edges of the cornfields before the reaper binder arrived still drawn by a pair of horses and then catching the rabbits that ran from the diminishing standing corn. When summer storms laid the corn flat, what was left behind had to be reaped by hand. Thick hedges, laid by hand and billhook, were there to shield the corn from damage. No combines had yet come to empty the fields of people.[26]

In the town, public utilities became more organised. In 1927 an all-night telephone exchange was introduced. As for water, many houses had their own wells, though many more shared a pump in the yard and a washhouse. Latterly some houses had their water pumped from the well into a water tank from which household taps would be fed.[27] It was in 1936 that a system was built to supply the whole town pumped from a well close by. (In 1962 the town was connected to the mains supply.) In 1927, the contract was signed for electrical cables to be laid in the town.[28] The new houses were supplied with electric light; older houses took time to be connected. Until then only a few houses like Mayshiel had their own generators to charge storage batteries, which were still in use in the early 1930s.[29]

Sugar beet on the Quay in the 1920s. Railway wagons could be brought right down to the quayside at that time.

The health of the town had been improving for some time. Various measures seem to have lowered the rate of infant mortality from its appalling levels in the early and mid-nineteenth century. Whereas in 1824, of sixty-five burials twenty-eight were of infants, the number had fallen to ten by 1875 and in the year of Peel's first election five children under the age of one died out of thirty-two burials, and three the following year. There was much to be done but that same year fourteen people died aged between the ages of seventy-one and ninety-four.[30]

As one of the smallest Urban Districts, Wells was in danger of losing its status and therefore its considerable powers as part of the revision of local government in 1929. It might have reverted to being made a civil parish. It seems likely that without Peel's efforts to make the council able to run its own services this might have happened. In the event it survived until the wholesale abolition of such councils in 1974.

Peel stood for the County Council in 1919, giving up his place on the UDC in 1943, two years after taking on the major responsibility of Chairmanship of the Education Committee. At that time almost all Norfolk children were educated in all-age schools.[31] Wells was therefore in the vanguard in having a new so-called Central school built in 1929; the old Board school became an infant and junior school. Central schools provided an improved general education of a practical character, sometimes with a slight industrial or commercial bias, for pupils between the ages of 11 and 14 or 15.[32]

The rise of the town as a seaside resort resumed after the war with assistance from the railway. Lacking hotel accommodation it proved more attractive to day trippers from Norwich and Dereham, and from an early date this was how it was advertised by the railway companies. Paid holidays for working men and women and the advent of the summer Bank Holiday on the first weekend in August, enacted in 1871, gave people more time to travel. Those arriving at the station were met by enterprising locals who provided a taxi service from the station to the beach. Days out by charabanc became popular. The town was never developed as were, for instance, Hunstanton and Cromer. At Hunstanton the L'Estrange family promoted the development of the new resort and at Cromer the Bond-Cabbells of Cromer Hall were similarly active; the Cokes were more interested in agriculture. Wells Quay was lined with maltings and public houses not hotels and a promenade; it was essentially an industrial town. It may have been for that reason that it was omitted from the maps of resorts advertised by the LNER, the successor company to the Great Eastern, in 1931. The more occasional pilgrimage traffic to Walsingham was by then a bigger draw attracting pilgrims from London and further afield.[33]

Warfare resumed

The Second World War impinged upon the town in a quite different way from the first. Airfields proliferated all around: Docking, Raynham, Sculthorpe, Langham and North Creake. North Creake airfield was actually in Egmere, a stone's throw from Wells. Built originally as a decoy base for Docking in 1941 it became operational in December 1943. Its staff numbered nearly 3,400 personnel who were dispersed around the perimeter of its three intersecting runways. Its use was largely confined to countering enemy radar operations, dropping metallic reflective material called 'window' to confuse radar reception and, more dangerously, flying ahead of bomber squadrons across the channel with radar jamming equipment on board. In the process seventeen aircraft were lost, eight Short Stirlings and nine Handley Page Halifaxes. The airfield buildings bestraddled the Fakenham Road which nevertheless remained open to the public, (except when a Halifax ran off the runway and caught fire when it hit a tree).[34]

Wells was in a small way involved in the Dunkirk evacuation in 1940. Lifeboat coxswain Ted Neilsen, a Dane who had come to live in the town, took a number of vessels from Wells to assist in bringing British servicemen from the French coast. Only one vessel from Wells, the *Bessie,* made the crossing. After the evacuation, Wells was one of the places to which displaced servicemen were sent. Several air-sea rescue vessels were moored in the harbour. Later, the lifeboat crew was often put on standby, sleeping in the lifeboat house, when bombing raids were launched from Lincolnshire so as to rescue crews of aircraft unable to make landfall.[35] Ted Nielsen was to receive an award for going aboard a Lancaster, which had crashed into the sea, in search of survivors.[36]

The fear of invasion was most acute early on in 1940. Initially, official estimates were that Wells was not a likely invasion point but even so two six-inch naval guns were brought in and set up on the beach, peering over the barbed wire entanglements replete with landmines. Their crews were billeted in a camp in the Pinewoods. The beach was off-limits except to fishermen whose permits were inspected by a sentry and few saw Mosquito aircraft practising with dummy highball bouncing bombs off Holkham.[37] The beach huts, untended, lost their roofs and doors in storms and filled with sand. The regular crump of guns firing at a target towed along the coast from Weybourne and Stiffkey could be heard for miles.[38]

Perhaps because of the number of airfields, north Norfolk suffered several air raids. Incendiary bombs fell harmlessly around the town in August 1942. A year later, on 18th August 1943, the harbour was brought to a standstill by a raid deploying so-called butterfly (antipersonnel) bombs. A team led by Captain Edward Bourne detonated thirty-one of these particularly unpleasant devices, doubtless saving the lives of those who might be attracted by their brightly painted colours. Bourne was awarded the George Medal.[39] Bourne was not the only person to be decorated: Frank Taylor, who was to become a respected harbour master, was awarded the DSM for his exploits with the Naval Intelligence Department landing French resistance fighters in occupied France; escaping capture, he had to be smuggled back to England via Algeria. Charlie Platten got the DCM; Billy Butters got the

MM, as did Robert Churchill; William Deeks got the DFC; Graham Cawdron got the DFM; others were mentioned in despatches.[40] Many stories remain untold. The air raid shelters on the Buttlands were put to use. Unexploded ordnance became a temptation to young children, some of whom, too adventurous for their own good, were lucky to escape with their lives.[41]

A Handley Page Halifax amidst the haymaking.

Wells became a garrison town. Pupils had gas mask practice at school. As D-Day drew near convoys of American army lorries supported by tanks would arrive, driving down the Quay, chewing up the roadways with their tracks, their crews throwing chewing gum to eager local children.[42] The girls, it is said, had never had so much choice; the Regal cinema on Clubbs Lane became a Mecca for off-duty servicemen. The story goes that on the eve of D-Day, many of the service personnel from Egmere were in the cinema and a message was flashed onto the screen requesting them to return to the base immediately.[43] Earlier in the war the manager succeeded in emptying the place by interrupting the film with the news that German paratroopers had landed at Blakeney.[44] There were many war scares in those days. The Regal had opened some time before 1929 as the Electric Palace and was renamed the Central Cinema in 1932 before becoming the Regal in 1937. The Park Cinema, a converted warehouse on the west end of Mill Road, opened in 1931 and closed in 1948. The Regal closed on 31st March 1975.[45]

Many young men had gone away to fight, leaving the fishing to their elders; thirty-four of them didn't come back (three were buried by the Burma railway;

Frank Southgate's painting of the tug Marie.

six died in the navy). The remaining fishermen were able to take advantage of the absence of trawlers to engage in line fishing for white fish which proved highly successful, negotiating their way through the narrow gap in the invasion defences to get out to sea. The war, of course, brought an end to cross-channel traffic and

The motor lifeboat Ernest Tom Nethercoat, *a 37 foot Oakley class boat, making her way to Wells for the first time in 1965.*

few vessels of any kind used the harbour. The only substantial traffic that the war brought was shipments of cement, some thirty of them, for the runways of the North Creake airfield in 1943. It closed in 1947. (Many of the airfields, notably Sculthorpe, were US bases and some local girls became GI brides. Sculthorpe was to become one of the largest nuclear bases in Europe during the Cold War.)

Within living memory

The war cost the country dear and rationing handed control over many commodities to local shopkeepers; the existence of rabbits and wildfowl probably helped feed some families. Rationing finally came to an end in 1954. Some aspects of life improved; others declined.

A trench for sewer pipes on Church Street, 1950.

After a long delay, in 1951 Wells finally got a proper sewerage system. The streets suffered dislocation for some months as the new sewerage pipes were laid under all the main streets, replacing the old 'combined' system, with a so-called 'separate' system by which surface water was allowed to drain into the harbour but foul water was taken via newly constructed pipes to a new treatment works north of Freeman Street. A pump on Knitting Needle Lane was built to take the waste from the south side of the town over the hill. It signalled the ending of the weekly visits of the night carts with their noisy iron wheels emptying privy buckets and, more important, raw sewage was no longer discharged into the harbour. (The treatment works was rebuilt in 1993.)[46]

After the war also the town got its gas lamps replaced by electric street lighting; little by little the houses did so too. Latterly, it ceased to be an act of bravery to leap out of bed and get dressed in winter: the plumbers had brought us central heating. High Street was still replete with shops: ironmongers, hair-dressers, tailors, home furnishings, a bicycle shop, a boot and shoe shop, grocers, bakers and, latterly, an antique shop. Ramm's butchers shop front was hung with carcases of beasts and birds; subsequently owned by Howell's, it would be the last to go. Some shop windows remained after their premises became private houses but the traces of others would quite disappear. The shops in Staithe Street remained, but changed

162

hands and uses to reflect the changing clientele.

On the passing of the 1944 Education Act when the school leaving age was raised to 15, it became clear that yet another school was required. On the opening of Alderman Peel Secondary Modern School in Market Lane in 1963, the 1929 building became the infant and junior school. Peel, by now an Alderman of the County Council, attended the opening; it was his last public engagement. He died in 1964.

One unlooked-for setback for the town was the so-called east coast flood. Wells had always been subject to flooding, as far back as the thirteenth century to our certain knowledge. The thirteenth-century surges which endangered Peterstone priory must have virtually swamped the town of Wells way beyond anything within living memory. Mary Hardy, brewer, farmer and diarist of Letheringsett had reported that in 1808 a storm surge had resulted in the inundation of Wells Quay and the swamping of the Royal Standard Inn.[47] Three hundred sheep were lost on the marshes in a gale in July 1817. The great storm of 1897 carried vessels onto the harbour tramway. Tides are the work of the mysterious forces of sun and moon, of wind and weather. Spring tides, as every sailor knows, come not seasonally but every fortnight when the twin forces of sun and moon in alignment pull the seas more strongly. If coupled with strong northerly winds, a tidal surge down the narrowing length of the North Sea exposes the Norfolk coast to the risk of sudden and severe flooding.

The most devastating of such events in modern times took place on the night of 31st January 1953 when 307 people died in England and many more were saved by the heroism of rescuers. In Wells the west bank of the channel was breached in three places, while floodwaters came also from Burnham Overy where the banks were also breached; the sewage treatment works were put out of action as a result.[48] The former motor torpedo boat launch *Terra Nova* was left high and dry on the Quay wall. A breach in the east bank let water up the old creek, flooding the railway station, past the church and as far as Two Furlong Hill. Another flood occurred in January 1978 which again breached the beach bank (and left a coaster, the *Function,* on the Quay). The damage was less severe but as a result the bank was strengthened, and in 1982 this line of defence was completed by the building of flood-gates across the west end of the Quay for protection should the Quay again be flooded. It proved effective in December 2013 when another storm surge higher than that in 1953 nevertheless wrecked many premises on the Quay and houses on the east end.

The harbour was slow to revive after the war: three coasters in 1946, six in 1947, two in 1948. Some wheat went to Scotland, barley to Suffolk, in the early 1950s. The

Above: *Holidaymakers watch the Dutch coaster*
Raket *mooring up about 1972. She had probably
brought a cargo of fertiliser.* Below: *Another coaster
moored by F. & G. Smith's granary.* Opposite:
*From the east end in June 2001. Service tenders are
grouped in the foreground; in the background the*
Albatros *has already taken up residence but the
floating pontoon has not yet been constructed*

growing road haulage trade turned its back on the sea and also confined itself to general carrying. The nationalisation of road transport left small carriers, like Barkers' and Granges', who had depots in the town, unable to carry parcels to and from Norwich which was more than the maximum twenty-five miles allowed for private carriers. The limit was subsequently lifted but with further changes in the licensing system and the decline in specialist industries in the city the general carrying trade fell away.[49]

It was at that point, about 1960, that imports, notably of fertiliser, caused a revival of the port. Barkers became shipping agents to carry the cargoes in both directions. In 1964 there were thirty-four ships bringing in fertiliser and animal feed, and taking out grain. In 1967 the number of vessels doubled to seventy-three ships bringing 5,000 tons in and taking out 3,000 tons. Fertiliser shipments increased from the late fifties; salt was imported as the barley exports began to decline – it had its revivals in the sixties seasonally but by

Top: *The bank breached in 1953.* Middle: *The former motor torpedo boat* Terra Nova *deposited high and dry on the quayside after the 1953 floods.* Bottom: *Coasters rafted together at the quayside in the 1980s.*

Top: *Tony Jordan was one of those who worked their whelkers out of Wells in the 1960s. He stands in front of his Lynn registered* Sally. Bottom: *The whelk coppers were kept busy boiling the whelks ready for market, photo from 1963.*

Looking up the channel at Wells from the lifeboat house in 2007, prior to the building of the outer harbour. Over the centuries, vessels would have to look carefully for the markers, thin withies placed in the sand and moved when the channel moved, to navigate the deep water on the way up to the Quay.

1971 it had all but ceased; animal feed, latterly soya, became the mainstay of the port. Small amounts of fishmeal and other fertilisers came in. For a short while outgoing vessels carried peas and sugar beet pulp. At one time, as many as eight vessels lay in the harbour, double banked. Most were unloaded by crane and grab directly onto lorries into temporary storage at Great Snoring or to the feed mills.[50] In 1980 Barkers built a storage facility on the old Leicester Lime works which had closed the year before.

By 1982 there were 258 inward movements almost all departing in ballast, empty. The port was very busy in those years employing stevedores on a casual basis as well as a staff of some thirty people. The iconic granary on the Quay used a suction hose (which produced less dust than a grab) but it was arguably under-used. Favor Parker had bought the Granary from Vynne and Everett in 1961; from there they transported soya to their animal feed mill at Stoke Ferry; they were to close down the Wells operation in 1991. Numbers of vessels had diminished, at first gradually, until 1991 when only fifty-five vessels came. Before that in 1988 Barkers ceased operating as shipping agents. In March 1992 the *Othonia* was the last motor vessel bringing cargo to Wells, leaving the *Albatros*, a Dutch sailing barge now familiar to Wells visitors, to continue until 1996.[51] She was to return at first offering leisure trips and subsequently as a floating pub and restaurant. She had first come to Wells in 1986. Another sign of the times was that in 1939 almost all the vessels carried a British flag; by 1954 most were Dutch. German, Dutch and Danish vessels predominated by the 1960s.

The new lifeboat, the *Cecil Paine*, arrived on station in 1945, followed in 1965 by the *Ernest Tom Nethercoat*. (This boat returned to the town in private ownership in 2012.) For the majority of her time on station the coxswain was David Cox who served the station from 1960 to 1986, having taken over from his uncle. She was the last open boat on the station though she latterly acquired a collapsible canopy over her cockpit. Prior to that the lifeboatmen stood in the open, often washed by continual breaking waves, navigating only with a compass and a watch until 1977 when radar was first fitted. It mattered a good deal that the crew were all fishermen who knew the waters well. The arrival of her replacement in July 1990, the much larger and faster Mersey class boat the *Doris M. Mann of Ampthill*, necessitated the reroofing of the station.

Wells next the Sea, town, channel, embankments and marshes, looking westward.

As for the fishing, as always the fishermen would exploit whatever they could. Dredging for oysters continued for a while; long line fishing in the channel has been long practised. In the 1970s sprats were found. Vessels such as the *Romulus* and *Remus* came from Whitstable or Faversham; their owners eventually settled here. Using electronic aids and otter trawls, they achieved some 400 tons of fish a year – often pair-trawling, two vessels sailing side by side. The fish were boxed in ice and mostly sent off for canning 200 miles away in Scotland; some were taken directly to Grimsby to be made into fish meal. In winter they fished for whitebait which went to Coles of Lowestoft. In summer they caught thornback rays, known locally as roker. Whelking continued after the war. There were several whelk boats and the occasional shrimper which went out as far as the Dudgeon light ship. Whelks found their way by railway inland to Manchester, Birmingham and Leicester, and beyond.[52] Some were used as bait by the long-line fishermen along the coast and were sold to them as such. Lining was not dissimilar to the practices off Iceland long before when hundreds of baited hooks were attached to a line held to the sea floor with anchors. Allegedly, Wells didn't go in for lining: 'they were too busy whelking!' (Wells' fish and chip shops, it was claimed, were supplied from Sheringham.)[53] Mussels were harvested from the harbour, grown from seed mussels brought from up the coast. Fishermen helped unload the ships that came in on the tide as casual labour. It was intermittently a busy place. Crabbing and lobster fishing began in earnest only in the 1980s but, by that time, the trawling was gone.[54]

The Eastern Counties Farmers Cooperative had come to Wells in 1935 and moved its milling operation here after the bombing of its Yarmouth depot in 1941, buying the No 2 Malting on Staithe Street.[55] It brought in grain from local farms in its lorries to the grain store on Staithe Street, from which the grain went on to the boats or the maltings, or else was ground into animal feed and returned, sometimes to the same farms. From its headquarters in Ipswich, E.C.F.C. was a major presence in the town. It was, at one time, the largest cooperative in Europe. However, the Wells premises were never large enough to meet demand and promises from Ipswich of modernisation were never fulfilled. It closed in the early 1970s.[56] The cooperative itself went bankrupt. The mill was demolished and became a car park. The Leicester Lime works was another big employer in the 1950s, providing local farmers with lime to sweeten the soil; its closure in June 1979 left another gap in the town.

As for malting, it had changed: in Ryburgh Smiths had begun to use more mechanised, less labour-intensive methods of manufacture; Pauls experimented at the old maltings in Wells with chemical treatments of the malt to shorten the cycle.[57] As production capacity increased demand fell. New production methods shortened the cycle from twelve days to two. The huge pneumatic maltings at Great Ryburgh were from a different world. Pauls withdrew in 1961. The buildings given to other uses, such as grain storage, were eventually demolished and replaced by houses.

Dewing and Kersley's mill by the railway station was a victim of the same process. In the 1960s it was still producing a range of flours for retail sale, distributed by its lorries to Norwich and further afield. 'Sunshine Flour' it was called. The company also had premises in Fakenham. The wheat came mostly from East Anglian farms and it made little use of the railway. It came to an end in 1980.

The railway had proved very useful for transporting material to the airfields during the Second World War but increasing competition from road transport and government indifference to railways resulting in lack of investment were to result in the eventual loss of the service. The harbour branch, whose goods movements must have interrupted the lives of those living on the Quay, finally closed in October 1952. In summer the pilgrimage excursion trains to Walsingham were stored there so as to free up the station for other traffic.[58] The Heacham branch was closed to regular passenger traffic in May 1952; after the 1953 floods which washed the line away east of Burnham Market no attempt was made to restore it for freight traffic. The last years of the Dereham branch saw the introduction of diesel railcars in 1955 providing the best service the town had ever seen: ten trains a day ran to Norwich. The 6.55 am for Norwich arrived there at 8.34 am, in good time for a 9.00 am start to the working day. It was a good way for children to get to school in Fakenham. Freight traffic from Wells to the Ryburgh malting increased. Whelks and timber were among the freight items which left the station yard. Holiday-makers came. The Wells branch was profitable. However, the larger network was not so and after the 1963 Beeching report, which recommended the cutting of 5,000 miles of passenger line countrywide and the closure of nearly half the stations, the last train ran from Wells on Saturday 3rd October 1964. Goods traffic continued for a further month.[59]

The harbour was not just a means of income. The sailing club, which began officially in 1913, was sailing Sharpies before the war, boats almost unknown now on the international circuit, but once an Olympic class. Hydroplane races, for twenty years or so in the 1950s and 60s, were major events in the harbour; crowds came to watch them on a Sunday afternoon. The heyday of waterskiing has probably passed; at one time half a dozen boats pounded up and down the channel pulling their intrepid skiers along; windsurfing is a hair-raising sport occasionally practised in high winds beyond the lifeboat station. The water has its manifold and alluring attraction. In tandem with this, the leisure industry, driven by the desire of inlanders for holiday homes, grew further; the Pinewoods caravan park added to

171

Top and Bottom: *Over the last hundred years the importance of tourism to the town has grown steadily.* Opposite: *The lifeboat* Doris M. Mann of Ampthill *launches on the 125th anniversary of the* Eliza Adams *disaster.*

the numbers of beds available for visitors.

The rise of the leisure industry, dependent as it was upon the preferences of those who had now all become customers – no longer primarily citizens – became a major source of income. A transformation of the Quay took place as shops and amusement arcades began to appear, taking the place of garages, pubs and industrial premises. Two families of showmen, part of the travelling community, the Grays and the Underwoods, set up at either end of the Quay, followed shortly by a third, John Gizzi, where Tom Grange's garage had been. Seaside rock and ice cream, bingo and various kinds of slot machines became a feature.[60] Children's buckets and spades could be bought. The travelling fair which had first brought the showmen to Wells had visited the town for years and continued on the Quay until new regulations put an end to the exhilaration of swinging out over the water on the rides. Grays arcade, next to the Granary, burnt down in 2005.

The rise of the leisure generation coincided, among other things, with the decline in church attendance. Hitherto, such men of the town as Frederick Smith, Tom Grange, Sam Peel and many others had been notable by their membership and even leadership of the various churches (just as their predecessors of the nineteenth century like Chapman, Southgate and Rump had been). Churchgoing revived after the war; congregations were still numbered in hundreds. By the 60s the young especially were doing other things and memory of godly duty began to fade. The same process eventually began to affect even secular organisations like Scouts and Guides, which had once provided a jostling partnership with the churches as well as tapping the energies of the young.

For the rest, the rise of second home ownership, infilling with extensive bungalows, the demolition of industrial buildings or their conversion into flats, the commercial development of the harbour to support the building and maintenance of the offshore wind farms; the rise of the shellfish fishery: these and many others are stories of the living which should be recorded, not yet as history, but as the raw material for a later history of what was once called 'the eye of Norfolk'.

10. Epilogue

History merges into memory. The previous chapter covered a period remembered by some locals, some of whom have recorded their reminiscences on paper or who have shared them with me. Some stories cannot be printed anywhere at least for the present. On the other hand, there is a danger that the record of some events even of quite recent date will be lost as people die and memories fade. Because people like to see where they fit into the mosaic of the life of the town and the community, to see themselves somewhere in the corner of the picture, it would have been possible to gather more of such stories. My task here has been a different one, that of trying to provide a longer perspective. One of the authors quoted wrote that we tend to think of the state of affairs that we first remember as the norm, whereas it was also the end of someone else's life experience. There is always change; it may help to see where we have been and to try to think about where we should be going and why.

The trouble is that the past is hard to find. In the long ago past available facts are few and far between and what we know may not be typical of what actually happened. Chance alone has preserved some records for us. More recently, the problem is the profusion of material and the difficulty of making sense of it all. This book would never have been finished had the publisher not given a completion date – and in truth no history book is ever finished. From the huge amount of information facts had to be selected and others left out in order to tell a story. Inevitably different people will tell the stories differently. A writer's interests, not to say his or her prejudices, are likely to be evident. For that reason it has been important, where possible, to let people speak for themselves. Conclusions have to be tentative. These are some of them.

First, it seems likely that Wells has played a significant and not always a minor part in the history of this land: fishing and malting in particular. One observer a hundred and seventy years ago was amazed that what he called 'a common little town' was capable of generating such 'disproportionate' amounts of commerce. That gave it perhaps more of an international flavour than it has now. The Dutch, Flemings and Icelanders were living here from the fifteenth century, as the records show. We traded with South America, the Mediterranean and the Baltic. The sea was a gateway.

Secondly, the independent character of the town seems to have been influenced by the fact that it exists between two worlds, the land and the sea. No one can choose only one of them, though some have tried to. The resulting instability has produced a lively dynamic which has often been very productive. When matters are uncertain, the exercise of wise judgement, courage and skill has made the difference between want and prosperity, and sometimes life and death.

Thirdly, attitudes and opinions have changed and changed often. It is not, as the television people sometimes try to suggest, that our forebears thought like us, they just wore funny clothes. They had similar basic needs of course, but their

Whatever the origin of the name and its previous use – see page 42 – the Buttlands remains a pleasant and green open space in the town.

view of the world was not the same as ours and their views themselves changed many times over the centuries. If there is any thread that runs through the story it could be that the sea gave them a sense that they were not in control of events and that they relied on the natural order in a way that supermarket shoppers will find it hard to understand. Landsmen knew this as well. The harvest was all. They thought of themselves primarily as members of communities and only secondarily as individuals. This does not mean that life was essentially stable; on the contrary, even in the absence of extreme events, every year brought forth the unexpected. Scarcity was the common experience of many people during most of our story. In that respect they were like many people alive today in other parts of the world. In spite of this, some may think, our forebears were much more religious than we are; though as always religion was sometimes used to coerce others rather than as something which directed their own conduct; they bargained with God as well as trusting in his benevolence or seeking to do his will. More latterly, a belief in Providence was combined with a belief that science held the solution to all problems, and this drove the decision makers. Providence itself has more recently been replaced by a belief in the power of the market and in human entitlement to personal fulfilment; on both those issues we may now be having second thoughts.

In particular, it is now clearer that the sea too has a history and that we cannot treat it simply as a boundless resource. The idea that it would endlessly provide was a survival of an older way of thinking no longer combined with the biblical notion that we were stewards, accountable for our use of its riches. We thought we could take from it because we did not think it belonged to anyone. On the contrary we can surely benefit from a better knowledge of the past, based upon knowledge of how the world got to be the way it is, and an understanding of the danger of losing what we fail to look after. Some say that the latest threat comes from what we are putting into the sea as much as from what we have long excessively taken out.

Lastly, like all communities Wells has been a place of competing interests. Not everyone thinks the same or wants the same; conflict of some sort is part of being human. Different interests were sometimes resolved but when they were not, dissent went underground. Acts of destruction, whether of manorial records or threshing machines, smuggling and other breaches of laws, have been part of the pattern. A lot of the time dissent was unseen; it emerged only from time to time as sometimes creative chaotic acts from secret lives of which history knows only a little. The resolving of conflict remains one of the most significant of all human activities. After all, the best about human nature is revealed when people collaborate in a common enterprise and attempt to see beyond difference. It is important that the fish be caught, the grain harvested, the family made safe and warm, but these are never the sum total of human aspiration. The larger issues of fairness, mutuality and who made the world and why still remain.

Looking south at low water illustrates the difficulty of the channel at Wells and why it has remained a small town rather than a major port.

Notes

ABBREVIATIONS:
CCR = *Calendar of Close Rolls*
CPR = *Calendar of Patent Rolls*
CSPD = *Calendar of State Papers Domestic*
NCC = Norwich Consistory Court (will registers at the NRO)
NRO = Norfolk Record Office

1. Introduction

1   Bolster, pp. 20–1.

2. The Making of a Community

1   Oppenheimer, p.192.
2   Records of land holdings in a nearby village testify both to their age and character. See Hesse, pp. 81ff.
3   Higham & Ryan, pp. 13ff; Blanchard, p. 180.
4   The word 'carucate' comes from the word for a wheeled plough and means the amount of land which eight oxen could plough in the season, something like 120 acres.
5   Blomefield & Parkin, vol. 9, p. 282.
6   Miller, pp.70ff., 74.
7   Bryant, p. 37.
8   Blomefield & Parkin, vol. 9, p. 283; Blomefield calls it Stafford's Manor but in the 1813 Enclosure Award it is called 'the Manor of Wells late the Dukes', referring presumably to the Duke of Norfolk.
9   Blomefield & Parkin, vol. 9, pp. 285, 235.
10 It formed the basis of *Cur Deus Homo*, the most outstanding scholarly treatise of the eleventh century, by St Anselm, Archbishop of Canterbury.
11 Blomefield & Parkin, p. 284.
12 Southern, p. 244.
13 A fifteenth-century copy of the 'Norwich Domesday' is held by the cathedral library.
14 The four main orders of Friars were the Franciscans, the Dominicans, the Carmelites and the Augustinians. Augustinian Friars need to be distinguished from Augustinian Canons whom we have already met.

15 Pantin.

16 Bedingfield, p. xxi.

17 Bennett, pp. 155ff.

18 See e.g. CCR 25 Ed. I vol. 4 (1906), p. 101.

19 Statute of Exeter 1285; Clanchy, p. 47.

20 Blomefield & Parkin, vol. 9, p. 283

21 Bennett, p. 196. The word is Saxon and means 'to take a thief'.

22 Orme.

23 The Virgin Mary teaching Jesus to read and St Anne teaching the Virgin Mary were both popular images by the fourteenth century: Orme, p. 60.

24 Clanchy, p. 13.

25 Bennett, p. 199.

26 Blanchard, p. 191.

27 Blanchard, p. 189.

28 Campbell et al., p. 33.

29 Prothero, p. 14.

30 Letters.

31 Mason, p. 37.

32 Purchas, p. 64.

33 Unger, pp. 58, 138f.

34 Blanchard, p. 102.

35 Ayers, pp. 67ff.

36 Pooley, p. 5; the records for the period are mostly lost.

37 Banham, p. 3; even as late as 1782 there were signs of a channel which ran up to the Church.

38 Oksanen, p. 185.

39 Campbell et al., pp. 48, 69.

40 Blanchard, p. 353; of the four main markets, Billingsgate with its gild of cornmongers, and which lay by the river, dealt with coastwise traffic: Campbell et al., p. 30.

41 Campbell et al., p. 85; *Calendar of Letters*, p. 12.

42 Carus Wilson, 'Medieval Trade', pp. 182ff.

43 Hipper, p. 11.

44 Lloyd, p. 306.

45 Carus Wilson, 'Medieval Trade', pp. 189, 197.

46 CPR, 37 Ed. III vol. 12 (1912), p. 324.

47 CPR 1 Rich. II, vol. 1 (1895), pp. 96–7.

48 Bolster, p. 29.

49 CPR 4 Ed. II (1311) vol. 1 (1894) p. 372.

50 Bede, p. 228.

51 Bolster, p. 28.

52 Childs, 'Fishing and Fisheries', p. 19.

53 CPR 36 Hen. III vol. 4 (1901), p. 147.

54 CPR 3 Ed.I vol. 1 (1901), p. 111.

55 Childs, 'Fishing and Fisheries', p. 20; Childs, *Internal and International Fish Trades*, p. 31.

56 CPR 6 Ed. II (1313) vol. 2 (1898), p. 194.

57 Woolgar, p. 36.

58 The *Eleanor* of Heacham, valued at £60, lost £110 worth of fish in February 1344 when it was attacked and sunk by Flemish pirates off the coast: Hooton, p. 36.

59 CCR 25 Ed. I vol. 4 (1906), pp. 82, 101, 121.
60 CCR 19 Ed. II vol. 4 (1898), pp. 183, 641.
61 Hassall & Beauroy, pp. 451–2.
62 The weight of a vessel is not its 'dead weight' but the weight of cargo which it is capable of carrying, originally measured in terms of the number of tuns (barrels) of wine. 'Tun' eventually became 'ton'.
63 CCR 11 Ed. III vol. 4 (1900), pp. 356, 402.
64 CPR 3. Ed. I vol. 1 (1901), p. 115.
65 CPR 1 Ed. II vol.1 (1894), p. 89.
66 CPR 50 Hen. III vol. 5, p. 653.
67 CPR 29 Ed. I vol. 3 (1895), p. 619.
68 CPR 3 Ed. II vol. 1 (1894), p. 248.
69 Harriss, p. 212.
70 Harriss, p. 217.
71 Miller, p. 96 n.7.
72 McKisack, p. 321.
73 CPR 10 Ed. II vol. 2 (1894), p. 684.
74 Bryant, p. 45.
75 Mason, p. 208.
76 Outbreaks occurred in 1361, 1369 and 1375: Harriss, p. 222.
77 CPR 43 Ed. III vol. 15 (1914), p. 22.
78 *Inventory of Church Goods*, pp. 93–4.
79 Harriss, p. 229.
80 Powell, pp. 34–5.
81 R. H. Britnell in Miller (ed.), *Agrarian History*, pp. 622–3.
82 Childs, 'Fishing and Fisheries', p. 23.
83 Page, p. 391.
84 McKisack, p. 203.

3. The Parish and its World

1   Childs, 'Fishing and Fisheries', p. 30.
2   Childs, 'Fishing and Fisheries', p. 22.
3   Hooton, pp. 50, 55.
4   CCR 47 Ed. III vol. 14 (1913), p. 30.
5   *Hamilton Papers*, no. 193.
6   *Libelle of Englyshe Polycye*, p. 41.
7   Carus Wilson, *Medieval Merchant Venturers*, pp. 108ff.
8   Ibid., p. 128.
9   Ibid., p. 138.
10 Childs, *Internal and International Fisheries*, p. 32.
11 Malster, p. 23.
12 Jones, p. 106.
13 Friel, *Maritime History*, pp. 50ff.
14 Friel, *Maritime History*, p. 52.
15 CCR 11 Ed. III vol. 4 (1900), p. 402.

16 CPR 23 Ed. I vol. 3 (1895), p. 151.

17 Friel, *Good Ship*, p. 149.

18 Barber, pp. 178ff.

19 CCR 13 Ed. III vol. 5 (1901), p. 513.

20 CPR 7 Ed. III vol. 2 (1901), p. 323.

21 CPR 3 Rich. II vol. 1, p. 475.

22 CPR 15 Hen. VI vol. 3 (1909), p. 42.

23 Thomas Walsingham, *Chronicon Angliae* ed. F. Maunde Thompson (Rolls Series) (London, 1874), p. 170 quoted in Childs, p. 32.

24 Ibid.

25 Friel, *Good Ship*, p. 35.

26 Childs, p. 22.

27 CPR 28 Hen. VI vol. 5 (1909), p. 319.

28 Friel, *Maritime History*, p. 85; by the early fifteenth century 80% of royal ships used a lead while only a quarter carried a compass. What fishing vessels carried is anyone's guess.

29 Carus Wilson, pp. 106f. A pew end at St Nicholas' church, Kings Lynn, dated 1419, showed such a vessel.

30 Friel, *Good Ship*, p. 85. Columbus averaged 3.5 knots when he sailed from Spain to the Bahamas.

31 Galloway, p. 21.

32 Fraser. The weight of a chauldron was to increase over time to two tons by the end of the century!

33 'One might accurately term the vessels plying between the Tyne and the Wash "grainships" as call them "colliers"' (Williams, *Maritime Trade*, p. 153).

34 Stirling, p. 156: the remark was apparently made by Lady Audrey Townshend to the wife of Thomas Coke, prior to her arrival in Norfolk after her marriage in 1718.

35 Allison, p. 17.

36 Moreton, *Townshends*, p. 162.

37 Moreton, *Townshends*, pp. 164ff.

38 Ramsay, p.10.

39 Moreton, *Townshends*, p. 150.

40 The best modern account of the life of a rural parish in those years is Duffy, *Voices of Morebath*.

41 Blomefield, p. 284.

42 Blomefield, p. 286.

43 See p. 53.

44 Blomefield, p. 286.

45 The dedication survived until the nineteenth century (Blomefield, p. 286); when it was changed to St Nicholas is unknown.

46 Bryant, p. 41.

47 Bryant, p. 39.

48 Bryant, p. 40.

49 Pantin, pp. 239ff.

50 I.e. the Virgin Mary: Will of William Clubbe 1528 (NCC Haywood p. 170); also Hugh Colkyr 1456 (NCC Brosiard 67/8); Hugh Tydde, 1471 (NCC Jekkys 263); William Clubbe 1501 (NCC Popy 71).

51 Margaret Ponyor, 1529 (NCC Mingaye 42); Stephen Massh 1465 (NCC Cobald 46).

52 Gospel according to St Matthew chapter 25.
53 Bainbridge, pp. 54, 60.
54 Williams, *Maritime Trade*, p. 192; its guildhall still stands in the Saturday Market Place.
55 Duffy, *Saints*, p. 59; Alice Briggs gave money to the Wells rood in 1514 (NCC Coppinger 60).
56 Duffy, *Stripping*.
57 Duffy, *Saints*, p. 62; Bainbridge, p. 54.
58 As above; see also Thomas Fuller 1471 (NCC Jekkys 255/6); Richard Sutton 1391 (NCC Harsyke 178).
59 Duffy, *Stripping*, pp. 170–2; a quarter of dedications were to martyr saints: Bainbridge, p. 64.
60 Hugh Tydd 1471 (NCC Jekkys 263).
61 Ibid; see also Sir John Bell 1510 (NCC Johnson 39) – Bell asked for forty-five masses to be said for his and his friends' souls.
62 Will of Thomas Waddilove, 1532 (NCC Mingaye 34).
63 He appears on the rood screen of Barton Turf; see Cotton.
64 *Dictionary of National Biography* (1895–1900), vol. 32, p. 347.

4. The Breaking of the Mould

1   The rectory of Wells was valued at £27 12*s* 5½*d* with its deductions; it appears to have been owned by the Friars Minor of Walsingham at the time. National Archives E 344/20/3, fol. 57.
2   Moreton, 'Walsingham Conspiracy'.
3   Swales, p. 262.
4   Letters Patent by Henry VIII to Thomas Paston (NRO MS 28543C6) 1541.
5   NRO will (NCC Coppinger 57; Coppinger 69; Mingaye 34).
6   Duffy, *Stripping*, p. 450.
7   Haigh, *English Reformations*, p. 134.
8   Walters, p. 227.
9   Duffy, *Saints*, p. 116.
10 Duffy, *Saints*, p. 111.
11 The Inventory of 1368 by William de Swnyflete, Archdeacon of Norwich reveals many more items than those on the 1552 list. Even allowing for the passage of time the suspicion must remain that some precious items were concealed. *Inventory of Church Goods*, pp. 93–94.
12 Duffy, *Saints*, p. 121; some was shipped to France through local ports.
13 Bryant, p. 40.
14 Haigh, 'Church of England', pp. 196ff.
15 Duffy, *Saints*, pp. 127f.
16 Bryant, p. 42; NRO PD679/1.
17 Wright, p. 50; at least three candidates refused.
18 Hassell Smith, p. 203.
19 Hassell Smith, p. 135.
20 Bacon, *Papers*, vol. IV, p. 105.
21 Mason, p. 577.
22 Hassell Smith, p. 201.
23 *Bishop Redman's Visitation*, p. 59.
24 Williams, 'Episcopal Visitation', p. 82.
25 Bacon, *Papers*, vol. V, p. 204; the matter was reported by William Halman, constable of the town.

26 Thomas, especially p. 307.

27 Thomas, p. 294.

28 Friel, *Good Ship,* pp. 93ff.

29 There are Dutch gables in several buildings locally including the Fleece Inn, one of the oldest in the town, and several buildings in Walsingham and Houghton; arguably the ubiquitous pantiles originate in Holland – the word 'pan' is Dutch for tile.

30 Laughton, p. 144.

31 Bacon, *Papers* vol. IV, p. 72.

32 Bacon, *Papers* vol. IV, p. xxxiii.

33 No one was impressed from Holkham; other ports where the press gangs operated included Cromer (11), Cley (11), Blakeney (8), and Morston (3). The press gangs were back for more in 1602: Bacon, *Papers* vol. IV, pp. 94 & 265. Impressment continued into the eighteenth centuries until a standing navy was formed.

34 Bacon, *Papers* vol. V, p. 7; Elphick, 'Press Gangs'.

35 Hassell Smith, p. 284.

36 Hassell Smith, p. 239.

37 Bacon, *Papers* vol. IV, p. 117.

38 Slack, 'Poverty and Social Regulation', pp. 221, 226. The act, the Statute of Charitable Uses, was the first attempt to regulate and protect charitable funds so as to ensure their efficient distribution.

40 Heal, especially p. 388.

41 Hooton, p. 75; State Papers 12 vol. 38, No. 8, p. 13; Muster Roll 1565. The total population of Lynn in 1377 is estimated to be in the region of 6,000.

42 Harrison, pp. 195ff.

43 Tarlow, pp. 171ff.

44 Jones, p. 106.

45 Jackson, p. 47.

46 Jones, p. 107.

47 Jones, p. 109. Effective trawling came only in the late eighteenth century.

48 Wells Parish Registers NRO MF 585 (1585–1671).

49 Williams, *Maritime Trade,* p. 241.

50 Thomas, p. 315.

51 Thomas, p. 2.

52 Bacon, *Papers* vol. V, p. 78.

53 Jones, p. 107.

54 Metters.

55 Williams, *Maritime Trade,* p. 90.

56 Hooton, p. 71.

57 Bacon, *Papers* vol. IV, p. 288.

58 State Papers of Charles I, vol. 200 (1631).

59 Bacon, *Papers* vol. IV, p. 236.

60 Mason, p. 324.

61 Jones, p. 110.

62 Millican, p. 84; Bacon, *Papers* vol. III, p. 111.

63 Bacon, *Papers* vol. III, pp. 138, 326.

64 Wells Port Books PRO E190/435/7 (Wells Local History Group Archive).

65 Jones, p. 107.

66 Robb Robinson in Starkey, p. 145.
67 House of Commons. 'First Report'.
68 Jackson, p. 50.
69 Carus Wilson, p. xxxiii.
70 Williams, Maritime Trade, p. 53.
71 Bacon, Papers vol. II, p. 146; Williams, Maritime Trade, p. 219.
72 Williams, Maritime Trade, p. 12.
73 Hassell Smith, p. 137.
76 Hooton, pp. 81f. Francis Shaxton, customs official at Lynn, forged the matrices of the seals which were attached to licences on his own behalf and that of many others. See also Williams, Maritime Trade, p. 26.
77 Hassell Smith, p. 235.
78 Williams, Maritime Trade, p. 131.
79 Metters, p. 2; the remaining records, victims of damp, mould and vermin, force us to guess. Of the seventy-six port books which must have existed from 1603 to 1640 only nine have survived.
80 Metters, p. 33.
81 Williams, Maritime Trade, p. 101.
82 Metters, especially p. 200.
83 Metters.
84 Francis, p. 23.
85 Metters, p. 149.
86 See above, p. 000.
87 Wells Port Books PRO E 190/435/7 (WLHG Archive).
88 Williams, Maritime Trade, p. 246 n.90.

5. The New Men

1   Dowsing, p. 449.
2   CSPD Interregnum (23rd August 1650), p. 535.
3   Wells Parish Register 1547–1689.
4   Blomefield, p. 285. It was lost in the 1879 fire.
5   Garlick is mentioned in a lease of property in Binham in that year.
6   Ketton-Cremer, pp. 47, 49.
7   Jewson, p. 9.
8   CSPD Charles II (1662–3), 7th January.
9   Mason, p. 429.
10 Paston, p. 243; NRO: BL/Y 1/159.
11 Wade Martins, Coke of Norfolk, p. xxx.
12 Hiskey, No. 35, April 2007.
13 Bacon, Report, p. 127.
14 Shovell is reputed to have been killed for an emerald ring on his finger when he was found exhausted on the shore after shipwreck off the Scilly Isles.
15 Mason, p. 154.
16 King Lynn Port books with Wisbech, Wells and Burnham: National Archives E190/435/7.
17 NRO FX245/12/14.
18 See p. 199 below.

19 15 Charles II (1663) c. 4 (Wells Local History Group Archive). Charles had been on the throne only since 1660, a period of three years, but the Restoration government did not recognise the existence of the Commonwealth. In its view, Charles had reigned since 1649, when his father was executed.

20 Bacon, *Papers* vol. V, p. 219.

21 Hooton, p. 123.

22 Report of John Smeaton, in Tidal Harbours Commission p. 451.

23 Bacon, *Papers* vol. I, pp. 65–6; Elphick, 'Early Use', p. 9.

24 The various engineers, Hodskinson and Smeaton, who reported in 1782 prior to one of the trials disagreed about date of the erection of Freston's sluice: Tidal Harbours Commission App. B, pp. 447, 451.

25 Report of Joseph Hume in Tidal Harbours Commission p. 79a; the bank is now called 'North Point' but since it does not point north it was probably originally the 'Nose' point.

26 9 George III (1769) c. VIII (Wells Local History Group Archive).

27 Ibid.

28 Barney, pp. 13ff.

29 Barney, p. 24.

30 See p. 34.

31 In the late seventeenth century twice as much barley as wheat was grown and half as much again as oats: Mathias, p. 388.

32 55,300 quarters to 106,960: Mathias, p. 429. A quarter was originally a measure of volume not weight (see above, p.).

33 *Norwich Mercury* 18th May 1786, 8th April 1786: taken from advertisements for their sale. Brancaster could steep 5,000 quarters a year.

34 Brown, pp.60–1.

35 Mathias, p. 432.

36 In 1744 Capt Hornby of the Wells vessel *Wrighton* en route for Rotterdam beat off and sank the French Privateer the *Marquis de Brancas* despite being heavily outgunned: *Newcastle Courant* 16th June 1744.

37 House of Commons Journal (February 1770) in Matthias, p. 431.

38 Elphick, 'Nicholas Jickling', p. 11.

39 In 1796, reported exports of malt from Wells totalled a mere 10,464 quarters, compared with 58,376 quarters of barley: Kent, p. 148.

40 From 106,960 quarters to 3,300 quarters: Matthias, p. 429; Clarke, p. 18.

41 Barney, p. 11.

42 Mathias, p. 437; it was called 'round the land barley'. Such trips would avoid the hazard of sea journeys in wartime.

43 *Norfolk Chronicle* 20th August 1842.

44 *Norwich Mercury* 29th March 1729; poor weather would lengthen or prevent the journey altogether.

45 Riches, p. 30.

46 Bowden, p. 70.

47 Trinity House Board minutes 1736; the first was at the Nore in the Thames Estuary.

48 Benham, p. 79.

49 Benham, p. 66.

50 Aldcroft & Freeman, pp. 91–2.

51 Aldcroft & Freeman, p. 3.

52   A carpenter earned about ten shillings a week in 1796 according to Nathaniel Kent.
53   Francis Rootley went bankrupt in 1749, Lawrence Rous in 1767, Thomas Jones in July 1785, John Buck in 1788 and Robert Haycock in 1797. There were more to come.
54   Wilson, p. 230.
55   Garry, p. 93.
56   Garry, pp. 111, 158.
57   Garry, p. 131.
58   Garry, p. 223.
59   Tarlow, p. 174; the difference in manufacturing methods is described on p. 65 above.
60   Holmes, p. 8.
61   Benham, p. 163.
62   Holmes, p. 7.
63   Holmes, p. 102; the Fleece, the Bowling Green and the Fighting Cocks (under the name of the Edinburgh) are still in being.
64   Holmes, p. 117.
65   Holmes, p. 79.
66   Holmes, p. 87.

6. Revolution Deferred

1   Knights, p. 182.
2   Thompson, p. 131.
3   Letters from Lord Townshend to the Duke of Portland, 16th and 22nd December 1795; Mason, p. 478; National Archives HO 42/37/306–8.
4   Ibid; letters of 22nd and 23rd December 1795.
5   Garry, p. 220.
6   Mason, pp. 460, 465, 468.
7   Joseph Arch, the first president of the National Agricultural Labourers Union founded in 1872, was a Primitive Methodist lay preacher. He became a Liberal MP for North West Norfolk in 1885.
8   Purchas, p. 36.
9   Wells Inclosure Act 1811 51 Geo III (Wells Local History Group Archive).
10   Allison, pp. 25ff.
11   Neeson, pp. 50ff.
12   Tarlow, p. 68; Wade Martins, *English Model Farm*, pp. 41ff.
13   Wade Martins, *Coke of Norfolk*, p. 114.
14   Purchas, p. 103; Map of the Manor of Wells 1668: NRO MS 21131, 179X4. This system still operates on the Gower peninsula in south Wales.
15   Extract of the Wells and Warham Enclosure Award 1813.
16   Parker, p. 96.
17   Thatcher, p. 1.
18   Parker, p. 165.
19   Bacon, *Papers* vol. IV, p. 192.
20   NRO PD 679 4th November 1754.
21   Crowley & Reid, pp. 27, 32.
22   Archer, p. 143; *Bury and Norwich Post* 9th February 1820.

23 *Norwich Mercury* 28th January 1830.
24 Hobsbawm & Rudé, pp. 55ff.
25 *Norfolk News* 30th December 1830.
26 Lee, p. 204.
27 [Charity Commission], p. 679.
28 Gregg, p. 183.
29 Digby, p. 13.
30 Digby, p. 4.
31 White, 1836, p. 629.
32 Arguile, p. 52.
33 Digby, p. 105.
34 Lee, p. 208; the words are those of an unsympathetic Suffolk clergyman, A. B. Henniker, in 1837.
35 Extract of the Wells & Warham Award 1813. R. F. Gerken, a retired Ordnance Survey cartographer, drew a map of the town from the award and its accompanying map in 1990.
36 Fryer's relationships with Bligh are a matter of some disagreement.
37 Opposed Private Bill Committee Evidence, 1844, volume 6, p. 14. The witnesses included James Chapman, Joseph Southgate, Robert Hudson, Captain Ryley and Nathaniel Beardmore
38 Ibid; evidence of James Chapman, p. 50.
39 Ibid., p. 160.
40 Chambers, p. 614.
41 Wells Parish Registers (Wells Local History Group Archive).
42 *Norfolk Chronicle* 22nd January 1820.
43 White, 1845, p. 617.
44 Aldcroft & Freeman, p. 50.

7. Prosperity

1   *Norwich Mercury* 22nd December 1831, in Hooton, p. 217.
2   Opposed Private Bill Committee Evidence, 1844: evidence of James Chapman, p. 70.
3   Aldcroft & Freeman, p. 157, Table 24; malt exports were small by comparison: just 3,300 quarters; but see p. 110.
4   Barney, p. 27.
5   6 & 7 Will. IV (1835) c.48 (Wells Local History Group Archive).
6   Tidal Harbours Commission, Appendix B, p. 438.
7   Stammers, *Victorian North Norfolk Sailing Ships*, p. 21.
8   Opposed Private Bill Committee Evidence,1844.
9   7 Vic. (1844) c. 93 (Wells Local History Group Archive).
10 Ibid. Schedule B.
11 Opposed Private Bill Committee Evidence, 1844; evidence of Revd Thomas Robert Keppel, p. 101.
12 Ibid. p. 130.
13 7 & 8 Vict. (1844) c. 94 (Wells Local History Group Archive).
14 Researches of David Perryman; there were also many 'dead' wells into which effluent was allowed to flow and, of course, to leak into the groundwater.
15 Minutes of the Wells Improvement Commissioners 1844–1874 NRO MC18/4/1.

16 Hiskey, No 20.
17 7 & 8 Vict. (1844) c. 94 ss. CXCIV–CCVII.
18 In this respect they were unlike the Improvement Commissioners who were required to live in the town.
19 Tidal Harbours Commission, pp. xiv–xv and Appendix; Barney, p. 30.
20 White, 1845, p. 682.
21 Tidal Harbours Commission, Appendix A, pp. 79ff.
22 Ibid., pp. 81–2a.
23 Barney, p. 30.
24 *Norfolk Chronicle* December 1862; Barney, p. 31.
25 Stammers, *Shipbuilding*.
26 Malster, p. 73.
27 Stammers, *Shipbuilding*, p. 3.
28 Ibid., pp. 18ff.
29 The largest ever built at Wells was the 334 ton vessel *Guadalete* in 1854.
30 Walker.
31 White, 1845, p. 682.
32 Stammers, *Shipbuilding*, pp. 23–27.
33 Stammers, *Victorian North Norfolk Sailing Ships*.
34 Wives are not usually described as working.
35 Wells 1851 census (Wells Local History Group Archive).
36 Tarlow, p. 176; the window tax was repealed in 1851.
37 Wells 1851 census.
38 Ibid; Stammers, 'East End to the Buttlands', pp. 3–5.
39 Evans, p. 244.
40 Evidence of James Everitt to the Select Committee on Malt Tax (12th June 1868), paras. 1491f. & 1514; the best malt was made in November, February and March: ibid., para. 1599. Ambient temperatures had to be between 50 and 58 degrees Fahrenheit.
41 *Norfolk News* 26th January 1861 in Stammers, 'East end to the Buttlands', p. 3.
42 Ibid., p. 5.
43 Ibid., p. 3.
44 Ede & Virgoe, pp. 280ff. Remarks from most of the churches were to the effect that attendance would have been higher but for the weather, illness, restrictions of space, ongoing repairs or 'several circumstances'.
45 At Fakenham Independent chapel a witness noted that half of those at an evening service had attended previously: Ede & Virgoe, p. 18.
46 Ede & Virgoe, p. 280.
47 A fight was advertised at the Fleece in 1808.
48 Tuck, p. 5; Field.
49 Welland, 'The Globe', p. 6.
50 White produced his Gazetteer and Directory for the county in 1836, 1845, 1864 and 1883; Kelly's Directory, first produced in 1835 and reaching Norfolk first in 1875, was the longest lasting: its final county directory was in 1937.
51 House of Commons, *Grain*, pp. 22, 40.
52 Mathias, p. 392.
53 Clark, p. 14.
54 From an average of under 1,000 quarters in the early 1820s rising to 15,757 quarters in 1838:

House of Commons, *Accounts of Grain.*

55 In 1810 harbour dues stood at £419 2*s*. They peaked at £601 10*s* 5*d* in 1841 before falling to £532 10*s* in 1843: Opposed Private Bill Evidence, testimony of Joseph Southgate, p. 76ff.
56 Barney, p. 32.
57 National production levels rose from just under 3, 000,000 quarters in 1839 to nearly 6,000,000 quarters in the 1870s: Brown, p. 25.
58 House of Commons, *Report from the Select Committee on Malt Tax,* Minutes of Evidence, p. 52.
59 NRO BR 320/1–9.
60 *Norfolk News* 25th March 1863; Clark, p. 92;Wharton, p. 11.
61 Stammers, *Victorian North Norfolk Sailing Ships,* p. 14;Finch & Benham, p. 45
62 Finch & Benham, p. 195.
63 Hipper, p. 165.

8. A Narrower World

1   Barney, p. 32.
2   Jenkins, p. 28.
3   Wells Harbour Office: records of Harbour Commissioners; finance records and printed reports in Barney, pp. 31–2.
4   Jenkins, p. 29. The Wells directors accused the Eastern Counties of swindling them.
5   Stammers, 'Operating'.
6   Jenkins, p. 37.
7   Clark, p. 23.
8   Clark, p. 53; House of Commons *Select Committee on the Malt Tax*, p. 52.
9   Wharton, p. 10.
10 Clark, p. 21.
11 Clark, p. 92; F. & G. Smith Ltd Directors Minute Book 26th January 1895.
12 Wharton, p. 32.
13 Wharton, p. 32.
14 Stammers, 'Anthracite', p. 77.
15 Royle, p. 173.
16 Ramster, pp. 179f.
17 Buckland, pp.48ff.
18 Ibid.
19 Buckland, p. 58.
20 Bolster, pp.2ff. Though primarily about the experience of North American fisheries it makes the point that it is the same ocean which washed European shores and the declines in fish, east and west, mirror each other.
21 Benham, pp. 100–103.
22 Walker, p. 23.
23 Walker, p. 28.
24 Leach & Russell, *Wells-next-the-sea Lifeboats* (Stroud: Tempus, 2006), p. 13.
25 *Norfolk Archaeology* vol. XXXIII p. 322.
26 Arguile, p. 58.
27 Its full title was the British and Foreign School Society for the Education of the Labouring and Manufacturing Classes of Society of Every Religious Persuasion! Gillard, ch. 2.

28 Gregg, p. 478.
29 Wells UDC Minutes. NRO: DC 18/4/3, 21st October; Report of R. H. Silcock DC18/4/5, p. 183.
30 NRO DC 18/4/4 (1904) p. 423.
31 Wharton, pp. 34–5.
32 Clark, p. 123.
33 Wharton, p. 36.
34 Clark, p. 62; the 1903 purchase increased the capacity by 243 quarters: Wharton, p. 32.
35 *Eastern Daily Press* 13th January 1894.
36 *Eastern Daily Press* 16th May 1918.
37 *Norfolk News* 11th November 1866.

9. A Small Town

1   NRO DC 18/4/3–5 Medical Officer of Health Annual Reports.
2   1911 census (Wells Local History Group Archive).
3   Wild, p. 9.
4   Wild, p. 40.
5   Wild, p. 37.
6   Wild, p.40.
7   Wild, p. 56.
8   *Local Government Journal* 4th November 1916.
9   7 & 8 Geo.5 Cap.xxxv (Wells Local History Group Archive); Wild, p. 61.
10 British and Empire killed were nearly a million; French nearly a million and a half; German and Austrian casualties were nearly three million. A total of over eight million soldiers died across the world with over 22 million wounded.
11 Jenkins, pp. 53, 58.
12 Clark, p. 138.
13 Howkins, p. 173.
14 Wild, p. 85.
15 Edwards, p. 22.
16 Howkins, p. 153.
17 Clark, p. 158; the company continued until 1962 when it merged with John Crisp who, in the name of Crisp Malting, are still in business.
18 F. & G. Smith, 26th January 1929, 25th March 1929.
19 Wharton, pp. 39, 52.
20 F. & G. Smith, especially 9th December 1939.
21 The bottles describe the works as being on Park Road; they were on what is now Mill Road. Street names were often changed by local usage.
22 Perkins, *Wells.*
23 Woods, p. 41.
24 Featherstone, p. 9.
25 Woods, p. 17.
26 Woods, pp. 34ff.
27 Perryman.
28 Wells Urban District Council minutes NRO DC 18/4/6.

29 F. &. G. Smith 28th June 1930.
30 Wells Burial Register (Wells Local History Group Archive).
31 Wild, p. 97.
32 Gillard, ch. 4.
33 Jenkins, p. 71.
34 Bartram, p. 33.
35 Conversation with David Cox.
36 Purchas, p. 82.
37 David Cox.
38 Woods, p. 47.
39 Supplement to the *London Gazette* 23rd December 1943.
40 Geoff Perkins, *Some More Wells People* and *Heroes*.
41 Geoff Perkins, *When I was a Young Lad*, p. 40.
42 Conversation with Ted Everitt.
43 Bartram, p. 19.
44 David Cox.
45 Welland, 'The Quay'.
46 Conversation with David Perryman.
47 Hardy, vol. 4, p. 385.
48 Letter dated 17th February 1953 printed in *Wells Local History Group Newsletter* No. 26, p. 4.
49 Barker, p. 55.
50 Records of Barker and Sons Ltd.
51 Jarvis.
52 David Cox.
53 Weatherhead, p. 107.
54 Weatherhead, pp. 110–111, 152.
55 F. & G. Smith, 14th May 1941.
56 Conversation with John Tyson.
57 The cycle was reduced from two weeks to nine to ten days. Malt quality was improved, the labour force halved and production doubled: Clark, p. 188.
58 Jenkins, p. 158.
59 Ibid. pp. 165ff.
60 Festing, ch. 5.

Bibliography

D. Aldcroft & M. Freeman (eds), *Transport in the Industrial Revolution* (Manchester: Manchester University Press, 1983)

K. J. Allison, 'The Sheep-Corn Husbandry of Norfolk in the Sixteenth and Seventeenth Centuries', *Agricultural History Review* 5(30), 1957, pp. 12–30

J. E. Archer, *By a Flash and a Scare: Incendiarism, Animal Maiming, and Poaching in East Anglia 1815–1870* (Oxford: Clarendon, 1990)

Roger Arguile, *A Church in a Landscape* (Wells: Jubilee Publications for S. Creake Parish Church, 2011)

Brian Ayers, 'Cities, Cogs and Commerce', in *East Anglia and its North Sea World in the Middle Ages* ed. David Bates and Robert Liddiard (Woodbridge: Boydell Press, 2013)

Nathaniel Bacon, *The Papers of Nathaniel Bacon of Stiffkey* 5 vols. (Norwich: Norfolk Record Society, 1978–2010)

Richard Bacon, *Report on the Agriculture of Norfolk* (1844)

Virginia Bainbridge, *Gilds in the Mediaeval Countryside 1350–1558* (Ipswich: Boydell, 1996)

Eleanor Banham, 'Wells next the Sea, A Re-located Town', *Wells Local History Group Newsletter* April 2011.

Richard Barber, *Edward III and the Triumph of England* (London: Allen Lane, 2013)

Brian Barker, *Norfolk Carrier: Memories of a Family Haulage Business, Barker & Sons, Wells-next-the-sea* (Wells: David Lowe, 2003)

John Barney, *The Trials of Wells Harbour* (Norwich: Mintaka Books, 2000)

Len Bartram, *R.A.F. North Creake, Egmere, Norfolk, 1940–1947: A Brief History* (Hunworth: Len Bartram, 1999)

Bede, *A History of the English Church and People* (Harmondsworth: Penguin, 1955)

A. L. Bedingfield, *The Cartulary of Creake Abbey* (Norwich: Norfolk Record Society, 1966)

Hervey Benham, *Once upon a Tide* (London: Harrap, 1954)

H. S. Bennett, *Life on the English Manor* (Cambridge University Press, 1937).

Bishop Redman's Visitation 1597 (Norwich: Norfolk Record Society, vol. XIX, 1946)

Ian Blanchard, *The Twelfth Century: A Neglected Epoch in British Economic and Social History* (available at www.ianblanchard.com).

Francis Blomefield & Charles Parkin, *An Essay Towards a Topographical History of the County of Norfolk*, Vol. 9 (London, 1806).

W. Jeffrey Bolster, *The Mortal Ocean* (London: Belknap, 2012)

Peter J. Bowden, *The Wool Trade in Tudor and Stuart England* (London: Frank Cass, 1971)

Jonathan Brown, *Steeped in Tradition: The Malting Industry in England Since the Railway Age* (Reading University, 1983)

T. H. Bryant, *Norfolk Churches: Hundred of North Greenhoe* (Norwich: Norwich Mercury, 1898)

Frank Buckland, *Report on the Fisheries of Norfolk* (House of Commons, 11th August 1875)

Calendar of Close Rolls 1216-1509 (London: Public Record Office, 1904–27)

Calendar of Letters from the Mayor and Corporation of the City of London 1350–1370 ed. R. R. Sharpe (London, 1885)

Calendar of Patent Rolls 1216–1452 (London: Public Record Office, 1894–1909) (access to the Patent Rolls was obtained through a digitised version produced by the University of Iowa as part of a historical project)

Calendar of State Papers, Domestic series (London, 1856–)

Bruce M. S. Campbell et al., *A Medieval Capital and its Grain Supply: Agrarian Production and Distribution in the London Region c. 1300* (London: Historical Geography Research Group, 1993)

E. M. Carus Wilson, *Medieval Merchant Venturers* (London: Methuen, 1954)

E. Carus Wilson, 'The Medieval Trade of the Ports of the Wash', *Mediaeval Archaeology* (1962)

John Chambers, *A General History of the County of Norfolk,* vol 2 (1829)

[Charity Commission.] *Further Report of the Commissioners Inquiring Concerning Charities: County of Norfolk, City of Norwich* (London, 1833)

W. R. Childs, 'Fishing and Fisheries in the Middle Ages' in *England's Sea Fisheries: The Commercial Sea Fisheries of England and Wales since 1300* ed. David Starkey, John Ramster and Chris Reid (London: Chatham, 2000)

W. R. Childs, *The Internal and International Fish Trades of Mediaeval England and Wales* (London: Chatham, 2000)

M. T. Clanchy, *From Memory to Written Record* 2nd. ed. (Oxford: Blackwell, 1993)

Christine Clark, *The British Malting Industry since 1830* (London: Hambledon, 1998)

Simon Cotton, 'Mediaeval Roodscreens in Norfolk: Their Construction and Painting Dates', *Norfolk Archaeology 40* (1987), pp. 44–54

Jerry Crowley and Andy Reid (eds), *The Poor Law in Norfolk 1700–1850* (Ely: EARO Resource and Technology Centre for Norwich Teachers' Centre, 1983)

Anne Digby, *Pauper Palaces* (London: Routledge and Kegan Paul, 1978)

William Dowsing, *The Journal of William Dowsing* ed. Trevor Cooper (Ipswich: Boydell, 2001)

Eamon Duffy, *The Stripping of the Altars* (London: Yale University Press, 1992)

Eamon Duffy, *The Voices of Morebath* (London: Yale University Press, 2001)

Eamon Duffy, *Saints, Sacrilege and Sedition* (London: Bloomsbury, 2012)

Janet Ede & Norma Virgoe, *Religious Worship in Norfolk: the 1851 Census of Accommodation and Attendance at Worship* (Norwich: Norfolk Record Society, vol. LXII, 1998)

George Edwards, *Crow-scaring to Westminster* (London: Unwin, 1922)

Peter Elphick, 'An Early Use of the Name Wells Haven', *Wells Local History Group Newsletter* No. 45

Peter Elphick, 'Nicholas Jickling and the Customs Service at Wells', *Wells Local History Group Newsletter* No. 43

Peter Elphick, 'Press Gangs', *Wells Local History Group Newsletter* 35 (April 2007)

George Ewart Evans, *Where Beards Wag All: The Relevance of Oral Tradition* (London: Faber & Faber, 1970)

F. & G. Smith Ltd Directors Minute Books (2 vols.)

Deryck Featherstone, 'Wells, a Kind of Paradise', *Wells Local History Group Newsletter* No. 41

Sally Festing, Showmen: *The Voice of Travelling Fair People* (Shaun Tyas, 2012)

Moira Field, *The Lamplit Stage: The Fisher Theatre Circuit, 1792–1844* (Norwich: Running Angel Press, 1985)

Roger Finch & Hervey Benham, *Sailing Craft of East Anglia* (Lavenham: Terence Dalton, 1987)

Sally Francis, *Saffron* (Norfolk: Sally Francis, 2011)

C. M. Fraser (ed.), *The Accounts of the Chamberlains of Newcastle upon Tyne, 1508–1511* (Newcastle upon Tyne: Society of Antiquaries of Newcastle upon Tyne, 1987)

Ian Friel, *The Good Ship: Ships, Shipbuilding and Technology in England 1200-1520* (London: British Museum Press, 1994)

Ian Friel, *Maritime History of Britain and Ireland* (London: British Museum, 2003)

Robert Galloway, *A History Of Coal Mining in Great Britain* (1882)

Mary-Anne Garry, *Wealthy Masters: 'Provident and Kind'* (Guist: Larks Press, 2012)

Derek Gillard, *The History of Education in England* (www.educationengland.org. 2011)

Pauline Gregg, *A Social and Economic History of Britain* (London: Harrap, 1956)

Christopher Haigh, 'The Church of England, the Catholics and the People' in *The Reign of Elizabeth I* ed. C. Haigh (Basingstoke: Macmillan, 1984)

Christopher Haigh, *English Reformations: Religion, Politics, and Society under the Tudors* (Oxford: Clarendon, 1993)

The Hamilton Papers: Letters and Papers Illustrating the Political Relations of England and Scotland in the XVIth century ed. Joseph Bain, vol. III (Edinburgh: H.M. General Register House, 1890)

Mary Hardy, *The Diary of Mary Hardy* ed. Margaret Bird (Kingston upon Thames: Burnham Press, 2013)

William Harrison, *A Description of England (1587)* (Cornell University Press, 1968)

Gerald Harriss, *Shaping the Nation: England 1360–1461* (Oxford: Clarendon, 2005)

W. O. Hassall & Jacques Beauroy (eds), *Lordship and Landscape in Norfolk 1250–1350: The Early Records of Holkham* (Oxford: Oxford University Press for the British Academy, 1993)

A. Hassell Smith, *County and Court: Government and Politics in Norfolk, 1558–1603* (Oxford: Clarendon, 1974)

Felicity Heal, *Hospitality in Early Modern England* (Oxford: Clarendon, 1990)

Mary Hesse, 'Medieval Field Systems and Land Tenure in South Creake, Norfolk', *Archaeology* vol. XLIII (1998)

Nicholas Higham and Martin J. Ryan, *Landscape Archaeology of Anglo-Saxon England* (Ipswich: Boydell, 2010)

Kenneth Hipper, *Smugglers All* (Guist: Larks Press, 2001)

Christine Hiskey, 'Notes from the Holkham Archives', *Wells Local History Group Newsletter* (various issues)

E. J. Hobsbawm & George Rudé, *Captain Swing* (Harmondsworth: Penguin, 1973)

Nigel Holmes, *The Lawless Coast* (Guist: Larks Press, 2008)

Jonathan Hooton, *The Glaven Ports: A Maritime History of Blakeney, Cley and Wiveton in North Norfolk* (Blakeney: Blakeney History Group, 1996)

House of Commons. *Accounts of Grain, Malt and Flour, Shipped from and to the Several Ports of England*, 1824, 1828, 1839 (House of Commons Papers)

House of Commons. 'First Report from the Committee Appointed to Enquire into the State of the British Fisheries – 1785', *Reports from the Committees of the House of Commons, Miscellaneous Subjects*, vol. 10, 1785–1801 (London, 1803)

House of Commons. *Grain, Malt and Flour Exported from England, Scotland and Ireland 1819–24* (House of Commons Paper 21st June 1824)

House of Commons. *Report from the Select Committee on Malt Tax* (1867)

Alun Howkins, *Poor Labouring Men* (London: Routledge, 1985)

Inventory of Church Goods temp. Edward III transcribed by Dom Aelred Watkin (Norwich: Norfolk Record Society, vol. XIX, 1947)

Gordon Jackson, 'State Concern for the Fisheries 1485–1815' in *England's Sea Fisheries: The Commercial Sea Fisheries of England and Wales since 1300* ed. David Starkey, Chris Reid and Neil Ashcroft (London: Chatham, 2000)

P. R. Jarvis, *Port of Wells Shipping Register 1939–1996* (unpublished)

Stanley C. Jenkins, *The Wells next the Sea Branch* (Usk: Oakwood, 2011)

C. B. Jewson, 'Return of Conventicles in Norwich Diocese', *Norfolk Archaeology* XXXIII (1965), pp. 6–34

Evan Jones, 'England's Icelandic Fishery in the Early Modern Period' in *England's Sea Fisheries, The Commercial Sea Fisheries of England and Wales since 1300* ed. David Starkey, Chris Reid and Neil Ashcroft (London: Chatham, 2000)

Nathaniel Kent, *General View of the Agriculture of Norfolk* (1796)

R. W. Ketton-Cremer, *Norfolk in the Civil War* (London: Faber and Faber, 1968)

Mark Knights, 'Politics, 1660–1835' in *Norwich since 1550* ed. C. Rawcliffe and P. Wilson (London: Continuum, 2004)

J. K. Laughton (ed.), *State Papers relating to the Defeat of the Armada* (Navy Records Society, 1894)

Nicholas Leach & Paul Russell, *Wells-next-the-sea Lifeboats* (Stroud: Tempus, 2006)

Robert Lee, 'Customs in Conflict: Some Causes of Anti-Clericalism in Rural Norfolk 1815–1914', *Rural History* 14:2 (2003)

Samantha Letters, *Gazetteer of Markets and Fairs in England and Wales to 1516* (List and Index Society, 2003; updated version available at http://www.history.ac.uk/cmh/gaz/gazweb2.html)

The Libelle of Englyshe Polycye: A Poem on the Use of Sea-power, 1436, ed. George Warner (Oxford: Clarendon, 1926)

T. H. Lloyd, *The English Wool Trade in the Middle Ages* (Cambridge: Cambridge University Press, 1977)

Mary McKisack, *The Fourteenth Century 1307–1399* (Oxford: Oxford University Press, 1959)

Robert Malster, *Maritime Norfolk* Part One (Cromer: Poppyland, 2012)

R. H. Mason, *A History of the County of Norfolk* (1884).

Peter Mathias, *The Brewing Industry in England 1700–1830* (Cambridge: Cambridge University Press, 1959)

Metters, G. Alan (ed.), *The King's Lynn Port books, 1610–1614* (Norwich: Norfolk Record Society vol. LXXIII, 2009)

Edward Miller, *The Abbey and Bishopric of Ely* (Cambridge: Cambridge University Press, 1951).

Edward Miller (ed.), *The Agrarian History of England and Wales, vol. 3: 1348–1500* (Cambridge: Cambridge University Press, 1991)

P. C. Millican, 'Christ's Dole', *Norfolk Archaeology* XXVIII (1945), pp. 83–86

C. E. Moreton, *The Townshends and their World: Gentry, Law, and Land in Norfolk c.1450–1551* (Oxford: Clarendon, 1992)

C. E. Moreton, 'The Walsingham Conspiracy of 1537', *Bulletin of the Institute of Historical Research* 63 (1990), pp. 29–43.

J. M. Neeson, *Commoners: Common Right, Enclosure and Social Change in England 1700–1820* (Cambridge: Cambridge University Press, 1993)

Elijas Oksanen in *East Anglia and its North Sea World in the Middle Ages* ed. David Bates and Robert Liddiard (Woodbridge: Boydell Press, 2013).

Nicholas Orme, *Mediaeval Schools: From Roman Britain to Renaissance England* (London: Yale University Press, 2006).

Stephen Oppenheimer, *The Origins of the British* (London: Robinson, 2007)

Opposed Private Bill Committee Evidence, 1844, volume 6 (Wells Lighting and Improvement Bill). Parliamentary Archives: HL/PO/PB/5/10/6

William Page (ed.), *The Victoria History of the County of Norfolk* vol. 2 (London, 1906)

W. A. Pantin, *The English Church in the Fourteenth Century* (Cambridge: Cambridge University Press, 1955).

R. A. C. Parker, *Coke of Norfolk* (Oxford: Clarendon, 1975)

Robert Paston, *A Whirlpool of Misadventures: Letters of Robert Paston, First Earl of Yarmouth 1663–1679* ed. Jean Agnew (Norwich: Norfolk Record Society, 2012)

Geoff Perkins, *Heroes and Fighting Men and Women of Wells-on Sea* (Wells: Geoff Perkins, 1992).

Geoff Perkins, *Some More Wells People* (Wells: Geoff Perkins, 2009)

Geoff Perkins, *Wells on Sea: A Town and its People – as it once was* (Wells: Geoff Perkins, 1996)

Geoff Perkins, *When I was a Young Lad: Boyhood Memories of Wells on Sea* (Wells: Geoff Perkins, 2000)

D. Perryman in *Wells Local History Group Newsletter* No. 16

Graham Pooley, *The Port of Wells: 1100 Years of History* (Fakenham: Graham Pooley, 1992)

Edgar Powell, *The Rising in East Anglia in 1381* (Cambridge, 1896)

R. E. Prothero (Lord Ernle), *English Farming Past and Present,* 4th ed. (London, 1927).

Arthur W. Purchas, *Some History of Wells next the Sea* (Ipswich: East Anglian Magazine, 1965).

G. M. Ramsay, *The English Woollen Industry 1500–1750* (London: Macmillan 1982)

John Ramster, 'Government, Science and the Fisheries' in *England's Sea Fisheries: The Commercial Sea Fisheries of England and Wales since 1300* ed. David Starkey, John Ramster and Chris Reid (London: Chatham, 2000)

Naomi Riches, *The Agricultural Revolution in Norfolk* (London: Frank Cass, 1967)

S. A. Royle, 'The Development of Small Towns in Britain' in *The Cambridge Urban History of Britain vol. III 1840–1950* (Cambridge: Cambridge University Press, 2000)

Paul Slack, 'Poverty and Social Regulation', pp. 221, 226 in *The Reign of Elizabeth I* ed. C. Haigh (Basingstoke: Macmillan, 1984)

R. W. Southern, *Western Society and the Church in the Middle Ages* (Harmondsworth: Penguin, 1970).

Michael Stammers, 'Anthracite for Wells-next-the-Sea: A By-way of the Swansea Coal Trade', *Cymru a'r Mor/Maritime Wales* vol. 20 (1999)

Michael Stammers, 'East End to the Buttlands: A Snapshot of a Rural Port in the mid-19th Century', *Wells Local History Group Newsletter* No. 51 (2012)

Michael Stammers, 'Operating the Wells and Fakenham Railway', *Great Eastern Journal* (October 2008)

Michael Stammers, *Shipbuilding in Wells in the 18th and 19th Centuries* (Wells: Wells Local History Group, 2012)

Michael Stammers, *Victorian North Norfolk Sailing Ships* (Norwich: Milepost Research, 2012)

David J. Starkey et al. (eds), *A History of the North Atlantic Fisheries* vol. 1 (Bremen: Verlag H.M. Hauschild, 2009)

A. M. W. Stirling, *Coke of Norfolk and his Friends* (1912)

T. H. Swales , 'Opposition to the Suppression of Norfolk Monasteries', *Norfolk Archaeology* XXXIII (1965), pp. 254–265

Sarah Tarlow, *The Archaeology of Improvement in Britain 1750–1850* (Cambridge: Cambridge

University Press, 2007)

Kevin Thatcher, 'Wildfowling at Wells', *Wells Local History Group Newsletter* (2011)

Keith Thomas, *Religion and the Decline of Magic* (Harmondsworth: Penguin, 1973)

E. P. Thompson, *The Making of the English Working Class* (Harmondworth: Penguin, 1968)

Tidal Harbours Commission, *Second Report* (1846)

John Tuck, 'The Fisher Theatre at Wells 1812 to 1844', *Wells Local History Group Newsletter* No. 44 (April 2012)

R. W. Unger, *The Ship in the Mediaeval Economy 600–1600* (London: Croom Helm, 1980)

S. Wade Martins, *The English Model Farm* (Macclesfield: Windgather, 2002)

S. Wade Martins, *Coke of Norfolk (1754–1842): A Biography* (Ipswich: Boydell, 2009) p. xxx.

Graham Walker, *The Memoirs of William John Harman 1854–1944: Shipwrecks and Rescues off Wells-next-the-sea, Norfolk* (Walker, 1995)

Henry Beauchamp Walters, 'Inventories of Norfolk Church Goods (1552)', *Norfolk Archaeology* XXVIII (1945), pp. 7–22, 89–106, 133–180, 217–228

Fran Weatherhead, *North Norfolk Fishermen* (Stroud: The History Press, 2011)

Mike Welland, 'The Globe Hotel', *Wells Local History Group Newsletter* No. 35 (2006)

Mike Welland, 'The Quay', *Wells Local History Group Newsletter* No. 55 (2011)

Betty Wharton, *The Smiths of Ryburgh* (Great Ryburgh: Crisp Malting, 1990)

William White, *History, Gazetteer and Directoryof Norfolk* (1836, 1845)

Susan Wild, *Sam Peel: A Man who Did Different* (Wells: Wells Local History Group, 2013)

J. F. Williams, 'An Episcopal Visitation in 1593', *Norfolk Archaeology* XXVIII (1945)

N. J. Williams, *Maritime Trade of East Anglian Ports 1550–1590* (Oxford: Clarendon, 1988)

Richard Wilson, 'The Textile Industry' in *Norwich since 1550* ed. C. Rawcliffe & R. Wilson (London: Hambledon, 2004)

Sheila Woods, *Out with the Tide: Recollections of Wells-next-the-sea* (North Walsham: Poppyland, 1989)

C. M. Woolgar, 'Take this Penance now and afterwards the Fare will Improve: Seafood and Late Medieval Diet' in *England's Sea Fisheries: The Commercial Sea Fisheries of England and Wales since 1300* ed. David Starkey, Chris Reid and Neil Ashcroft (Chatham, 2000)

John Wright, 'The Tudor Period' in *Stiffkey with Cockthorpe: A Story of Norfolk People* (Cromer: Poppyland, 2013), pp. 43–69

Units of measurement

Pre-metric systems of length, volume, weight and currency obtained for almost the whole of the period. None were standardised until the 18th or 19th centuries. I have attempted to simplify the descriptions to make the reader's task simpler.

GRAIN AND MALT

Grain and malt were measured by volume until the twentieth century. Standardisation only came latterly.

Four bushels = 1 comb
Two combs = 1 quarter
1 quarter of malt = 336 lb (pounds)
6.67 quarters of malt = 1 ton (Imperial)
6.56 quarters of malt = one tonne (metric)
1 quarter of barley = 448 lb = 203 kg
5 quarters of barley = one ton
4.92 quarters of barley = 1 tonne
10 quarters = 1 last
1 last = approx. 2 tons

COAL

Coal was measured in chauldrons, a unit of weight. This varied over time but was equivalent to just over a ton in the earlier period. Some guidance is given in the text.

CURRENCY IS REFERRED TO BY THE PRE-DECIMAL DIVISIONS:

12 pence = 1 shilling
20 shillings = 1 pound

Topography

The town faces the sea to the north, its marshes lying a mile and a quarter seawards. A channel runs from the Quay to the sea through the marshes, the west marsh having been drained. It is now farmland. A number of streets run southwards up the hill into the town, the most significant being Staithe Street where most of the shops now are. It meets an east–west road, variously named, which runs along the top of the ridge leading to Holkham. From it southwards lie the Buttlands, a green space and, a little to its east, High Street which runs down the hill to the church. Maps of various dates can be found in the text. Many road names changed often.

Index

Note: Page locators in *italics* denote illustrations.

204

Turner family 75, 78, 79, 80
turnips 94, 128
turnpikes 86, 107–108
Twight, Ann 106
Tydd(e) family 47, 53–54, 56, 57, 59
Tyrrell, Henry *13*, 115, 122–123, 123
Tyzack, James 115
Tyzack, William 123

Underwood family 174
units of measurement 199
Urban District Council 143, 150–152, 158

Vikings 15–16
Vincent, Patrick 124
volunteer corps 92
Vowell, Richard 56
Vynne and Everett 155, 168

Waddilove, Thomas 57
waggons 86–87, 104
Walden, John 106
Walpole, Robert 89
Walsingham conspiracy 55–56
Walsingham priory 20
Walsingham Union 100–101
war memorial 153
Warham Slade 78, 79, 81, 110
Warner, Henry Lee 79
Warren, Mr (engineer) 115
weaving 28–29
wells 11, 116, 157
    becomes an independent port 77–78
    name 11
    topography 11
whaling 32–33
Wheatley, William 74
whelks 156, *167*, 170

Wiggen, Thomas 73
Wighton 18, 19, 34, 48
wildfowling 97
Wilks, Mark 91
Williams' blacksmiths yard *149*
wind farms 14, 174
windmills 84–*85*, 146
windows 65–66, 88
    stained glass 148
witchcraft 61, 66, 67
Wiveton, embankment 78
wool 28–29, 43, 48, 85–86
Wordingham, Charles 139
workhouses 98, 100–101, 124
World War I 153
World War II 158–160
worsted 87
wrecks 19, 32, 86
    manorial claim to 19, 64
Wright, Thomas 103

Yarmouth
    barley exports 129, 138
    bombed 153, 155
    fisheries 30, 66, 70
    Flemish merchants 35
    gilds 52
    harbour 72
    Icelandic fishery 69
    and pirates 32, 68
Young, Arthur 94
Young, James 115